So They Remember

So They Remember

A Jewish Family's Story of Surviving the
Holocaust in Soviet Ukraine

Maksim Goldenshteyn

UNIVERSITY OF OKLAHOMA PRESS : NORMAN

Publication of this book is made possible through the generosity of Edith Kinney Gaylord.

Library of Congress Cataloging-in-Publication Data

Names: Goldenshteyn, Maksim Grigoriyevich, 1988– author.
Title: So they remember : a Jewish family's story of surviving the
    Holocaust in Soviet Ukraine / Maksim Grigoriyevich Goldenshteyn.
Description: Norman : University of Oklahoma Press, [2022] | Includes
    bibliographical references. | Summary: "Holocaust survival story of
    Motl Braverman and his family at the Pechera death camp in Soviet
    Ukraine. The camp was established in 1941 by Romanian dictator Ion
    Antonescu, one of Hitler's closest allies. Drawing on survivors' stories
    and secondary literature, the author reconstructs life at the camp with
    the contradictions that defined the camp experience and shows how
    the events of eighty-plus years ago continue to shape the identities of
    survivors and their descendants"—Provided by publisher.
Identifiers: LCCN 2021023221 | ISBN 978-0-8061-7606-2 (paperback)
Subjects: LCSH: Braverman, Motl, 1929–2015. | Jews—Ukraine—
    Chernivtsi—Biography. | Holocaust, Jewish (1939–1945)—Ukraine—
    Transnistria (Territory under German and Romanian occupation,
    1941–1944)—Biography. | Peciora (Concentration camp)
Classification: LCC DS135.U43 B7327 2022 | DDC 940.53/180922477—dc23
LC record available at https://lccn.loc.gov/2021023221

The paper in this book meets the guidelines for permanence and
durability of the Committee on Production Guidelines for Book
Longevity of the Council on Library Resources, Inc. ∞

To my children

Contents

Acknowledgments

By the time this book is published, nearly a decade will have passed since my maternal grandfather, Motl Braverman, first shared his memories with me. For that, I am forever grateful. I am also indebted to the other Holocaust survivors who have entrusted me with their stories: my maternal grandmother, Anna Braverman, my great-aunts Etel and Luba,[1] my grandmother's cousin Eva Poliak, and my grandfather's good friend Boris Sandler. I also wish to thank Svetlana Voskoboynik for telling me about her late father, Aleksander.

For years, I found all sorts of excuses to delay this project. I am grateful to the small group of family, friends, and colleagues who helped me overcome my self-doubts to see this book to completion. My mother, Svetlana Braverman, has answered hundreds of my questions over the years and was the first to document my grandfather's experiences. From the time we first met, my wife, Megan, has encouraged me to put words to paper. She has supported me throughout this journey. My mother-in-law, Jodi Sanchez, and my former college journalism colleagues and friends William Mari and Allen Wagner have long offered words of encouragement. A special thanks to the cartoonist Amy Kurzweil, whom I first met on a college trip to Israel and who recently published a graphic memoir about her own family's story, *Flying Couch*, for helping me find a clearer focus.

While writing this book, I had the privilege of speaking to Holocaust survivor Moris Bronshteyn. Moris, now a Bay Area resident, was born in Dzhuryn, Ukraine, a town that plays an important role in this book. Beginning in 1994, Moris conducted video interviews with seventy-four Holocaust survivors in Ukraine, many of them survivors of the Pechera camp, for what is now the USC Shoah Foundation's Visual History Archive. In doing so, he helped preserve their stories for generations to come. Moris's video interviews and his book of interview transcripts, *Dead Loop*, allowed me to add texture to the scenes my grandfather and great-aunt described to me a decade ago.

I am also grateful for the work of the scholars cited throughout the book, people who painstakingly documented a chapter of Holocaust history that has long been overlooked. This includes leading historian Radu Ioanid, who found time to speak with me just as he was transitioning to his new post as Romania's ambassador to Israel. I also wish to acknowledge Rebecca Golbert, who in 2004 authored the first comprehensive study of the Pechera camp, and Jeffrey Veidlinger, whose work documenting the towns and villages of Ukraine's Vinnytsia Province has greatly contributed to my understanding of my family's past.

While writing my manuscript, serendipity seemed to strike time and time again. This included a chance introduction, by way of email, to Tulchyn librarian Vladislav Vigurzhinsky, who supplied the photo of Tulchyn's School No. 1 that appears in this book. Well into the writing phase, I happened upon an unpublished memoir written by my grandmother's cousin Eva Poliak, which revealed that my family's ties to the village of Pechera were more extensive than I could have imagined.

I was also fortunate to receive assistance from the professional staff and researchers at a variety of institutions, each of whom went out of their way to answer questions, provide access to archival materials, and grant the necessary permissions—all during a global pandemic. These include (in no particular order), the Judaica Department within the Vernadsky National Library of Ukraine's Manuscript Institute; Yad Vashem, the United States Holocaust Memorial Museum; USC Shoah Foundation, Leo Baeck Institute; National Museum in Kraków; Jagiellonian Library at Jagiellonian University; and the State Archive of the Russian Federation. I would have been lost without the assistance of the Seattle Public Library system and its indefatigable interlibrary-loan team. I am also indebted to French organization Yahad-In Unum, founded by *Holocaust by Bullets* author Father Patrick Desbois, which granted me access to photographs from its 2018 trip to Pechera.

Finally, I wish to thank former University of Oklahoma Press editor-in-chief Adam Kane (now the director of Naval Institute Press), who first championed this project. I am grateful for the support of senior acquisitions editor Alessandra Jacobi Tamulevich and senior manuscript editor Stephanie Attia Evans, who along with the wider OU Press team shepherded this book to publication. Copyeditor Richard Feit helped improve the final manuscript in immeasurable ways. I am also grateful to my readers, including fellow OU Press author Barbara Rylko-Bauer, for their incisive feedback. I owe thanks to cartographer Erin Greb for designing the map.

I regret that some of the people mentioned in the preceding paragraphs are no longer with us. There is one other person: my father, Grigoriy Goldenshteyn, who died of ALS in 2019. In his last text message to me, on my thirty-first birthday, he told me he hoped my wishes would come true. In being able to tell this story, they have. I hope that my two young children, to whom this book is dedicated, will gain an appreciation for their heritage and for the people who sacrificed so greatly for them—and for me.

A Note on Transliteration and Toponyms

SCHOLARS HAVE USED A VARIETY of naming strategies when writing about the villages, towns, cities, regions, and rivers at the center of this book. Some have rendered their names using the Romanian transliteration, others the Russian, Ukrainian, and Polish variants. Occasionally, multiple approaches are used. Throughout this book, I use Ukrainian transliterations to reflect current usage. One obvious benefit is consistency. Another is allowing readers to more easily experience the places in this book (through Google Maps and the vast collections of online photos and videos that can be found for even the smallest, most remote of villages). There is, however, a downside. Many of the survivors I interviewed, or whose testimonies I have used, referenced these places by their Soviet-era Russian names. This was a difficult concession to make, but a necessary one.

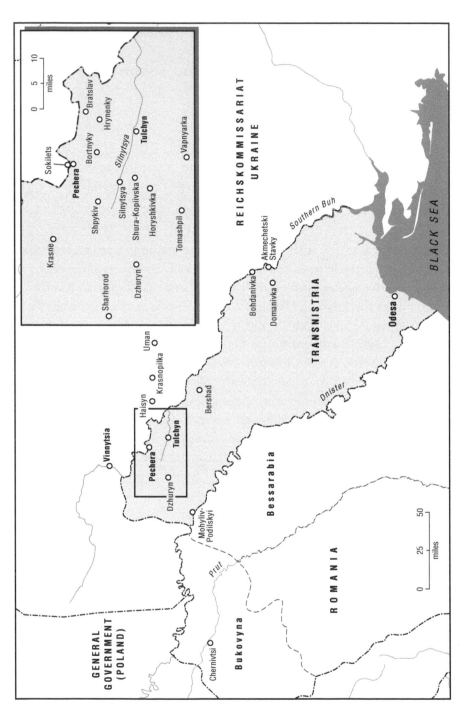

Transnistria (Romanian-occupied Soviet Ukraine), 1941–1944. Map by Erin Greb Cartography.

Prologue

I FIRST CAME TO HEAR THE STORY on a Saturday in spring 2012. That afternoon, the elevator in my grandparents' apartment building opened to a dimly lit hallway, which carried the muffled sound of a Russian daytime talk show. I followed the tired blue carpeting past the first row of doors until I reached their unit. Inside, they had assumed their usual places. My grandfather Motl, then eighty-three, sat on the far end of his prized sleeper sofa, a remote control at his side. The TV was now tuned to a Russian news broadcast. "Rockets Strike Southern Israel," the chyron read. My grandmother Anna, seventy-four, stood in the kitchen wiping down the stove, the water still running from the faucet.

My visit began as they usually would, with their chiding me for my choice in outerwear—I came wearing a thin sweatshirt—and for my weekend stubble. I then sat down to the dishes my grandmother had prepared and arranged on her dining table. As we got to talking, I turned to the subject that their daughter Svetlana, my mother, had mentioned to me in passing a week earlier, something about my grandfather's leading people to safety during the war. The revelation was so startling that I had since forgotten what prompted the conversation. When I looked up from my cucumber and tomato salad, my grandfather had already retrieved a large shoe box from his bedroom. Inside was a manila envelope with assorted newspaper clippings. There was also a thin, yellowing booklet, which he had kept inside a Ziploc bag. He explained that the pages held the stories of Holocaust survivors from Chernivtsi, Ukraine, the city where I was born and where our family had lived before emigrating to the United States as refugees in 1992. He leafed through it and found his picture and an accompanying

1

submission. He proceeded to read all six pages aloud. "The fascists entered and the tragedy began," he had once written.[1]

My first instinct was to record our conversation. I asked for permission, and he agreed. We spoke for several more hours that same day, he on one end of his couch and me on the other, my phone face-up between us. I came back to hear more on Saturday afternoons for the next few weeks, each time with a notebook and pencil in hand and in a familiar role. At twenty-three years old and now two years out of school, I had already had a brief and unremarkable career as a journalist. Beginning in college, I had written for newspapers across western Washington. My grandfather never approved of my first career choice and constantly harped on my low pay and the dangerous nature of the work (inspired by what he saw on Russian television, no doubt). Still, he stored each of my articles in a folder under his bed. My last reporting job had been at a small daily on Washington State's Kitsap Peninsula. Now, the story I found myself confronting was that of my own family, a past that had eluded me all these years.

During our interviews, my grandfather spoke with a certain detachment, as if relating someone else's experiences. Later, he assured me that the death camp he survived was never far from his mind. My questions, he said, had rekindled his long-dormant dreams. "Did I think about it after the war? For all these years I've thought about it," he told me. "How could it have happened? The Germans were a learned people. How could they have taken children and killed them? I can't understand it." Recently, he had seen a Russian television program about the German liner *St. Louis*. In 1939, more than nine hundred Jewish refugees boarded it in Hamburg and sailed across the Atlantic, only to be denied asylum—in Cuba, Florida, and Canada—and forced back to Europe, where 254 of its passengers later died in the Holocaust. "We think now, could something like this really happen again?" my grandfather said. "I get scared when I hear people say it. I remember that it really can. I start remembering everything in my head. And right away, I think of these camps and ghettos. It's frightening."

The ideas I had formed about the Holocaust, from books and movies, left me unprepared for what I was hearing. In late 1941, during one of the coldest winters of the twentieth century, nearly every Jewish resident of Tulchyn, my grandfather's small town in Soviet Ukraine, was sent to a camp in the remote village of Pechera, forcibly marched there on foot. The camp's originators were not Adolf Hitler's henchmen but Romanians sent by the dictator Ion Antonescu, Hitler's Romanian counterpart. The mode of extermination awaiting my grandfather's family and thousands like them was not Zyklon B but a more "experimental" method, as my grandfather and fellow survivors would often put it: starvation, disease, and exposure. The camp's setting was not an isolated complex found at the end of a rail spur, as were the Belzec, Sobibor, and Treblinka killing centers, but the grounds of a former manorial estate in an idyllic village.[2]

The story was full of paradoxes: Ukrainians who both saved and tormented Jews; guards who turned a blind eye to escaping prisoners; escapees who returned to the camp time and time again even after managing to flee. Although seven decades had passed, my grandfather still remembered the precise routes he traveled between villages to beg for food, the number of kilometers separating one village from the next, the names of the guards, the sequencing of key events. With a pencil in his unsteady hand, he sketched the camp's layout on the back of a blue index card. After the first interviews, I began triangulating these memories against secondary sources. I discovered that a report produced by an international Holocaust commission, formed in 2003 after a series of troubling public statements from the Romanian government and chaired by Auschwitz survivor, author, and Nobel Peace Prize laureate Elie Wiesel, concluded that Pechera was among the sites of the "most hideous murders committed against Jews anywhere during the Holocaust."[3] Until now, I had never heard of a place called Pechera, much less that my own grandfather had survived a death camp.

Sitting beside him that spring, I couldn't help but be reminded of the Liev Schreiber–directed movie *Everything Is Illuminated*, based on the novel by Jonathan Safran Foer. In it, the protagonist, played by Elijah Wood—an eccentric, bespectacled type who is also the author's namesake—visits Ukraine to plumb the depths of his family's past only to discover that his late grandfather's shtetl is long gone. The outcome loosely mirrors the author's own real-life trip to Ukraine, where he was disappointed to have found "nothing but nothing."[4] As I would soon learn, the story of Jewish life in my own grandfather's hometown did not end after the Holocaust, a fate often ascribed to small Eastern European communities with large prewar Jewish populations. When my grandfather and fellow survivors were liberated by the Red Army, they returned to places like Tulchyn and remained there for decades. Sometimes, they encountered the very camp guards who had so wronged them as children. Yet their memories of 1941–44 were repressed by a government intent on downplaying the singularity of the Jewish wartime experience. In doing so, the Holocaust was erased from public memory.

When survivors could finally begin speaking out during the late Soviet and early post-communist periods, much of the world had already decided what the Holocaust was. As historian Jeffrey Veidlinger notes, survivors who had left their ancestral homelands during the war or in the first years afterward gave the impression that Eastern Europe's Jewish communities were entirely "lost," that they had "vanished," and that they had been "erased," as prominent books from second- and third-generation survivors would sometimes suggest. Yet my own family's story, like those of tens of thousands of survivors who remained behind in Soviet Ukraine, did not fit this narrative.[5]

In summer 2012, my mother and I visited my eighty-five-year-old great-aunt Etel, my grandfather's older sister, long-since widowed and living alone. She, too, had survived the camp in Pechera. Photos of her son Mitya, her only child, killed in an unexplained military accident at the age of just twenty-one, adorned the walls. Mitya's death, Etel would explain, was one of the two defining tragedies of her life. At one point, she walked to the middle of her living room to demonstrate the effects of starvation on a teen-age body. She imagined the woolen dress she had worn to the death camp, pinched the end of it, and looped it around her waist three times. All these years later, she told us, she still saw German soldiers chasing after her in her sleep. It was strange to be sitting there, chatting and sharing a fruit tart with a woman I had known my entire life—a fixture at holiday gatherings and birthday parties—only to realize that I knew almost nothing about her. "Well go ahead," she said several times that afternoon. "Ask me more questions."

Most weeknights that summer, I walked from the office tower where I now worked to the University of Washington's Suzzallo Library. Under the vaulted ceiling of the famous reading room, I translated and transcribed my interviews, taking notes and highlighting passages. I bought a new backpack to carry the reading material I was now amassing. At home in my spartan apartment, I began listening to testimonies from other survivors interviewed in the late 1990s by the USC Shoah Foundation and the United States Holocaust Memorial Museum, some of whom, as I would later learn, had known my grandfather. I set out to write something—what exactly, I wasn't sure. Within a couple of weeks, the enormity of this undertaking began to weigh on me. I began to doubt that I was the right person for it, that someone else would be better suited for the work. My trips to the library became less frequent. Weeks away turned into months. At one point, my grandfather asked me what I planned to do with what I had learned. I didn't have the heart to tell him I had given up.

During the next few years, I focused on my career and started a family. But Pechera was never far from my mind. Only after becoming a new father did I begin to see the stories I had heard, the stories of child survivors, in a new light. I felt a growing responsibility to make sense of what had happened, to preserve a near-forgotten chapter of the Holocaust—or in the words of scholars Marianne Hirsch and Leo Spitzer, to perform a small act of repair.[6] My spark came late one night in early 2017 when I opened the scratchy audio recordings I had avoided since my grandfather Motl's passing. "You should write this so that no one forgets," I heard him telling me on that Saturday afternoon nearly five years earlier. "So they remember." With my wife and toddler asleep upstairs, I sat at our dining table until the early-morning hours, listening to his voice. My primitive smartphone had captured the hourly chimes of a wall clock, the din of the TV, and my grandmother Anna's occasional sighs from the kitchen. Difficult points during his retellings would sometimes end with her asking us to come to the table to eat or for me to translate a new letter that had come in the mail, details I had long forgotten. For the first time, I began to find the words I had been searching for.

In October 2018, while writing this book, I was reintroduced to Boris Sandler, my grandfather's friend, former schoolmate, and fellow survivor, whom I had first met at the unveiling of my grandfather's memorial a year after he died. When I arrived at Boris's apartment with my mother, he was surprised to hear that I was interested in his story; he had been expecting only to confirm that my grandfather, too, had been imprisoned in Pechera. Seated at his oak dining table, we spoke for two hours. "It was worse than you probably think," he told me at one point. A lap-sized dog flitted in and out of the room and occasionally brushed up against my legs. Boris's son, Sasha, sat on the couch a few feet away watching Russian television. He left the room several times to take phone calls from the patio. Later, unprompted, he told me that he'd never heard his father tell these stories.

At the end of the interview, I shook Boris's hand and thanked him for speaking to me. He then handed me a folder with some documents, including a lengthy newspaper article about his late sister Manya, published twenty years earlier.

"I hope I haven't burdened you today," I added while on my way out.

"No!" he replied in his booming, baritone voice. "You listened. This is a mitzvah."[7]

CHAPTER ONE

Beyond the Dnister

IN JUNE 1941, NEARLY TWO YEARS after the invasion and partition of Poland, three million German troops and hundreds of thousands more from Nazi-allied Romania and Finland launched Operation Barbarossa, a surprise attack on the Soviet Union that would be history's largest military operation. After seizing territories that Romania had lost to the Soviets a year earlier—northern Bukovyna and Bessarabia—Romanian dictator Ion Antonescu's men butchered tens of thousands of Jews living across these reclaimed borderlands. Those Jews who were not murdered outright were confined to ghettos and transit camps. Later that summer, Adolf Hitler granted his Romanian counterpart a neighboring strip of land in occupied Soviet Ukraine. It would be named Transnistria. The Romanians could now force surviving Jews from northern Bukovyna and Bessarabia farther east. There, they would join local Jews already languishing in ghettos and camps.

That summer in Transnistria, the residents of a town called Tulchyn found themselves living under both German and Romanian occupations. The Romanians would eventually expel Tulchyn's Jewish residents—including my maternal grandfather's family—to what became Transnistria's most notorious concentration site, known by its prisoners as the Death Noose. As Axis losses mounted in late 1942 and 1943, it became clear that Antonescu's plan to fully "cleanse" Transnistria of its Jews—by forcing them into Nazi-occupied Ukraine—would never fully materialize. Yet between summer 1941 and spring 1944, Antonescu succeeded in killing hundreds of thousands of innocent civilians while inflicting incalculable suffering on those who defied the odds and survived.

Even Adolf Hitler admired the barbarity of Ion Antonescu, marshal of Romania. On August 19, 1941, with the Axis campaign against the Soviet Union approaching its third month, Hitler observed to his propaganda minister Joseph Goebbels, "As far as the Jewish Question is concerned, it can now be stated with certainty that a man like Antonescu is pursuing much more radical policies in this area than we have so far."[1] Antonescu's regime had been killing Jewish men, women, and children of all ages and had already cleared entire Jewish communities.[2] Meanwhile, Nazi Germany's mobile killing units were targeting only Jewish men in their open-air massacres and needed ever more manpower to meet the growing expectations placed on them.[3]

Seven months earlier, in January 1941, Hitler had divulged to Antonescu the first phase of his then-secret ambitions, the planned Soviet invasion. In June of that year, Antonescu was briefed on Hilter's ultimate goal: extermination of European Jews. Germany and Romania were allied on both fronts. For Hitler, Romania's oil and other natural resources would be vital for the coming assault. For Antonescu, it would be a chance to recover the territories ceded in 1940: northern Bukovyna (present-day southwest Ukraine) and Bessarabia (split between Moldova and Ukraine) to the Soviets, and northern Transylvania to Hungary. This, combined with Romania's precarious position between Nazi Germany and the Soviet Union, Germany's recent victories against the French and British, and Antonescu's own deep-seated anti-Semitism, made the alliance a logical one.[4]

Hitler and Antonescu would meet at least ten times through the summer of 1944.[5] Press photos of the men often depict the five-foot-nine Hitler standing beside or opposite his much slighter, shorter, and older counterpart. It was during their third meeting, on June 12, 1941, staged in Munich just before Antonescu's fifty-ninth birthday, that Hitler confided in him the secret plan to annihilate Eastern European Jewry.[6] The next day, a photo of their handshake was published in the *New York Times*. The revelation showed the extent of the trust Hitler had placed in Antonescu. The men admired one another.[7] And until the late stages of the war, they enjoyed a close relationship—one in which Antonescu did not hesitate to speak his mind, even if that meant contradicting Hitler.[8]

Antonescu would not have to wait for the blueprints of Germany's "Final Solution to the Jewish Question" to be drawn at the Wannsee Conference in January of 1942. Instead, the Romanians drafted a secret directive of their own with its own barely disguised euphemism: the "Cleansing of the Land." The plan would complement Hitler's with a vision of Romania's making. As the scholar Jean Ancel has noted, the guidelines from Antonescu were a "Romanian euphemism for shooting tens of thousands of Jews [from the northern Bukovyna and Bessarabia countryside] and deporting the rest later." Of the countries aligned with Nazi Germany, only Romania initiated its own mass extermination program.[9]

That Romanians had not descended from "the Nordic race" as had Germanic peoples mattered little—at least not yet. To further ingratiate themselves with Hitler, both Ion and Mihai Antonescu, Romania's deputy prime minister and foreign minister, set out to prove that they were just as much anti-Slavic as anti-Semitic. Although these declarations were hardly sincere, they nonetheless won the respect of Hitler, who agreed that the Latin race to which Romanians apparently belonged should join the Germanic race in the war against Jews, Slavs, and Anglo-Saxons.[10]

Romania's path to genocide can be traced to the mid-nineteenth century and the country's modern origins. In 1878, at the Congress of Berlin, the European powers agreed to recognize Romania's independence from the Ottoman Empire on the condition that it extend civil rights to the growing Jewish population. Romania provided similar assurances for Jews and other minorities in 1919 by signing the Treaty of St. Germain with the Allied Powers and in 1923 by granting them citizenship in the new constitution. Romanian cultural and political elites resented these demands. They characterized the urban-dwelling Jewish minority, engaged largely in trade and commerce, as a threat to Romania's national and racial character. Much of the destructive rhetoric that followed, which placed the blame on Jews for the country's problems, persisted through the interwar years. Even in October 1942, Antonescu complained about the 1878 Treaty of Berlin and attempts by foreigners to meddle in Romanian affairs.[11] As leading scholars have noted, what changed over time "was not the nature of the antisemitism they espoused, but the fact that antisemitism had passed from the realm of verbal expression and occasional outbursts of antisemitic violence by private groups or individuals to the realm of government policy and state action."[12] During the Antonescu regime, anti-Semitic propaganda

would make much of the Romanian public indifferent to the killings perpetrated by their government; it also incited many every-day Romanians
to participate in the violence.[13]

Antonescu had long harbored toxic beliefs. The son of an army officer,
he began his military career in 1904. He served in the Second Balkan War
and again in World War I as a cavalry officer, showing great promise. He
would earn the nickname Red Dog for his hair color and volatile temperament.[14] While being considered for the position of Romania's military atta-
ché in Paris in 1920, French general Victor Pétin warned his minister of
war that despite his potential, "Antonescu is extremely vain as regards his
own person and his country, is chauvinistic, xenophobic and I am sure that
we cannot count on him." Antonescu was passed over for the job. Two years
later, he assumed the role anyway when his predecessor had to leave Paris.
Pétin again cited Antonescu's "extreme xenophobia" as among the defining traits "of this strange figure."[15]

Antonescu ascended to power in September 1940 alongside the Iron
Guard—a fascist political party and movement whose members were called
Legionnaires—and he inherited a homegrown anti-Semitic, nationalist ide-
ology. The Romanian Orthodox Church and the country's folklore tradition
had long promoted negative Jewish stereotypes. The church presented Jews
as "divinely accursed creatures ruled by the devil."[16] Other popular myths
about Jews persisted, including the notion that they were responsible for
the Soviet annexations of Bessarabia and northern Bukovyna in 1940, which
had been under Romanian control for more than two decades. Jews were
falsely accused of mistreating the Romanian Army during its withdrawal
from these territories—proof that they were more loyal to the Soviets.[17]

Under Romania's King Carol II and the leaders who preceded Antonescu,
Romania had already passed anti-Semitic laws that stripped many Jewish
citizens of their rights. After Antonescu and the Iron Guard forced Carol II
to abdicate in the wake of the country's humiliating territorial losses and
formed a new government, Antonescu added new laws to further exclude
Jews from Romanian society and to expropriate their property. After the
regime change, unchecked terror swept across Romania. Legionnaires and
mobs murdered, tortured, and humiliated Jewish civilians, enriching themselves by plundering Jewish businesses and confiscating Jewish property.
Antonescu supported the Iron Guard's aims, including the "economic dis-
possession of the Jews and their physical removal," but preferred that it be

done more methodically and "lawfully" and without wrecking the Romanian economy (good relations with Germany were contingent on the availability of Romanian oil).[18]

In January 1941, the Legionnaires staged a rebellion against Antonescu, whom they accused of being too sympathetic to the Jews. They then incited a three-day pogrom, or anti-Jewish riot, in Bucharest. Hundreds of Jews were robbed, terrorized, or savagely tortured and killed by Legionnaires and local citizens. Jewish homes, business, and synagogues were set ablaze. After suppressing the coup and repressing the Legionnaires, Antonescu controlled the government. The violent outbursts of the previous few months, which had now abated, would soon be replaced with a centralized, state-sponsored plan for mass death.[19] In April 1941, as Romania readied itself for war and to recapture northern Bukovyna and Bessarabia, Antonescu provided the clearest picture yet of his intentions: "I give the mob complete license to slaughter them [Jews]. I withdraw to my fortress, and after the slaughter I restore order," he said.[20] Though an obscure figure outside Romania, Antonescu would rank second only to Hitler for orchestrating the most Jewish deaths during the Holocaust: more than four hundred thousand in all.[21] Of the twenty-five thousand Roma also sent to Transnistria by the Romanians, eleven thousand died.[22]

In the early morning of June 22, 1941, 585,000 Romanian troops belonging to the third-largest Axis army joined German forces in breaching the Soviet border and opening an 1,800-mile front. Some of the Romanians were well-acquainted with the immediate terrain in northern Bukovyna and Bessarabia and the whereabouts of Jewish populations, having served in these rural areas as recently as the year prior, before Romania's exit. Their rapid advance preceded a first wave of violence. This plan was carried out by the Romanian Army and its gendarmes (military policemen), in tandem with the German Army and Einsatzgruppe D, one of the four mobile battalions formed to protect the rear and butcher Jews in the Soviet Union.[23] Antonescu's "cleansing" of Bessarabia and northern Bukovyna—by murder or detainment and deportation—was portrayed as a fight against communism, in which Jews were cast as the "the spearhead of Bolshevism."[24] It was enacted the moment Romanian forces arrived and "under no German pressure."[25]

Ion Antonescu's men used an improvised brand of terror in the East that contrasted with the industrial and bureaucratic method of mass murder that would be adopted in German killing centers, beginning in Chelmno, Poland, later that year. For the Romanians, this generally meant on-the-spot shootings of a town's Jewish inhabitants or their transport to a nearby site for slaughter (also carried out by individuals with firearms). This hands-on and personal method resembled Hitler's tactics in the Soviet Union, where nearly half of Nazi Germany's victims died, most often by bullets but also in gas vans.[26]

Yet as Holocaust historian Radu Ioanid explains in his revelatory book, *The Holocaust in Romania*, Antonescu's approach came from a government "hardly capable of organizing systematic extermination" and "indecision, contradictory orders, bureaucracy (in all of the negative sense of the word) . . . as well as the personal motivations of thousands of individual perpetrators." Ionid writes that Antonescu's methods more closely resemble those used in "Cambodia under Pol Pot or the ethnic cleansing of the Yugoslav wars than with the industrial killing processes of the Third Reich."[27] Even the stated goal of redistributing Jewish wealth to the Romanian state could not be fully realized, a result of widespread corruption starting at the lowest ranks; the gendarmes often robbed Jews and kept the spoils for themselves.[28]

Throughout the reclaimed territories, informants and volunteers turned on neighbors and became collaborators. In the Bukovyna settlement of Hertsa, a local fiddler pointed out the homes of 1,500 Jews. Elsewhere, priests did the same.[29] When Jews were identified, they were assembled or arrested and then massacred, often with the aid of local populations. The rape of women and girls became commonplace. Some Jews were rounded up and taken into the woods to be shot; others were gunned down near their homes. In one instance, a man's body "was cut into pieces, and his blood was smeared on the axles of carriages." The heinous nature of the killings drew the condemnation of the German Army.[30]

As the violence raged on into July, Mihai Antonescu addressed his fellow cabinet members. He reveled in the opportunity at hand:

> I don't know how many centuries will pass before the Romanian people meet again with such total liberty of action, such opportunity for ethnic cleansing and national revision . . . This is a time when we are masters of our land. Let us use it. If necessary, shoot your machine guns. I couldn't care less if history will recall us as barbarians. . . . I

take formal responsibility and tell you there is no law. . . . So, no formalities, complete freedom.[31]

The sheer number of victims soon presented a problem that the Romanians either had not anticipated or were not interested in addressing: burying the dead. This, combined with their habit of pillaging and accepting bribes from local Jewish populations, offended even German sensibilities; they routinely complained about the Romanians' conduct, going so far as to question whether their Romanian partners were right for the job. A German chief of the security police sent this missive to foreign minister Joachim von Ribbentrop:

The way in which the Romanians are dealing with the Jews lacks any method. No objections could be raised against the numerous executions of Jews, but the technical preparations and the executions themselves were totally inadequate. The Romanians usually left the victims' bodies where they were shot, without trying to bury them. The Einsatzkommandos issued instructions to the Romanian police to proceed somewhat more systematically in this matter.[32]

In Bessarabia, the task of burying the dead sometimes fell to the locals, who willingly assisted when invited by the gendarmes and town leaders to help. As columns of Jews were being marched to their deaths, peasants often followed close behind. Once the Jews were shot, the peasants would bury them with the tools they had brought from home. Clothes and other items recovered from the corpses were theirs to keep, while the gendarmes claimed money and valuables for themselves.[33]

The violence was not limited to Bukovyna and Bessarabia. Within Romania's prewar boundaries, Jews from the northeastern city of Iași (Jassy), one of the country's most important Jewish cultural centers, were subjected to some of the Holocaust's most heinous acts. Situated just ten miles west of the former border with the Soviet Union, half of Iași's prewar population of one hundred thousand was Jewish.[34] It was home to the country's oldest surviving synagogue, built in the late seventeenth century, and more than a hundred others. Days before an anti-Semitic fervor swept the city, the Romanian military coordinated the digging of two trenches in a nearby Jewish cemetery. Then, on June 24 and June 26, Soviet air raids sent the city into a panic. The attacks played into the hands of a national government already mobilizing hundreds of army personnel, gendarmes, and the city's police force for the chaos ahead. Uniformed Romanians and ordinary civilians alike were emboldened to commit barbaric acts. Mobs chased Jews from their homes so the abandoned houses could be more easily looted. In one instance, a hospital mortician gained entry to a Jewish home by clubbing a man and pulling his wife to the street by her hair. An actor with the National Theater requested that an entire family be massacred so he could take over a grocery store they operated next door to his business, which he had long coveted. Thousands of Jews, some in pajamas, were rounded up and marched to police headquarters, where they were gunned down. All personal effects—even down to even their pens—were later stripped from the corpses.[35]

Survivors were taken to the train station, where they were forced to lay face down on the platform. They were then packed into sealed trains that had been used to transport carbide and that still emitted an overpowering odor. One of the death trains followed the same route repeatedly in the summer heat, its purpose clear: to torture those aboard. These crimes resulted in the death of nearly fourteen thousand people.[36]

By July 30, hardly any living Jews remained in the 441 villages and small towns of northern Bukovyna and Bessarabia. Most Jews residing in villages were murdered. Tens of thousands of surviving Jews from towns and urban centers were imprisoned in ghettos or transit camps before they could be deported to the East.[37] As with other stages of the Romanian-led "cleansing," their internment was carried out haphazardly. The Romanian chief military prosecutor, describing the condition of the more than three thousand people he had observed in four Bessarabian camps, wrote, "There is no one to guard them. There is no one to feed them. Please tell [us] what to do with these Jews." Jews were forced to sell their things to locals in exchange for food or to subsist on puddle water and roadside plants.[38] Without food or water and with disease quickly spreading among them, more than seventeen thousand Jews died in August alone in transit camps or while being deported.[39]

In the immediate term, Antonescu's plan for the Jews of northern Bukovyna and Bessarabia assumed a rapid retreat by the Red Army, allowing him to drive surviving Jews farther east into occupied Soviet Ukraine before passing them off to the Germans. By August, the easternmost boundary under Romanian occupation—and the furthest that Germans would allow Antonescu to concentrate the deported—was marked by the Dnister River. On the river's eastern banks, the Einsatzgruppe D had decimated local Ukrainian Jews by the tens of thousands.

On August 30, 1941, in an agreement reached between the governments of Bucharest and Berlin and in appreciation of Romania's involvement in the Soviet invasion, Hitler gifted the Antonescu administration a sixteen-thousand-square-mile sliver of captured land in occupied Ukraine, a territory about twice the size of Massachusetts bounded by the Dnister River in the west, the Southern Buh River in the east, the Black Sea coastline in the south, and the Lyadova River in the north. The northern demarcation line was finalized in early September, when Hitler approved Antonescu's request to have the towns of Tulchyn, Mohyliv-Podilskyi, and Zhmerynka included on the Romanian side.[40] The resulting territory would be called Transnistria, meaning "beyond the River Nistru." Its borders, which were arbitrary, had no historical, cultural, or demographic basis.[41] Yet the Romanians now had the distinction of being the only non-German power to rule over a large swath of occupied Soviet land.[42]

The August understanding gave Antonescu permission to evacuate the Jews of Bessarabia and Bukovyna to Transnistria, but no farther east than the Southern Buh River to avoid overwhelming the Einsatzgruppen, which, along with the German and Romanian armies, had by this point executed more than one hundred thousand of Transnistria's 331,000 local Jews. The fate of the remaining Ukrainian Jews and the 150,000 deportees arriving from Bessarabia and Bukovyna in the months ahead would be sealed with an order from Antonescu in early October 1941: "All the Jews in Transnistria will be immediately imprisoned in the camps on the [Buh] established by the governor of Transnistria. . . . Their estates will be taken over by the local authorities." Antonescu made no arrangements for the Jews' basic needs during the deportations and internment of late 1941 and early 1942, with the expectation that "the Jews will live on their own."[43] The aim was extermination, if not by starvation, thirst, disease, and exposure then by the waiting Germans, for whom victory seemed assured and whose methods of assembly-line mass murder grew ever closer to implementation.[44]

CHAPTER TWO

The Death Noose

O N A THURSDAY MORNING IN SEPTEMBER 1942, a thirteen-year-old boy sat on the lawn of a death camp in the occupied Soviet village of Pechera, Ukraine, awaiting a long-rumored massacre. An hour later, still seated beside his family, he made one last plea: for God to steer the bullets through his head and heart first. Though he had never been more frightened, what the boy dreaded most was not his own death but the possibility of living long enough to see the gunfire consume the lives of his mother, brother, and two sisters before it ended his.

The boy, Motl Braverman, my grandfather, was growing restless. What remained of his muscle and fat stores did little to cushion him from the ground below. As he alternated between sitting and lying down, he scratched where the scabies mites had burrowed into his skin. Over his sore-pocked body were the clothes he had reduced to rags from continuous wear. His thoughts drifted to his missing father, to the home his family had been forced to leave behind, to the injustice of being marooned in this place. He had last eaten a day ago—two fistfuls of bread from the loaf a villager had slipped through a fence for his family—and now the familiar gnawing in his belly had returned. Many of the fellow prisoners sprawled out around him wept. Some prayed. Motl saw a man binding tefillin to his head and arm. He overheard a group whispering about the need for someone—anyone—among these thousands to live to tell their story.

From what the prisoners could tell, the camp's Romanian overseers and the German death squad that had arrived to carry out the massacre were at an impasse. No one seemed to know why. Survivors recalled decades later that at first, a single German lory idled at the entrance. Then, several more pulled in behind it. The first prisoners to board the trucks did so on their own initiative, volunteering to be shuttled to the execution site first, their will to live having long been exhausted. A mass of seated detainees now stretched from the interior courtyard to the guardhouse at the camp gate's main gate. They all waited to be sent to their deaths.

Just days earlier, a handful of the village's Ukrainian inhabitants had approached the camp's walls and gates to warn the likely victims, some of whom they had hired for odd jobs, others of whom they had befriended. They explained that three villages of people had been enlisted to dig trenches in some distant woods, and they described the processions of men and women carrying shovels. As one rumor had it, the camp's children would be shot and the adults trucked away by the Germans for labor. Other versions foretold a complete slaughter.

The camp stood on a wooded bluff overlooking the Southern Buh, along a stretch of river that kinked between the villages of Pechera and Sokilets. The river marked the boundary between Transnistria, the Romanian zone of occupation, and the vast German-controlled territory known as Reichskommissariat Ukraine. Stone walls that began near the riverbanks in Pechera sloped up the hillside and encircled the camp before meeting the iron gate that marked its entrance. The grounds had once belonged to one of Poland's most famous noble families, the Potockis, before mobs destroyed their palace in late 1917.[1] A government sanitorium was built on the foundation of the former palace and began serving Soviet war veterans stricken with tuberculosis, one of the three hundred sanitariums operating in Soviet Ukraine at the time.[2] According to the medical wisdom of the day, the restorative powers of unspoiled air and tranquil surroundings held the keys to recovery.

The property's prior uses stood in eerie contrast with the events of 1941–44, when about eleven thousand Jewish prisoners passed through the camp's entrance.[3] They were deprived of food, water, adequate shelter, medical care, and sanitation. The words "death camp" displayed on a wooden board above the iron gate made the Romanians' intentions clear to new arrivals.[4] The camp was one of two hundred concentration sites organized across Transnistria, each intended as temporary holding pens where populations would thin out on their own.[5] Romanian authorities trusted that further military momentum by their German allies would allow them to send survivors east across the Buh and into German hands, thereby clearing their newly gained Soviet territory of Jews.[6]

The camp's stranglehold on the prisoners confined there inspired a name that survivors would recall decades later: Myertvaya Petlya, or the Death Noose. As the story went, prisoners often descended to the Buh in groups to collect drinking water. Some were fortunate enough to have brought bottles, jars, and buckets. Others filled their shoes or steeped clothes that could be wrung out later. While on the banks, the prisoners reflected on camp life and almost always about the madness of being left to roam between the stone walls. One day, a young woman put words to the indignation they had all felt and coined the nickname. This was, after all, where the living were trapped and only the dead could leave.[7] The noose grew ever tighter around the necks of prisoners the longer they remained living. True to its name, four in five prisoners would perish.[8]

The first 3,005 Jews sent to Pechera came from the town of Tulchyn, fifteen miles to the south.[9] They included my grandfather Motl, along with his sisters, Etel, fourteen, and Manya, six; his brother, Lova, two; and his parents and maternal grandfather. Not long after they were herded to Pechera in December 1941, villagers approached the camp intending to barter with the starving Jews. Initially, this bazaar took place at the camp's main iron gate, in full view of the Ukrainian policemen, local collaborators who had been recruited to guard the camp, before being moved to a side gate.[10] For many Jewish families, trading away the last of their belongings for scraps of food was their only recourse. For the villagers, trading with Jews may well have been their only opportunity to find clothes, shoes, linens, and other fabrics, which were all difficult to come by in wartime. While this contact was not expressly permitted by the Ukrainian camp guards, it continued to take place, one of the many contradictions that enabled a small fraction of the prisoners to survive. At the gates, a family could turn scraps of fabric into two loaves of bread, or a gold ring into beetroot with bread and potatoes.

Some days, Soybil Braverman, Motl's mother, and Idel Braverman, Motl's father, would venture to the side gate to trade one of their few remaining items for food. They came especially early on a Monday morning in September 1942 with Idel's jacket. Their four children remained sleeping in room 37 of the main camp building, which they shared with a few dozen prisoners. The steady hum of the Buh's rapids was suddenly interrupted by a woman's piercing screams. Motl awoke to a fellow prisoner standing at the near window and pointing at German trucks entering the camp. They had just crossed into Pechera on a nearby bridge that spanned the Buh.

From his room's window, Motl and the others watched as the first lorry approached the camp's main square along a tree-lined driveway. This incited panic on the third floor. With his siblings still asleep just feet away and his parents nowhere to be found, Motl's first inclination was to run. Days earlier, his parents had reasoned that if the rumors were true, then only he stood a chance at escaping, and it would be better for just one of their children to survive than none at all. On this day, following through on his promise meant leaving his sleeping sisters and brother behind. In the corridor, it meant ignoring the outstretched arms of ailing prisoners who were slumped against the walls, pleading for food. And it meant averting his gaze from the swollen corpses piling up on the landings of the stairwell, which had become a makeshift morgue. On his way down to ground level, he passed other prisoners who were doing the opposite: retreating to their rooms and away from the Germans.

Once outside, he ran toward a familiar section of the camp's stone wall, near the stairs leading down to the Buh. But before he could reach it, he locked eyes with the camp guard Smetansky, a Ukrainian policeman who was patrolling the camp's rear on the footpath ahead. Although not especially tall or physically imposing, Smetansky was widely regarded as the most sadistic of the guards, a man with an explosive temper who seemed to truly delight in clubbing women, children, and the elderly for infractions real and imagined. He gained notoriety for shooting Jews attempting to accept food from villagers, including a Bessarabian prisoner buying a bucket of cherries, an incident long remembered by prisoners and non-Jews alike.[11]

Motl's family experienced Smetansky's wrath on several occasions. One episode was seared into Motl's memory—the time Smetansky threw him, his mother, and his mother's friend to the ground and bludgeoned them for attempting to escape, stopping only when he was too tired to continue. Soybil shielded her face as best she could, only for Smetansky to shatter the bones in one of her arms. Soybil's friend later died from her injuries, according to a separate retelling from Etel. When not in a murderous mood, Smetansky was known to knock buckets full of water out of the hands of weary prisoners to amuse himself, forcing them to muster what little energy they had left for another trip to the Buh and back.[12]

Although Motl was in full view of his tormentor once more, the man looked disoriented, as if the presence of a dozen or so Germans had taken him by surprise. Until now, the Germans had not been seen in the Pechera camp during its first months in operation. Like the Romanians, they feared catching typhus.[13] Sensing Smetansky's confusion, Motl bolted for a different a section of the wall. After clearing it, he skidded down the hillside toward the Buh. At the river's edge, he noticed a young woman, maybe eighteen at most, who sat reading a book.

"Save yourself! The Nazis are here!" he screamed.

She stared back at him with indifference, as if unaware that Germans perched on a hill across the Buh in Sokilets liked to use prisoners for target practice as they gathered water or bathed. He was struck by how well-dressed she was. And her hair—it was still being cared for.

"Girl, are you a Jew or not?" he finally asked her.

"What's it to you?" she shot back.

"It's nothing. Don't you know? The Germans are here."

He decided that she must have been one of the newcomers from the ghetto in Mohyliv-Podilskyi, a town in northwest Transnistria that had become a major transit point for Jews being forced across the Dnister. Three thousand of them had been transferred to the camp only weeks earlier.[14] It seemed to Motl that only a new arrival could still maintain some semblance of human dignity. Had their paths crossed under less dire circumstances, or even several months earlier, Motl may well have remained at her side, doing more to convince her to run. But now, attuned only to his own survival, he could think of only thing: reaching the opposite riverbank. He waded into the frigid waters alone, climbed atop a boulder jutting out from the current, and leapt across to a few others until he reached a river islet overrun by brush.

No sooner had he stumbled onto land than a man approached him. He helped Motl to his feet.

"Boy, where are you from?" the man asked while studying his ashen face and body.

"I'm from this side, from Sokilets. I was trying to fish," Motl said, his teeth chattering.

Only then did he realize that in his rush to escape, he had forgotten a shirt. His wet, tattered pants clung to his legs.

"Do you know what's happening up there?" the man asked, gesturing toward the camp.

"I wouldn't know. I only came to fish."

Sensing that the man's questions had been satisfied, Motl retreated into a dense thicket. He found a sturdy tree and hoisted himself onto a branch. He was now shivering uncontrollably from cold and fear. As the sound of shouting and gunfire echoed from beyond the river, he imagined the worst, that Lova and Manya were frightened and that he had seen his family for the last time. It was hard to gather much of anything from his vantage point.

Inside the camp, many prisoners' worst fears were being realized. The Germans had ordered everyone outside. Those too weak or too sick to leave their rooms or who had been found hiding in the cellars were executed on the spot. Everyone else was lined up and sorted. The most able-bodied men, women, and teenagers were singled out and ordered onto Germans trucks. Unbeknownst to them and any remaining loved ones, they were about to be transferred to slave labor camps east of the Buh, where they were almost certain to die in the months to come.

For the camp's survivors, that ill-fated day and its labor selections continued to evoke visceral memories decades later. "Puddles of blood, the thumping of the Germans' boots, the barking of the dogs, shots, Germans' screams," recalled child survivor Mikhail Bartik.[15] A recurring scene in survivor testimony is that of the death squad members pulling infants and toddlers from their mothers' arms. These Germans are remembered for kicking the children into the air or slamming them into walls and trees, with their mothers fighting in vain to free themselves from their captors and fellow prisoners looking on helplessly.

Fifteen-year-old Reizia Vainblat of Tulchyn was assigned to one of the groups marked for deportation. While seated inside a truck that day, she spotted her aunt near the fountain. "At that moment," she recalled, "my aunt crawls away from the fountain on all fours and screams, 'Rozochka!' as if to say goodbye to me, and a German takes out his gun and shoots her in the head. Brains fly in every direction."[16]

At dusk, Motl heard the German trucks roar to life. The soldiers were belting their brutish victory songs. Then came more screams. A few final shots rang out. Motl sat peering through the branches and waited until the last of the trucks crossed back into German territory. To his surprise, he began to see children and adults gathering across the river. But it was hard to be sure. He eased himself back to the ground and swam to them. He saw his friend Arkadii's mother in the crowd. She urged him to get back to Soybil, who had been searching for him on the grounds above.

At the foot of the former sanitorium building, another group was congregating. They watched fellow prisoners remove bodies that had been stacked near window wells to the basement, waiting, perhaps, to see whether their own loved ones would turn up among the dead. Motl began to stare too—until he saw the familiar outline of a woman in the growing crowd. It was his mother. He ran toward her and put his hand to her back. She grabbed him and wept, asking where he had been. She and Etel were convinced that Motl was in one of the mounds. As they staggered up the front stairway and back to their room, where the other Braverman children were waiting, Soybil described how some Germans had taken his father away. Twenty-eight people were shot for not reporting to the courtyard, she told him, and many of them in the head at close range.

The events of the following two days, a Tuesday and Wednesday, only heightened Motl's fears. Not only were there more Ukrainian policemen, but now, the place was teeming with uniformed Romanian gendarmes. In their coats, they were far more imposing than the Ukrainians, who dressed no differently than the male peasantry and were distinguishable only by their armbands.[17] The same week, he watched a new wave of prisoners— more than eight hundred in all—arrive from a ghetto in the village of Rohizna, where Jews from the town of Shpykiv, as well as Pechera's few Jewish families, had been held.[18] Motl saw them rejoice at the sight of their relatives and friends, probably, he guessed, because they were not yet privy to the Germans' plans.

In room 37, Soybil reminded Motl and Etel that should the Germans return, their odds of survival would be better if they ran than if they remained with their family. It would be pointless for her, in her weakened state, to attempt any kind of getaway with Manya and Lova in her arms, she said. She asked that her oldest children think only of themselves and to run as fast and as hard as they could from the armed men and not to look back. With luck, a compassionate family beyond the camp's walls would take them in, she reassured them. With that, they shared what may have been their last loaf of bread, a gift from a Ukrainian woman who had warned them about the trenches.

On Thursday morning, in room 8 of the main camp building, a mother and father were consoling their daughters, six-year-old Shelia Vaisman and her sister, Raisa. During the selection earlier that week, soldiers tore young children from their mothers' arms. One of the men proceeded to kick an infant into the air as if he were a soccer ball. The child fell to the ground and died. Seeing this, Shelia asked her father if she too would be killed this way. She then fainted at his feet. Three days later, Shelia and her sister were still distraught and refused to leave their corner of the room. Their parents' latest pleas were interrupted by the return of the Germans. Chaos engulfed the camp once more. In Shelia's room, an older girl from the Kamenbrodsky family, who was about sixteen at the time, announced that she intended to escape. Shelia's mother begged her to follow the girl. Crying and screaming, Shelia clung to the girl's dress as they both ran outside, where the older girl was shot dead before Shelia's eyes.[19]

As instructed, Motl and Etel planned to run for the wall just as Motl had done earlier that week. But when they emerged from their building's back entryway, they were overwhelmed by the number of armed men who had arrived to fortify the camp. Etel recognized some of the death squad members from the Monday selection. According to Radu Ioanid, they likely belonged to the SS-affiliated Sonderkommando Russland, an extermination unit comprised of local ethnic Germans whose families had settled in what became Soviet Ukraine in the eighteenth and nineteenth centuries.[20]

The men again proceeded to search the camp as they had three days earlier. Everyone was ordered to gather their things and to stack them near the stone fountain in the square. Outside, the engines started, the trucks lurched forward, and thousands of prisoners shuffled along behind them toward the gate. Soybil held Lova in her arms while the three older children walked beside her. Farther ahead, someone cynically addressed a prisoner named Yankel—a pious older man who had become known for little sayings that boosted camp morale—and asked for his assessment.

"Well, Reb Yankel, now you see that the end has come."

"We still don't know what fate has in store for us," he answered. "An hour before the evening is not yet evening."[21]

What happened next has long defied explanation. The Romanians locked the gate, and the trucks never left the camp. After hours of uncertainty,

Pechera's Jewish prisoners were spared. Motl later heard from other prisoners that the camp's Romanian commander, Sergeant Major Stratulat, was stationed nine miles away in Shpykiv when he was alerted to the Germans' plan. One prevailing theory shared by camp survivors was that Stratulat had fallen in love with the beautiful Paulina Zeltser, a prisoner from Bukovyna or Bessarabia known by her diminutive name Polya, and that she had convinced him to step in.[22] In his retellings, Motl was convinced that the reason it took Stratulat so long to halt the massacre was the time it took for him to drive to Pechera. After the war, many survivors also reported hearing that Stratulat personally appealed to Ion Antonescu himself. Others suggested that the gendarmes had called the local district prefect, who in turn called Transnistria's governor Gheorghe Alexianu for guidance.[23] One survivor reported that Stratulat went so far as to send King Mihai (Michael) of Romania a telegram begging him to end the bloodshed.[24] Historian Radu Ioanid attributes these theories to hearsay and doubts that Stratulat would have ever asked the king or the highest echelons of the Antonescu regime for permission to intervene. As a low-level official, it would not have been Stratulat's place to elevate the issue to Antonescu.[25]

Even without Antonescu's input in Pechera in September 1942, Stratulat may have been within his rights to thwart the Germans. Aside from the massacres taking place in southern Transnistria, the gendarmes were not beholden to "the wish of a dictator or the signature of a bureaucrat" when deciding if a group of Jews should live or die.[26] The Antonescu regime provided few specifics for how Transnistrian Jews should be treated. If orders were handed down, they were given orally or via handwritten correspondence, which mostly disappeared.[27] The whims of junior military personnel often provided all the justification that would be required. Such was the disordered nature of the Holocaust in Transnistria and the reclaimed territories, where Romanian and German orders could clash and where Romanian directives often conflicted with or contradicted one another.[28]

At any rate, with Polya standing behind him and acting as his translator, Stratulat addressed the surviving prisoners, many of whom had resigned themselves to dying.

"Home! To your homes!" Stratulat implored to the expressionless faces staring back at him.[29]

"None of us understood the Romanian. We didn't understand him, we were from Ukraine," remembered survivor Riza Roitman. "[Polya] then translated. She said in Yiddish, 'Jews, you have a mighty God. You were supposed to be annihilated, but you are left living. You can return to your places.'"[30]

For the time being, the mass graves remained unfilled. Instead of jubilation, there was silence.

"For a while afterward, people were hesitant to disperse," recalled Mikhail Bartik. "Many were hoping to have quickly parted with such a life. This wasn't a life—this was a tragedy."[31]

Privately, others rejoiced, eventually dedicating songs in tribute to Polya.[32] But there was also an immediate matter to attend to that Thursday afternoon: rummaging through the belongings that remained near the fountain, items that proved to be the difference between life and death in the winter months ahead.

CHAPTER THREE

Tulchyn

T HE WANING DAYS OF SPRING 1941 had been as carefree as any
for the two eldest Braverman children. With his fifth-grade year behind
him, Motl was rarely home for long. He and other boys living on Tulchyn's
Voikova Street often challenged rival factions from the surrounding neighborhoods to games of soccer. None of the boys had ever owned a ball—
that is, until one of them produced a stocking from his mother's wardrobe
and others filled it with their spare rags. Provocations during the matches
led to rock throwing and the occasional broken window. One day, the
Voikova boys decided to dam a nearby creek, which made for a memorable afternoon swim.

With his shock of coarse black hair—which often stood on end, as if
stiffened by electric current—and prominent eyebrows, he was just coming into his own. As much as he loved the warm summer months, Motl
already had grand ambitions for fall and winter. He thought often about
darting around on the pair of fence posts he had chiseled into skis. The
previous January, they had allowed him to conquer the snowy knolls on
the edge of town with his friends. He hoped to venture farther into the
countryside, where the steeper hills would allow for even more daring
descents.

Etel had been looking forward to traveling that summer, a well-earned
break from caring for Manya and Lova and from other household respon-
sibilities that she, like most first-born daughters in large Jewish families,
often assumed. That June, she visited her aunt Yeva in the city of Vinnytsia, nearly forty miles to the north. She wore one of her favorite dresses to
the bus station and applied a fresh coat of lipstick before boarding. Despite

being born into a family of modest means, she took great care to dress fashionably, a habit she would maintain into old age. It helped that her father, Idel, a tailor, occasionally salvaged spare cuts of fabric and repurposed them into garments for his wife and children. She wore the few outfits that she owned with immense pride.

Just past noon on June 22, as the petite, dark-haired Etel sat on a park bench with her family in Vinnytsia, a man came bounding down the street in their direction. "War! War!" he shouted at anyone who would listen. News of the day's early-morning invasion, which saw Axis troops cross unimpeded into Soviet territory, had just reached the public that afternoon, a full eight hours after it began. Stalin, who sounded "disoriented and incoherent" when he was first notified by telephone, deferred to his foreign minister to make the first announcement by radio.[1]

"The government of the Soviet Union expresses the firm conviction that the whole population of our country . . . must now stand solid and united as never before," Vyacheslav Molotov said. Afterward, as "lighthearted" songs filled Soviet airwaves,[2] many state officials abandoned their posts or prioritized the evacuation of industrial plants over that of civilian populations.[3] Jews living in the border regions were unaware of the grave danger that specifically awaited them. A German intelligence officer stationed in Belorussia later said as much in his report, adding that Soviet Jews "believe . . . that we shall leave them in peace if they mind their own business and work diligently."[4]

"My goodness, how scary it was," Etel said of her reaction to learning of the attack that summer day. "Right there, I immediately yelled to my aunt, 'I want to go home!'"

"We need to evacuate, Etel," her aunt Yeva said.

"I screamed, 'No, I don't need any evacuation. I want to go home.'"

Yeva brought her to the bus depot the next morning, though no buses came. Her uncle Misha, who would also soon be deployed to the front, spent the next night in line and managed to buy her a ticket for the last bus to Tulchyn. That afternoon, she arrived to find that most of the town's storefront windows had been smashed. Jewish shops and homes were being looted. She watched as residents dragged sacks of stolen goods behind them.

Days before the start of the German occupation in July 1941, unending columns of retreating Soviet troops—filthy, dejected, and often wounded—coursed through the town of Tulchyn. Seated on her living room sofa more than seventy years later, Etel recalled how one of the men described the battlefront: "He said he'd just returned from a burning meat grinder." Yet the town's Jewish residents, like millions of Soviet citizens huddled around their radios, were reassured that the Axis invasion would soon be quelled.

In a July 3, 1941, radio address, Soviet leader Joseph Stalin claimed that "the best German divisions and air force units had already been smashed and had found their grave on the fields of battle."[5] In Tulchyn, the low-flying German planes Etel saw suggested otherwise. Plumes of smoke billowed from burning factories and distant military posts, likely a product of Stalin's scorched-earth policy. Germany and its Axis allies had already traveled 350 miles into the Soviet interior.[6]

The Molotov-Ribbentrop Pact signed by Hitler and Stalin two years earlier—before their joint attack on Poland launched World War II on the European continent—was supposed to have preserved peace between the superpowers. Instead, the German-led invasion caught both the Red Army and civilian populations by surprise. Heeding the lessons of Napoleon's defeat nearly 130 years earlier, Hitler intended to conquer much of the Soviet Union in a matter of months, and crucially, before the onset of winter. In Tulchyn, the gravity of the moment became apparent when the older boys and men were drafted into the Red Army, leaving a town of mostly children, women, and the elderly to fend for themselves.[7] Like most Soviet Jewish populations, Tulchyn's residents had little to no knowledge of how Jews in Germany and Poland were being treated.[8] That was no accident. The Molotov-Ribbentrop Pact mandated that all criticism of Germany be censored within Soviet borders.[9] For many people, hearsay from neighbors and other residents was considered more reliable than what was transmitted over the radio.[10]

Amid the confusion in the first days of war, Tulchyn's streets and the roads leading out of town were choked with horse-drawn carts and people. The Soviet government and the local administration provided little guidance on whether to evacuate.[11] Tulchyn's Jewish families agonized over the decision.

"We wanted to evacuate. But where to? It wasn't possible," Etel recounted. "Mom went to an acquaintance who worked for the town council. He says to us, 'No one is going to harm you. Stay where are you. Take a bag of flour.'

Even if we wanted to leave then, we couldn't. Those that could have left already had."

As German forces neared Tulchyn, twelve-year-old Mikhail Bartik crossed paths with a family friend and conscript who was headed to the war front. A coachman by trade, he shared some parting words with Mikhail and a few others nearby, which a tearful Mikhail recounted during a 1994 interview.

"My dear people," he announced that day. "A black plague is coming. We are all goners. Salvation is unlikely. Run, save yourselves."

"But there was nothing to save ourselves with," Bartik said. "It was a hopeless situation."[12]

In Tulchyn, which had no train station, many tried to flee. Eleven-year-old Boris Sandler and his family left for Zhuravlivka, about ten miles west, hoping to catch a train. Hearing that the station had been overwhelmed by Soviet conscripts, they attempted to reach a train station in Demkivka, where someone announced over a loudspeaker that the crowd should disperse because the station was likely to be targeted in an air raid. After being forced back to Tulchyn, Boris's family was undeterred. They evacuated again ten days day after the outbreak of war. Boris, his fifteen-year-old sister Manya, his one-year-old brother Pyotr, and his parents all boarded a horse-drawn carriage. This time, the Sandlers journeyed to the east, braving uneven terrain and steep ascents. Bombings by German aircraft left their ears ringing. Artillery shells whirred overhead. Bodies dotted the countryside. Occasionally, they encountered charred Soviet military trucks on the roadside. The route they had chosen led them through Haisyn and Uman, both of which would soon fall to Nazi forces. Along the way, they picked up Boris's older cousin.[13]

One night, the Sandlers came to a small bridge. By the looks of it, the original span had collapsed under the weight of a tank. A flimsier replacement made of timber nearly buckled under the Sandlers' cart. A steady rain fell on the travelers in the darkness. Some days later, they passed a series of food stands along a dirt road. The locals were selling bread and cheese, but they refused to accept the Sandlers' Soviet rubles and insisted only on bartering. With nothing to offer them, Boris and Manya's parents had no choice but to press on.

"This was our first taste of hunger," Boris recalled.

Weeks into their journey, they managed to reach a town along the Dnieper River, near Kremenchuk, where gunfire seemed to emanate from all sides. Their cart overturned, and the Sandlers found themselves in an open field. Dazed, they watched as two uniformed Red Army officers approach them. The men asked for any spare civilian clothing that the Sandlers might have. In return, they introduced the Sandlers to a woman living in a nearby home, who emerged with a warm kettle of borscht. Under her care, the Sandlers remained in hiding for the next three days. On the fourth, the woman's husband had a change of heart.

"That's it. Pack up, *zhidy*," he insisted, using the Russian pejorative for Jews. "The Germans are here to take care of us. For you, there's no salvation. Go where you want."

With nowhere to turn, the Sandlers purchased a blind horse and cart from a garbage collector. They were intercepted by Germans almost immediately and were forced to turn back, a common outcome for evacuees.[14] They then joined the masses of captured refugees on the road home. Germans aimed their whips at passing carts and hurled insults at the passengers. But the occupying soldiers saved far worse for the growing number of local Jews over whom they now presided. As the Sandlers passed through Kirovohrad (now Kropyvnytskyi), Boris heard someone yell out, "Get going! What are you waiting for?" Thousands of the city's Jewish residents would soon be slaughtered in the first of several planned mass-murder operations, which would destroy a community that was once home to fourteen thousand Jews.[15]

During the month-long return trip to Tulchyn, the Sandlers proceeded through Uman's still-smoldering woods. From his seat, Boris could see bodies strewn about on the road. Peering deeper into the forest, the extent of the carnage came into focus. The dead littered the landscape. The Sandlers' passage had coincided with the end of the disastrous Battle of Uman, which saw the Germans encircle and destroy the Sixth and Twelfth Soviet Armies, kill more than seventy-nine thousand soldiers,[16] and capture another hundred thousand prisoners of war.[17] Yet the fighting continued around them. Like Kirovohrad, Uman's local Jews would also be massacred in a series of murder operations beginning in the late summer of 1941.

"We passed through with such difficulty, through fire and bullets," Boris said of the journey home.

By the time the Sandlers returned to Tulchyn, they discovered that their home on Stalin Street had been claimed by Germans. They moved in with a pair of wealthy Jewish families who had been sharing a home left vacant by other evacuees. Like the Sandlers, at least half—and as many as three-quarters—of Jews from the now-occupied territories of Ukraine either chose to remain in their homes or could not elude the occupiers while on the run.[18]

Tulchyn teenager Svetlana Kogan-Rabinovich and her family also made an unsuccessful evacuation attempt. Svetlana, the grandniece of renowned Yiddish writer Shalom Rabinovitz, better known by his pen name, Sholem Aleichem, would later describe fleeing Tulchyn for Haisyn, a town thirty-five miles to the northeast where her grandparents lived. "During the bombings, people would scatter into the forest," she would recall. "The horses were exhausted and hungry—there was no time to let them graze, and peasants didn't give them fodder." Yet on July 25, they found themselves under German occupation. Some of the Germans spotted Svetlana while she was walking to a river to fill her kettle. After she was forced to clean their motorcycle wheels, Svetlana's parents decided to hide her in her grandfather's attic. The Germans came looking for her the next day.

"Our hunchbacked [neighbor], Shlima, got frightened and pointed out where I was hiding," she said. "A German dragged me from the attic by my braid. Mother ran after him and begged him to take her to work instead of me, but the German drove her away. He beat me with a ramrod."

Svetlana and others who had not reported for work were brought to trenches near a bathhouse to be killed.

"Armed Germans and Ukrainian *polizei* [local policemen recruited by the Nazis] . . . were already standing there. I knew one of them; he used to work as a street sweeper," she said. "They made us stand in a row before the trenches. As we were waiting for the shot, we suddenly saw a tall, skinny red-haired German running toward us without his field tunic, waving his arm. He asked if anyone knew how to mend socks. Along with seven other people, I raised my hand. We were taken away. The others were shot." Like so many others, Svetlana and her family were then forced back to Tulchyn.[19]

The Germans first occupied Tulchyn in late July 1941. Hundreds of miles into their incursion, they happened upon a town where time had stopped. Tulchyn's location on a river and the presence of a Polish palace and Roman

Catholic church mirrored other former Pale of Settlement communities nearby. These shtetls, or *shtetlach*, had sizable Jewish populations that often lived in their own enclaves, dense Jewish neighborhoods that still retained the urban characteristics of medieval European towns.[20] In Russian, they were known as *mestechki.*

Tulchyn's Jewish population in 1939—5,607 Jews, or 42 percent of all residents—was concentrated on the urban streets surrounding the market.[21] The other inhabitants, Ukrainians, were Orthodox Christians. Jews were primarily craftsmen, working as tailors, glazers, coopers, and barbers. They also constituted most of Tulchyn's musicians. Hardly any worked in agriculture or on the railroad, a point of distinction between the Jews and Ukrainian peasants who lived in the countryside and worked the land. These differences were as much tied to the identities of both groups as their language and religion.[22]

Poverty pervaded shtetl life. Tulchyn's Jewish houses were primitive wood-frame dwellings with thatched roofs that were prone to leaking.[23] Few homes followed any sort of building convention, because none existed.[24] Later in life, Etel found parallels between the Tulchyn of her youth and the shtetl of popular imagination and Yiddish literature, in which streets meander aimlessly and homes cant to one side or the other.[25] Motl described neighborhoods with rows of tightly-packed houses, their architecture distinctly Jewish, as Jews and non-Jews would have been keen on pointing out.[26] He remembered that children seemed constantly to be spilling out of each. Their neighborhood was only blocks from the Potocki palace, which had belonged to the town's former Polish owners, the eighteenth-century Cathedral of Christ's Nativity, and the Silnytsya River, which was prone to flooding with arrival of the fall rains.

Motl and Etel's childhood home on Voikova Street had a typical floor plan for the time. The front door opened to a short hallway, which led to a living room that also served as a bedroom and workshop for their father, Idel, a tailor. A ladder led to a small loft. There was also a separate kitchen, dining room, and bedroom. During one of his retellings, Motl emphasized that husbands and wives slept in separate beds in those days. He and Lova shared the living room with their father, while Soybil and the girls slept in the other room. The home's elegant furniture was a point of pride. One of the children's grandfathers, an upholsterer, built them a divan for the living room. Soybil sometimes lamented to her eldest daughter that she would have preferred a smaller home, one that needed less upkeep. Idel worked long days at a sewing factory and often continued to tailor clothing well into the evening after the children were asleep. The home was where they expressed their Judaism with holiday meals and other traditions, not unusual for Jewish families in the Soviet Union, where the authorities were intent on eliminating religious life and forced synagogues to close.[27]

In 1926, the year before Etel was born and when Tulchyn was still the capital of its namesake district, just one in ten households had electricity.[28] Etel and her classmates were old enough to remember living through the Great Famine of 1932 and 1933, when millions starved to death as a result of Stalin's collectivization policies. Yet by her early teens, Etel sensed a new vitality in Tulchyn. There was live music in the central park, dancing in the town square, and a theater that hosted frequent performances. Idel, who was thirty-nine before the start of the war, and Soybil, who was thirty-six, made a point to see every new film playing in the town's cinema (with Etel tending to Manya and Lova at home).

"It was an extremely joyous, happy atmosphere," Etel recalled. "People were always out and about on Lenin Street. It was impassable sometimes. I would need to run to the store for Mom, and I couldn't get through."

Like nearly all Jews living in the region, Yiddish was the Braverman children's first language. It was the primary language spoken in their household and between the town's Jewish children. While neighbors conversed in their mother tongue, they shifted to Ukrainian when addressing the non-Jews who lived on the town's periphery. The two groups converged once each week for market day, where relations were often warm. Some Ukrainians even picked up on Yiddish. Yet longstanding interethnic tensions and resentment quietly simmered in the interwar years, the result of a strained and often turbulent history.[29]

Jewish migration to Eastern Europe and what is now Ukraine—the "borderland"—accelerated beginning in the 1300s as Jews were being banished from Western and Central Europe. With the merger of the Crown of Poland and the Grand Duchy of Lithuania into the Polish-Lithuanian Commonwealth in 1569, Poland reestablished control over a region of west-central Ukraine called Podolia, a land of windswept plains, forests, and deep river valleys that would become one of the cradles of Hasidism in the eighteenth century and constitute much of what is now Vinnytsia Province and Tulchyn.

Nearly all Podolian land was sold to a handful of powerful Polish families, who ruled from the comfort of their estates and oppressed the Ukrainian peasants working the land in the shadow of their manors and palaces.
Polish landowners had enticed them to move to their private towns with
"obligation-free" land leases of fifteen or twenty years to fuel their grain
trade. When these leases expired, landlords exploited peasants with crushing demands that amounted to serfdom, a practice that was being phased
out in Western Europe. Jews often worked as merchants, artisans, and mon-
eylenders. While Jews could not own land, they could lease it from Polish
noblemen. Often, they exploited the peasants working the fields.[30] In Podolia, Jews sometimes worked as rent and tax collectors on behalf of the Polish ruling class. New laws stipulated that the peasantry could frequent
only the taverns and mills belonging to the Polish gentry. The nobles
assigned Jews to manage them. In this way, wrote journalist Anna Reid,
Poles, Jews, and Ukrainians were for centuries "locked together in a frozen web of mutual dependence and resentment."[31]

In 1648, most of Tulchyn's two thousand Jewish residents were murdered
during the Cossack uprising against Polish colonialists and their Jewish
intermediaries.[32] Tulchyn, a fortified town, was besieged by Cossacks and
peasants. About 1,500 Jews and hundreds of Polish noblemen vowed to
defend it together. "The Jews, stationed on the walls of the fortress, shot at
the besiegers, keeping them off from the city," wrote historian Simon Dubnow. After being thwarted, the band of rebels negotiated with the Polish
inhabitants and their leader, Count Chetvertinski, telling them they would
be spared if they sacrificed the Jews.[33] He agreed. A Rabbi Aaron urged the
town's Jews not to retaliate and to choose martyrdom instead: "Listen, my
brethren! We are in exile among foreign peoples. If you attack the *szlachta*
[the Polish nobility], other countries will soon be aware of it, and they
will—God forbid—avenge themselves upon our brethren there. If this is a
decree from heaven, we must accept it in love and trust God's mercy. How
are we better than our brethren in [Nemyriv]?"[34]

The Cossacks then entered the town, seized Jewish property, and
forced the Jews into a garden. They unfurled a banner declaring that anyone willing to convert to Christianity would be spared. Not one of the
1,500 Jews accepted the offer. They were then slaughtered. Later, the
Poles—including Count Chetvertinski—were also killed by another band
of Cossacks.[35]

In 1793, the Russian Empire annexed Right-Bank Ukraine through the Second Partition of Poland. Episodic violence and terror continued in Tulchyn into the eighteenth and nineteenth centuries.[36] In 1918 and 1919, 519 Jewish residents were murdered in a series of civil war pogroms.[37] While Christian clergy attempted to shield the town's Jews from the marauders, an investigation found that most of Tulchyn's non-Jewish residents had acted indifferently toward the violence. Some did try to hide their Jewish neighbors.[38]

In the days before the Germans' arrival, the Bravermans spent much of their time hiding in a neighbor's cellar. Then, on July 23, Etel and Motl happened to be outside when the first German arrived by motorcycle, perhaps on a scouting mission. The rest soon followed in other motorcycles and trucks. Their appearance left an indelible impression on the town's Jewish children. Many of their fathers worked as coachmen—it was still one of Tulchyn's most common occupations—and travel by horse-drawn cart was the region's primary method of transportation. The Germans' dramatic entrance made the Red Army's shortcomings all the more evident.[39] It was difficult for survivor Mikhail Bartik to imagine how downtrodden Red Army soldiers like the kind he saw in retreat—many in rags, and some barefoot—would defeat menacing Germans of this caliber. They were well-groomed, well-nourished, well-dressed, and well-equipped, he said.[40]

Upon entering Tulchyn in the summer of 1941, the Germans were spotted bathing in the Silnytsya River at the edge of town. Next, they went door to door, ransacking Jewish homes in search of valuables. No item was safe. When they came to the Braverman home, they demanded the spools of thread sitting on Motl's grandfather's workbench. When survivor Riza Roitman, then twenty-three, returned to Tulchyn after a second evacuation attempt, she walked through her front door to find Germans playing classical and Soviet tunes on her family's gramophone. They left shortly thereafter with the gramophone and the accompanying record collection in hand.[41] Jewish homes were soon marked with a Star of David to distinguish them from the town's Christians.[42] Motl remembered non-Jews marking their own homes with crosses.

In August, Idel and Soybil decided to bury an assortment of valuables and fabric rolls under their wooden floorboards. At the direction of his father, Motl covered the hole with plywood and spread dirt around the top. Doing so would have come instinctively. Without refrigeration, families like the Bravermans often stored pickled vegetables and preserves underground. These spaces were abundant beneath Tulchyn's houses and could also double as hiding places. Even underground networks that linked homes were common under busy shtetl streets. Yet by burying some of their possessions, Soybil and Idel knew they were taking a risk. Shtetl Jews often believed that peasants were aware of secret chambers in Jewish homes.[43]

For Motl, the reality of life under the occupation did not fully register until a frightening ordeal outside the town's cinema. The Germans had rounded up Jewish boys and elderly men and were forcing them to push a truck weighed down by boulders. To further their amusement, the Germans flogged them as they struggled. Motl learned later that the brakes were being applied within the cab. Another time, he saw a pair of Germans force an elderly Jewish man to his knees in the street before taking a knife to his beard. Watching such abuse being leveled so callously against his people, Motl would later explain, marked a turning point: the end of his childhood and the beginning of a nightmare.

After nightfall, Tulchyn was beset by drunken soldiers in search of young women and older girls. They pounded on the doors of Jewish homes and sometimes forced their way in. When word of these night prowls spread, Soybil refused to let Etel leave her sight. She was no longer allowed outside the home, lest someone discover where she lived. Some parents had their daughters sleep in fields and gardens as a precaution.[44] One day, a schoolmate of Motl's was stopped by two Germans. They asked about his parents, who they were, and where they lived. He replied that his father had been conscripted and that he lived with his mother. He would later confide to Motl that the Germans had followed him home and raped her.

Late one evening, the Bravermans awoke to the sound of shattering glass. Soldiers had broken into the house behind theirs, which Motl's uncle was renting to a woman and her two daughters. Motl and Etel watched flashlight beams rove across their windows. Suddenly, they heard footsteps above them. Soybil started up the ladder to the attic and found the two neighbor girls huddling behind the Bravermans' chimney stack. They had evidently crossed on a wooden plank connecting the two homes to evade the men. Sensing the danger of the moment, Soybil rushed Motl and Etel up to the same hiding place. Flashlights from across the alley now cast a glow around the brick column that obscured them from view. Cradling their knees, the children closed their eyes and measured every breath. They remained there until early the next morning, when rain began to pelt the tin roof overhead, gently rousing them awake.

On August 31, the Romanian takeover of Transnistria was formalized through the Tighina Agreement with Germany, which recognized Romania's intent to eventually clear Transnistria, Bessarabia, and northern Bukovyna of its Jews, but only after the Soviet Union was defeated (a foregone conclusion at the time). The Germans hoped it would prevent the Romanians from flooding the lands east of the Buh with more deportees until they had the capacity to receive them. The German and Romanian armies would soon clear the territories west of the Southern Buh, leaving them to the Romanian gendarmerie units to oversee.[45] For the occupiers, Transnistria would also serve "as an enormous farm," which would help offset the costs of a war that would last far longer than expected. Farmers would be exploited, and most of the crops would be shipped to Romania.[46]

Also in August, new directives for Transnistria called for evicting Jewish residents from their homes and confining them within ghettos, setting the stage for the tragic months to come. A bulletin posted in three languages warned that leaving these areas was punishable by death. It also forced Jewish inhabitants to report to local authorities for their new housing assignments within ten days.[47] Though the concept of a Jewish ghetto originated in sixteenth-century Venice and would later spread throughout Western Europe, they were novel to Antonescu's Romania, and they were new to Ukraine. Late that summer, an advisor of Antonescu's visited Warsaw to observe the Nazi ghetto model firsthand. Whether the advisor ever shared his learnings with Romanian leadership and whether it influenced their decision-making is unknown.[48]

The Romanian authorities never bothered to define ghettos and often referred to ghettos and camps interchangeably.[49] These Romanian sites differed from the better known German sites of forced concentration in Poland. Transnistria's were smaller; most housed between a few dozen and many hundreds of Jews. Depending on the location, Jews might be restricted to living on a single street, a neighborhood, or some other defined residential area in their hometowns and villages.[50] Unlike the closed Warsaw and Łódź ghettos of Poland, the Romanian sites were more porous—often without walls and fences or marked only by barbed wire—which allowed for interactions and trade with non-Jews.[51] In the case of some ghettos, there was no barbed wire at all. In the north of Transnistria, barbed wire was only added in fall 1942.[52] The Romanian gendarmes overseeing them were willing to relax the rules and turn a blind eye to violators in exchange for bribes. Nonetheless, ghetto conditions were miserable.

On September 22, a Colonel Lazar ordered the Tulchyn ghetto to be formed, restricting Jewish movement and forcing residents to carry identifying papers. The ghetto was established on October 1, which fell on the Jewish holiday of Yom Kippur. It was located in the loosely defined eastern neighborhood known as Kaptsanovka, just south of the Potocki palace, where impoverished Jews tended to live.[53] Many of Tulchyn's Jews were forced to abandon their homes and to crowd into vacant ones or to move in with other families, as the Bravermans were forced to do. As many as fifteen people were crammed into each. Although barbed wire now marked the ghetto's perimeter, it was still possible to exchange goods and to interact with former non-Jewish neighbors.[54] Jews were required to wear yellow stars on the left side of their chests "composed of two cloth triangles 7 centimeters in diameter—on a black background."[55]

The Romanians and the remaining Germans frequently scoured the town in search of laborers. If spotted in the open after 6 A.M., Jews aged fourteen to sixty were at risk of being forced into hard labor or to complete any number of unpleasant tasks.[56] Despite her best efforts to go unseen, Etel was standing in an open doorway one afternoon when she heard the words "*komm, komm, komm*" being directed at her. An armed soldier, who was watching her from a distance, gestured for her to follow him. He led Etel and ten others to an army garrison where wounded Soviet soldiers were being brought to die. She recoiled at both the odor and at the sight before her.

"My God. How they laid on the floor," she said. "If there was straw underneath, they were fortunate. Others were placed across beams. They were dying. No one tended to their bandages. It smelled of rot."

That day, Etel's job was to care for the men in the absence of nurses. She brought them water and tried to comfort them. Despite the language barrier, she inferred that she would be shot if she failed to return to work the next day. Instead, she remained home in hiding. Her friends were forced to scrub floors in buildings where the Germans were staying and to wash away the grime and sweat from their uniforms.

"That's the kind of life it was," Etel said, something she would often repeat during her retellings.

Though underage, Motl was assigned to a kitchen run by a Hungarian. He was a nice enough fellow, and he rewarded Motl and his friends with leftovers after their shifts (they mostly peeled potatoes). One day, after finding themselves short of produce, the boys accompanied the Hungarian on a walk to a nearby neighborhood. They found a garden and began harvesting the potatoes. A German stormed out of an adjacent home and gave the Hungarian a verbal lashing. After composing himself, the man led the boys to the next garden, which they quickly raided.

For added manpower, the Germans and Romanians organized some of the local Ukrainian men into the collaborationist *polizei*.[57] By September 1941, their recruitment became standard practice across Transnistria.[58] As an extension of the gendarmes, *polizei* were called on to guard the camps and ghettos, where they sometimes assisted with mass executions.[59] Many of Transnistria's *polizei* had previously been Soviet POWs captured during the initial stages of the war and released to work in police units based in their home communities. Some POWs were also used as farmhands to help offset the labor shortage created when the region's able-bodied men were sent to battle.[60] Those who became *polizei* were sometimes influenced by German propaganda claiming that the occupiers were there to rescue citizens from "Judeo-Bolshevism," a familiar antisemitic trope.[61] Some were motivated by material gain, others by antisemitism, still others merely to protect their interests during the occupation.[62]

In occupied Soviet Ukraine, siding with the enemy was less suspect than in other parts of occupied Europe where collaboration also took place.[63] Stalin was, after all, the architect of the Holodomor (the Great Famine) in 1932–33 and the Great Terror in 1937–38. In some parts of Ukraine, locals showered the arriving Germans with flower bouquets and treated them to bread and salt for saving them from the Bolsheviks. Veterans of World War I still had a positive perception of the Germans from prior dealings with their army.[64]

In Tulchyn, the *polizei* had been ordinary men before the war. The town's Jewish children would remember them as neighbors, as the fathers of their classmates, or as their friends' older brothers. One—Mishka Ivanov, the patriarch of the only non-Jewish family from their street—had lived next door to Mikhail Bartik. By all accounts, Mishka had been a decent person. His two daughters spoke Yiddish as well as their Jewish peers. That all changed when he decided to don an armband.[65]

Within weeks, overcrowding and unhygienic conditions in the Tulchyn ghetto and throughout Transnistria had created the ideal breeding grounds for typhus, the deadly bacterial disease spread by body lice. Romanian officials, like the Germans, believed that Jews were its primary carriers.[66] In October, as part of an attempt to stem the outbreaks and to protect his men and supply lines, Antonescu ordered local Jews and the growing number of deportees from northern Bukovyna and Bessarabia to be isolated in towns and villages along the Romanian side of the Buh "in view of exterminating them."[67] For the Antonescu regime, the slow creep of disease and starvation became the preferred method of "cleansing" northern and central Transnistria. This differed from the systematic massacres in the southern districts.

In late 1941, Franklin Mott Gunther, the U.S. ambassador to Romania, confronted Ion Antonescu and Mihai Antonescu. They pleaded ignorance. Afterward, in November 1941, Gunther wrote to the State Department about the atrocities that had come into his purview.

> During the past three weeks evidence has been accumulating . . . that [what] remains of the Jewish population in [Bukovyna] and Bessarabia is being evacuated eastward into the war-devastated territory of the Ukraine under conditions so appalling that they would seem to afford a substantial share of the evacuees little chance to survive. . . . This modern Captivity would seem deliberately calculated to serve a program of virtual extermination. . . . As you know, I have constantly and persistently held before the attention of the highest Rumanian officials the inevitable reaction of my Government and the American people to such inhumane treatment, and even outright slaughter, of innocent and defenseless people, citing at length the atrocities committed against the Jews of Rumania. . . . The program of systematic extermination is continuing none the less, and I see little hope for the Rumanian Jews as long as the present German controlled régime continues in power.[68]

The following month, Romania declared war on the United States, severing diplomatic ties. Gunther died only ten days later while still in Bucharest.

CHAPTER FOUR

The Road to Pechera

BETWEEN 1940 AND 1942, a series of interrelated climate anomalies wreaked havoc across the far corners of the globe. Flooding plagued Peru. Vast areas of Africa, Central Asia, and Australia experienced catastrophic droughts. Record-high temperatures in Alaska contributed to widespread wildfires. Across much of Europe, the period produced the coldest two winters of the twentieth century.[1]

Snow blanketed Transnistria in November 1941. Temperatures plummeted to −22°F, ensnaring tens of thousands of Jews being herded by foot to concentration sites along the Southern Buh River. Many of those crossing Transnistria would freeze to death, often after trading away layers of clothing to local peasants in exchange for food. Their guards, meanwhile, led convoys in shifts to preserve their strength.[2] Along the way, Jews were beaten and robbed by Ukrainian mobs and the gendarmes. The *polizei* and gendarmes routinely raped girls and women. They shot laggards. Jews were forced to sleep in open fields and collective farms with no protection from the elements, while the Romanians sought refuge in the villages.[3] *Polizei* who knew the terrain helped the gendarmes lead the way. Some were already numb to the heinous duties that collaboration entailed, having helped Einsatzgruppe D killing squads carry out their mass executions. Just as the Germans used vodka and schnapps for "selective disinhibition" at massacre sites, the *polizei* relied on *samogon*, a local moonshine derived from beets, for much the same reason.[4]

Romanian planners were only vaguely familiar with the names and locations of the designated concentration sites. The previous fall, after scouting potential routes and overnight stops in two Fords—a trip slowed by muds and flooding—they concluded that the winter deportations would be a logistical nightmare, to say nothing of the human cost.[5] The Romanians were unprepared for the number of Jews who now had to be accounted for, nor did they intend to sustain the populations they were uprooting and holding captive.[6]

By December 1941, the Jews of Tulchyn had spent two months in a crowded ghetto. There were already whispers of the earlier Romanian atrocities in Odesa. Some internees had reason to believe they were next or that they were going to be deported. One day, an acquaintance of the Bravermans, a Ukrainian woman who lived nearby, called for Soybil from across the strands of galvanized wire that now separated them. She asked if Soybil—or "her Sonia," as she insisted on calling her—had heard the rumors. When Soybil told her that she had, the woman offered to safeguard some of her household items until the Bravermans' eventual return, an inevitability in Soybil's mind. Soybil agreed.

In Tulchyn, many families' fears were confirmed in early December.[7] Jewish residents who had received advanced warning had already packed bundles of clothes and food to bring with them. Others were caught off guard when early one morning, the gendarmes and *polizei* signaled their arrival at homes across the ghetto with thunderous pounding of rifle butts on doors and window shutters. They informed the residents that they were to gather in the street and had only a few minutes to do so.

A gym teacher from Tulchyn named Stoyanov, who would figure prominently in survivor testimonies as the head of the local Ukrainian police, helped lead the expulsions with particular zeal. "During house searches, he would shoot into the air to signal that there was nobody left in the house," survivor Svetlana Kogan-Rabinovich recalled.[8] Dozens of the town's Jews were said to have died by suicide to avoid leaving Tulchyn and were later buried in the town's Jewish cemetery. Others had already been duped into turning over their valuables—even their own gold teeth—for the right to remain in their homes, an agreement that the Romanians now refused to honor.[9] Of the Jewish residents in Tulchyn, only 118 artisans were allowed to stay behind, largely because the Romanians decided that they still needed their specialty services.[10]

On the streets, the frigid temperatures of the previous month were beginning to moderate. Sleet and freezing rain fell throughout the morning as

Tulchyn's Jews were led inside a new two-story school near the ghetto, the town's School No. 1.[11] The doors and windows were locked behind them. The din of thousands of frightened children and adults overwhelmed the halls and classrooms of a building that was meant to handle perhaps a few hundred—"like herring into a barrel," as one Pechera survivor described it.[12] There was no sign of food or water. The youngest children wailed. Elderly people were overheard chanting the Shema Yisrael prayer in affirmation of their faith, expecting perhaps that the words would be among their last.[13] From the window closest to her, Etel could see some of the townspeople peering in from the street. They seemed to be pointing at the school building and asking the Romanians standing guard if they could bring the Jews something to drink. None were allowed in.

By the next morning, after a night spent on the floor of the school, the children had grown so thirsty that they were pressing their mouths to the condensation dripping down onto the windowsills. A hungry Lova, meanwhile, was inconsolable. His mother, Soybil, offered him a piece of bread from her bag—she had packed two loaves with her—but he batted it away and threw his head back in protest. "I don't want this bread. I want the bread from the cupboard!" Soon, the guards made an announcement: all males were to assemble on the first floor. Etel heard a teary-eyed Motl, standing between his father and maternal grandfather, telling Soybil goodbye.

"I remember the look on Motya's [the diminutive for Motl] face—what a man he was. All of twelve years old," Etel said. "He cried, 'Mama, they're taking all the men away.' And in front of Mom, he told her goodbye and wept. And did he ever cry."

The gendarmes led them to the nearby Jewish bathhouse several hundred at a time. Inside, they were told to undress and to pile their clothes together, supposedly so each garment could be inspected for lice and disinfected. Several hours passed before the men and boys in Motl's group could retrieve their things from the heap. The next day, every Jewish girl and woman was ordered to the bathhouse for the same reason.

"The Romanians surrounded us. We were undressed, standing naked. All the women. Can you imagine?" Etel said. "They roamed between us and tapped us on the rear with their clubs, laughing. I'm hiding there behind my mother, and I'm only fourteen. And some hours later, after they told us they had disinfected the clothes they threw the clothes back again. We dressed and went back to the school."

After the war, some of Tulchyn's survivors reasoned that the entire operation must have been an elaborate charade and that its real purpose was to allow the gendarmes to search the clothes for gold. Many recalled that the Ukrainian physicians of their youth oversaw the supposed disinfections alongside the Romanians, as if to legitimize the exercise. The depraved Dr. Beletsky, well-known in Tulchyn before the war, is frequently referenced in oral testimony as also having administered anti-typhus vaccinations in the bathhouse, though many survivors claim that the strange injections were meant to expose Jews to various diseases and to hasten their demise in Pechera.

Even if the local gendarmes truly wanted to delouse the clothing, they would have needed delousing ovens, which were in short supply. Beyond quarantining local Jews in improvised camps and ghettos along the Buh to protect German and Romanian personnel, Romanian authorities were willing to let typhus and other epidemics run rampant within the concentration sites themselves. Antonescu addressed the topic during a December 16 cabinet session, days after Tulchyn's Jews were ordered to leave their ghetto.

When they convened, Antonescu and his men debated how best to deploy their remaining delousing ovens. There were too few to go around, not enough even for the army. When Gheorghe Alexianu, a former law professor whom Antonescu had appointed to oversee Transnistria as its governor, requested "several" units, Antonescu responded that he should "let those people there [Jews] continue to die." Available ovens, Antonescu declared, should be reserved for Romanian troops in Bessarabia. At Alexianu's urging, Antonescu agreed to at least consider the matter and to provide "rudimentary ovens." Having seen firsthand the devastation wrought by typhus during World War I, Antonescu knew full well how the crisis would manifest along the Buh without new measures. "The disaster will come in February, when a person is weakened by the winter, because he has not fed himself properly and has not left the house," he said.[14] He was not far off. The epidemics arrived in northern Transnistria's camps and ghettos in late January.[15]

Tulchyn's Jews spent one final night in the school after returning from the bathhouse. The next day, still without food and water, they were ordered to line up in the street. Under the watch of the Ukrainian police and gendarmes, the massive column was slowly led out of Tulchyn and in the direction of Torkiv, a village eleven miles to the northwest. The unpaved roads were now swollen with melted ice and snow. Gusts tore across the region's plains and undulating river valleys.[16] Had Tulchyn's Jewish residents known in advance where they were being resettled, they may have wondered why the men leading them chose the course they did. They could have taken a more direct route to the village of Bortnyky—just north of Tulchyn—on the way to Pechera.[17] Instead, the Romanians needlessly extended the journey by veering west through the villages of Kopiivka and then Torkiv in heavy mud and under a steady rain, before reorienting to Pechera in the territory's northeastern reaches.

For several hours after departing Tulchyn, Lova and Manya rode in the back of a wagon with some of the family's belongings. Motl sat in the coachman's seat. Etel and her parents walked alongside them, wading through muck that sometimes reached their knees. A Ukrainian policeman led the horse by its halter. The gendarmes had seized the wagon and many more like it from the peasantry, among the few areas of planning that accounted for the needs of the children in the convoys.[18] The Braverman children's good fortune, if one could call it that, was short lived. The policeman who had been guiding their horse on foot suddenly lifted all three children out of the wagon and took Motl's place. Startled, the children stood rooted to the spot in the middle of the road, in full view of a few approaching gendarmes.

"I look up and Manya and Lova are in the deepest mud, weeping," Etel recalled. "My goodness, as soon as I saw this, I ran in front of the Romanians. I didn't want to know if they were going to kill me or not kill me, and I scream, 'My children, my children!' You can only imagine. I grab Lova. My mom hoists up Manya."

For the next few hours, Motl, his father, Idel, and his sixty-five-year-old grandfather carried the family's belongings, which amounted to a few bundles' worth of clothes and food. Idel also carried some possessions on his person. They occasionally passed groups of Ukrainian villagers standing on the roadside, some of whom were moved to prayer by the sight of the convoy. Others reached out to offer food. Tulchyn's Jews were prohibited from stopping for any reason, even to relieve themselves or to eat or drink, but many did so anyway. Soybil spotted a rusted metal pail along the road and used it to collect rainwater from a few hoofprints. All seven Braver-mans drank from it.

At some point before nightfall, the column came to a stop beside an open field. The *polizei* and the gendarmes told Tulchyn's Jews, whose clothes were sopping wet from the rain and caked in mud, that this was where they would be spending the night. A small stream running nearby provided Motl and many others their first drink of clean water in nearly a week. Early the next morning, they extracted themselves from the dirt and were forced to march on, now in the freezing rain. The elderly men and women were falling behind. At first, the gendarmes and *polizei* threatened these strag-glers with their clubs. Then they began shooting them. Some moribund Jews simply collapsed and never rose to their feet again. Devout elderly Jews who had refused to eat the non-kosher food offered by the Ukrainians fell to the mud wrapped in their prayer shawls.[19] Countless families had no choice but to leave their loved ones behind in the filth. As had been the case in Bessarabia and Bukovyna, the gendarmes left trails of corpses in their wake and refused to let families stop to bury their loved ones or to even say a prayer. This was perhaps the biggest violation of all. Jean Ancel writes that the painful experience of leaving the deceased behind "tested the Jew-ish community and its values. For many Jews, caught up in circumstances beyond their control, the abandonment of Jewish bodies eventually eroded a deep-seated respect for the dead. The crossing of this 'red line' scarred numerous survivors."[20]

When they reached Torkiv, a small village straddling the Shpykivka River, the gendarmes and their police escorts told the Jews that they would sleep inside an abandoned barn. Cold, hungry, and frightened, the first to enter it sought spaces along the outer walls, where there was still straw for them to rest on.[21] Motl recalled sleeping closer to the center of the barn, where dried animal waste still covered the ground. Sometime that night, in total darkness, some combination of Ukrainians and Romanians entered and began robbing the convoy. The hours before dawn were punctuated by groans, children's cries, and the occasional gunshot. In the dark, Reizia Vainblat's beloved grandmother, Leyka, known for her cooking and unmatched wit, became confused and agitated. Unable to make sense of her surroundings, she called repeatedly for someone to bring her a *samovar*, a kind of kettle, so she could drink some tea. She spent the night in a trough. Hours later, her family found her dead.[22]

The next morning, as the transport neared Pechera, a few children spotted some unpicked and still-frozen sugar beets. They ran and plucked them from a sodden field, even as the *polizei* rained blows on their heads and backs. Twelve-year-old Donia Presler came away with three of the precious roots, gnawing on them until the convoy entered Pechera.[23] When thousands of bedraggled men, women, and children came into view in a column that stretched more than half a mile, the locals looked on in terror. Three months earlier, in late September 1941, the village's few Jewish families disappeared, having been taken to a ghetto in nearby Shpykiv. Now, thousands of strangers entered their village. "So many people marched," recalled an elderly resident of Pechera decades later, who saw Tulchyn's Jews pass her home as a girl. "We didn't know who they were because they were surrounded by policemen. We were scared. We were scared to come out."[24]

When the last of the new prisoners were sent down the camp's alley, the gate was closed behind them. A handful of *polizei* positioned themselves in a hut near the main entrance and outside the stone walls. The new prisoners began to jockey for places to shelter. Barracks and storehouses could be found on either side of the courtyard, just in front of the abandoned sanitorium. There were also stables and underground cellars. Some filed into the former sanitorium building and took residence in the wards or in the basement. Mikhail Bartik and his family claimed a spot in a windowless dining hall, which would soon become known as the Refrigerator.[25] Motl's parents and grandfather ushered the children into one of the barracks, where they discovered a kitchen. They ventured farther down a narrow hallway, into what must have once been a changing room for the sanitorium's attendants and claimed it for themselves. Everyone slept on the exposed concrete floor that night except Motl's grandfather, who climbed atop a bay of lockers. Motl closed his eyes and fell asleep to the sound of the rushing Buh below.

During their first few days of imprisonment, Motl and other young prisoners roamed the grounds. They passed under the tree canopies, walked well-worn paths lined by garden beds, and inspected the high stone walls. Those who ventured to the Buh saw a three-part church and bell tower on a distant cliff, looming over the river valley. For Motl, the experience of acclimating to life within the camp was akin to being a spider trapped in a vivarium, an analogy he would draw decades later. Like Motl, many survivors would later emphasize the picturesque setting that they first encountered as child prisoners, as if unable to reconcile how a place so serene could have brought about such misery.

Pechera had long captured the imagination of visitors from far-flung places. By the late seventeenth century, the areas that became southwestern Ukraine had been scarred by war and repeated invasions. The Podolia region in southern Ukraine was largely deserted. In 1681, the Tsardom of Russia, the Crimean Tatars, and the Ottoman Empire signed a treaty that granted the Ottomans control over what was then Right-Bank Ukraine, including Podolia. A buffer zone was established between the Southern Buh, the serpentine river winding from the west of Ukraine to the Black Sea, and the Dnieper to the east.

The newly installed Ottoman ruler, Gheorghe Duca, chose Pechera as the new capital "of his Ukrainian domain," a village situated on the very edge, quite literally, of Ottoman territory.[26] He then had a stone castle built on a cliff above the Buh near an ancient settlement. According to village lore—teachings that were confirmed during archeological expeditions in the late 1940s—the area's long-ago inhabitants used caves and passageways in the rock to protect themselves from invaders (explaining how *pechera*, meaning "cave," became the village's name). In 1682, Duca arranged for a park to be built a half-mile downriver from his new outpost. He envisioned a rectangular plot running parallel to the Buh below. Linden trees were planted to frame the exterior of the park. Rows of lindens also lined an eight-hundred-foot alley that extended into the park from the entrance. Duca was so taken by his Ukrainian residences, one built near Pechera and others on the Dnister, that he planned to move his family to Ukraine from the Principality of Moldavia (now divided between Romania, Moldova, and Ukraine), where he had lived since his childhood. He quickly realized his goal of repopulating decimated towns and villages and attracting settlers from far and wide, and he created profitable enterprises in farming and animal husbandry that could be taxed. After his death in 1685, his successor moved the capital north to Nemyriv. In 1764, the abandoned castle was destroyed. Its stone ruins were used to build the foundation for a wooden church that would takes its place. A bell tower was added a century later from the same material.[27]

The work of enhancing and expanding Duca's nearby park was soon taken up by Jan Świejkowski, one of Pechera's successive landholders. He added trees and fashioned it in the style of the English landscape garden, a trend that had swept across Europe. A two-story neoclassical palace, commissioned in the early nineteenth century, rose on the same grounds, replacing a modest manor that once stood there. The palace was modeled after the so-called Podolsky Versailles—built by the Potocki family in Tulchyn—albeit half the size. At the front entrance, visitors passed under a portico supported by four Ionic columns. A terrace at the rear of the palace, with views to the Buh, was enclosed by a balcony balustrade. A spiraling staircase was built into the slope leading down to the riverbanks. Newly added marble statues adorned the landscape and the stairs, as did baths and grottos. Visitors could see the palace from the narrow iron gate that marked the property's entrance, which opened to the alley that Duca had laid more than a century earlier.[28]

The Potockis came to own twelve thousand acres of land and forests in Pechera in the 1840s, including what had been Duca's park, and began renovating the palace in 1874.[29] There was a grand ballroom with chandeliers, a tapestry room with a fireplace mantle commissioned by a famous French cabinetmaker, a room that housed rare weapons produced by Tulchyn's armory, carpets emblazoned with the family's coats of arms, and a family library containing thousands of volumes. The palace also held a large collection of Slutsk belts, worn by Polish noblemen over their *żupan* garments, as well as porcelain, crystal, and an eighteenth-century rampart.[30]

In the 1870s, Pechera enchanted the prolific Belarusian artist Napoleon Orda, who produced more than a thousand drawings and watercolors during his travels across what is now Belarus, Poland, Lithuania, and Ukraine. Breaking with tradition, Orda was careful not to embellish the landscapes and architecture he encountered, capturing them as they were.[31] His lithographic printings include a panorama of the Southern Buh valley, called "Peczara nad rzeka Bohem." Pictured is the bend separating Pechera and Sokilets, and perched high above one of the riverbanks, the Potocki family palace. The sketch depicts a wall that runs the length of the hillside before ending near the Buh. The blue Russian Orthodox church and bell tower, erected where Duca's castle once stood, can be seen in the distance. Orda had also produced a piece while presumably sitting in Sokilets and looking directly across the river at Pechera. The rear face of the Potocki palace and its colonnade rises above the forested hillside. (This was likely the same view afforded to Germans watching the camp's rear seven decades later.)

In a memoir, the nephew of the property's final heirs, Franciszek Potocki and Maria Radziwiłł, recalled visiting his uncle and aunt at their Pechera estate when he was just a child:

> Count Franciszek had a very large palace in [Pechera], overlooking the River [Buh], consisting of, I think, at least seventy or eighty rooms and, swarming with servants dressed up in the Cossack style, in yellow and blue uniforms, these being the Potocki colours and, incidentally, the Radziwiłł colours as well. The stables were full of Arab horses, amongst which there was an old stallion called Ahmed, a particular favourite of us children, who used to have felt shoes placed on his hoofs and was led in from time to time to the drawing-rooms for the entertainment of all guests.[32]

The Potockis would leave other imprints on the area, including a nearby mill built on the Buh, and in 1904, a family chapel and crypt in their park. Franciszek Potocki remodeled his palace once more between 1912 and 1915.[33] Yet just two years later, in late December 1917, dozens of drunken soldiers descended on the property. They demanded to be let into the cellar, where they drank spoiled wine. Afterward, they began plundering the palace. They also set fire to an outbuilding which had functioned as a hospital. When they found fireworks, they decided to light them in an office full of documents. With parts of the palace engulfed in flames, some of Pechera's villagers took part in the looting. Another mob stormed the palace in April 1918, breaking doors and windows, destroying the roof, plundering what was left of the valuables and alcohol, and setting fire to much of the building.[34] The Potockis would soon become one of the many Polish magnate families to lose their lands and fortunes in Ukraine in the aftermath of the Russian Revolution.[35] Eventually, Count Franciszek Potocki and Maria Radziwiłł returned to Kraków. They remained fixtures in the city's high society, even with their diminished wealth. In time, the lavish dinner parties they had once hosted in their Kraków palace—attended by other aristocrats, Polish elites, and foreign nobility—became much more modest.[36]

In 1928, when Polish art historian Antoni Urbański published the second edition of his book about the vestiges of Polish influence across its former borderlands, he noted that the ruins of the former palace were being "demolished at the brick" and taken downriver to Bratslav to build "some Bolshevik building."[37]

By December 1941, the opulence of the Potockis' former property had long faded. Debris and glass were scattered across the grounds, suggesting that the site had been damaged by war and the buildings ransacked. In the sanitorium, flooring materials had been stripped away, leaving only concrete. The prisoners now occupying every inhabitable nook scrambled to cover the window openings with blankets and rags to keep the frigid wind and snow from intruding. None of the plumbing worked.

From the perspective of its founders, the camp's remote location would prevent the spread of typhus beyond the Jewish population concentrated there. Yet according to local historian Faina Vinokurova, there was another benefit to the camp's placement on the far edge of Transnistria: it allowed the Romanians to plainly demonstrate their brand of depravity to the Germans watching the camp's goings-on from across the Buh, from the territory they controlled.[38]

The arrival of Tulchyn's Jewish community in December 1941 marked the beginning of a torturous existence. In their first hours and days, they came to a startling realization: they were being starved. Aside from a small stream that flowed near the stairs to the Buh and snow that could be melted, the Buh was the only source of drinking water. But to reach it, the captives had to descend a series of staircases coated in ice, an effort that was beyond the capacity of many who had been weakened by their ordeal. Etel often saw her father carrying buckets of water to and from the river for fellow prisoners, climbing some 160 steps to the camp on each return trip.

They were also learning the camp's unwritten rules. Once, early in their internment, Soybil hung some clothes out to dry, including a woolen dress of Etel's that her father had fashioned for her out of a tablecloth. It was quickly snatched. "She was under the impression that she was still home," Etel said of her mother's acclimation to camp life. Each new convoy of prisoners would learn the same lessons. Eight-year-old Arkadii Plotitskii of Shpykiv heard the word "stolen" for the first time during his first day in the camp, when two of his family's pea pies disappeared from their room in the former sanitorium building.[39]

The Ukrainian guards were also quick to demonstrate their cruelty. There was Smetansky, the unhinged drunk known to unfurl his whip at prisoners' legs with one hand and bludgeon their heads with a club held in the other—sometimes in one motion.[40] Motl also remembered two guards who were both named Mishka, a Mishka Odessit and a "Mishka with the Kubanka," who was rarely seen without his Kuban Cossack hat. At least one of the *polizei* guarding the Pechera camp, a Mikhail Stepanskii, had been a Red Army soldier held in a German POW camp. He found that collaboration, which Pechera's mayor had talked him into, was more palatable than enduring beatings at the hands of the Germans.[41]

When a few prisoners made the mistake of prying branches from the camp's trees or disturbing the hedges while gathering kindling for their fires, they were beaten by the *polizei*. The unknowing offenders were told that Jews could only gather fallen twigs and leaves. Some of the prisoners began to construct makeshift stoves out of the bricks and scrap metal they had found. The bricks formed the legs, and the metal was laid over them to hold the pots. Others simply set their pots or tin cans atop two small piles of brick, lighting the plant debris underneath to simmer what little food they had managed to bring from home. A fortunate few had somehow found pots or tin cans and charged fellow prisoners to use them. The stoves were built indoors and outdoors and in the alleys between the buildings. Soybil would prepare soups in much the same way. Each family member received the same small helping, in which they could expect to find the occasional lump of grain or a potato wedge. The *polizei* were known to kick the pots over, sending the precious contents spilling out into the snow. Survivor Ana Rozenberg recalled that unlike the Germans and Romanians, who never stepped foot in the camp for fear of contracting diseases, the *polizei* would enter often. As a result, many female prisoners were in constant fear of being raped.[42]

When their food ran out, Pechera's prisoners resorted to trading the last of their things. With shoes and clothing in short supply, non-Jews from surrounding villages journeyed to Pechera seeking bargains. Basic consumer goods were almost impossible to find on the shelves of general stores, which were often bare. There was no soap, matches, or even sewing material. The shortages, which were created by Stalin's disastrous five-year plans, were made all the worse when the retreating Red Army enacted its scorched-earth policy. Factories were destroyed, and industrial production was crippled.[43] In Pechera, the prisoners' dire circumstances gave their trading partners substantial leverage. Many Jews spent their final days barefoot, and if not completely naked, then nearly so, forced to decide between starving or and succumbing to the deep freeze.

Curiously, the *polizei* paid little attention to the bazaar, allowing it to take place for an hour each day, or to the frequent contact between Jews and outsiders. Their indifference to the risks of disease transmission likely alarmed the Romanian occupiers. Trade between Jews and peasants proliferated in places where Jews had been sequestered. Military personnel were convinced that the locals were courting disaster—often unwittingly—and that they were putting military supply lines and troops at risk. In southern Transnistria, a Romanian army commander lectured local residents about proper hygiene and of the dangers of buying "clothing full of lice." He noted later that they "lack even the most basic concept of personal and environmental cleanliness, and their health workers are no more enlightened. There is not a single doctor in the general vicinity, and there has been no soap for months."[44]

Yet even with the Jews at their most vulnerable, many of Pechera's villagers also hurled food over the walls out of compassion, especially when a distraught child could be heard on the other side. By doing so, they risked angering the guards, who were liable to kill anyone for the slightest offense. Those who did approach the camp's perimeter were sometimes shaken by what they saw and heard. Others came simply to gawk at the prisoners.[45] One day, Motl watched a stooped old man hobble toward the camp before peering in through a gate. He seemed to be relishing in the suffering.

"*Zhidy! Zhidy!*" he barked through a toothless scowl. "Your mothers! Thank God. Thank God. How long I've waited."

The Romanians' approach to Transnistria's Jews varied by region. Each camp, ghetto, and district seemed to operate under its own set of rules. The handful of makeshift camps were generally located away from the communities to which their prisoners had belonged. In contrast to the centrally planned Nazi camp network, there was no cohesive system that linked them or that dictated their inner workings. They sometimes comprised little more than stables, pigsties, or abandoned houses damaged by war. Unlike the German camps, Romanian authorities had no intention of providing sustenance for their victims nor barracks or latrines.[46] In northern and central Transnistria—where thirty-five thousand Jews still lived—there was no plan to methodically murder them.[47] Instead, the Romanians were content "to let nature take its course" and to force Jews to languish in place until any survivors could be handed off to the Germans, perhaps as early as spring 1942.[48]

Just thirty miles south of Pechera, in Vapnyarka, the Romanians organized one of the only other camps in northern Transnistria within the ruins of a former Soviet cavalry training base. Vapnyarka differed mainly in that the Jewish political prisoners interned there ate bread made from barley and straw. They were also served grass-pea soup, made from the peas that had been stored on base by the Soviets for use in a horse-feed blend. While the high-protein, drought-resistant crop had long been cultivated for human and animal consumption, it was known to cause paralysis of the lower limbs if eaten with enough regularity. The Romanians guarding the camp knew to stay away from it.[49] With more than a thousand prisoners held in Vapnyarka in September 1942, a Romanian commander assured a new transport that the inhabitants would "come out of this camp either on all fours or on crutches," which proved true for many.[50] Elsewhere, the Romanian authorities took a much more drastic and active role in the extermination of Jews.

The large camps of southeastern Transnistria, in a region that Jean Ancel would call the Kingdom of Death, included those of Bohdanivka, Akmechetski Stavky, and Domanivka, all located near the Southern Buh. In Bohdanivka, when starvation, disease, and exposure did not reduce their numbers quickly enough, forty-eight thousand Jews—mostly from Odesa and also from Bessarabia—were shot at the edge of a ravine under the pretense of typhus prevention. The bodies were then cremated by a team of two hundred Jews, most of whom were killed in turn. Five thousand Jews deemed unable to walk to the execution site had already been burned alive in two stables. The killings were conducted by the Romanian gendarmes and a mix of ethnic German and Ukrainian policemen.[51] Similar executions befell the prisoners of Domanivka. In nearby Akmechetski Stavky, a pig farm, Jews died of starvation, disease, and exposure. Farther to the south, in the Black Sea port city of Odesa, Jews living under the Romanian occupation were blamed for the bombing of Romanian military headquarters. In retaliation, thousands were hung, shot, or burned alive in warehouses. The remaining Jewish population was incarcerated in ghettos and deported to camps, including Bohdanivka, where they were shot at the edge of pits and where their bodies were incinerated.

Around the same time that Tulchyn's Jews were marched to Pechera in December 1941, a gendarme commander for the area claimed in a report that the typhus issue had now "been partly solved" in the north with the isolation of Jewish populations who "will be guarded by local police," and that as a result, "it had been possible to stop the typhus epidemic."[52] Inside the camps and ghettos, the opposite was true: conditions were all the more ripe for an outbreak. On New Year's Eve, a second wave of inmates totaling 746 Jews arrived in Pechera, mostly from the nearby town of Bratslav. Then came another transport with 450 Jews from Trostyanets.[53] In January, Jews from Ladyzhyn and Vapnyarka arrived, including those from northern Bukovyna and Bessarabia.[54] Within the increasingly overcrowded dwellings, a new routine emerged for many of the prisoners, foreshadowing the disaster ahead. They would rise from their resting places to shake the body lice off their clothing and into the snow outside.[55] Others spent their idle time picking lice off themselves or loved ones and crushing them between their fingers, staining their nails red.[56] Most would soon fall ill.

As hundreds of years of Eastern European history had shown, typhus infestations were a natural consequence of war, displacement, and overcrowding, when hygiene can no longer be maintained. The vermin responsible for transmitting typhus is the body louse, nearly identical to the head louse. Temperamental in nature and about the size of a sesame seed, body lice live in unwashed clothes rather than on human scalps, where it is too warm for their liking. They prefer feeding on the blood of human hosts with body temperatures between 98 and 102°F. Should they find that their hosts are too hot or too cold—if in the throes of a typhus-induced fever or because they have died—lice flee to more hospitable environments. After first latching on with a bite, body lice plunge their needles into the upper skin to feed while simultaneously excreting feces that contain *Rickettsia prowazekii*, the typhus-causing bacteria. For humans, what follows is intense itching at the site of the bite. By scratching or by smashing the louse, a person can unknowingly rub the feces into the bite or into the raw skin. Although infected lice always die from the very disease they are spreading, their feces remain a potent source of *Rickettsia prowazekii* long after they are gone. Infected lice can also travel as far as five feet per hour to find their hosts.[57]

In the overcrowded spaces where Pechera's starving prisoners now lived, laying side by side, the body lice that swarmed them could pass from host to host with ease. In early January, after developing sores from their scratching,

Motl and Etel began to experience the telltale symptoms of typhus, as did their younger siblings and grandfather. Their limbs began to feel numb. A rash formed on their torsos. They spiked fevers and complained of body aches. Eventually, they could do little but lay in place, lost in a stupor. Countless sick prisoners laying nearby, in neighboring rooms, and in other buildings suffered from the same cascading symptoms, along with the more pronounced ones, including hallucinations. Many sick prisoners who had taken refuge in the main three-story building were relegated to the basement, in an apparent effort to stem the tide of the outbreak on the floors above. Their distressed cries could be heard throughout the day.

With their own children in a state of delirium, a terrified Soybil and Idel applied cold compresses to their foreheads. What little food they had went to the children, whose mouths they forced open to spoon in nourishment. It occurred to Idel that if he could find a samovar, he could prepare his own soups for the children instead of relying on other prisoners and their cookware. He then approached the fence and asked if the local Ukrainians gathered there knew of a metalsmith who could help. Idel found a man who, for a fee, built him a cylindrical kettle made of tin. A small pipe extended into the middle of the samovar, where Idel could place burning twigs, pinecones, and leaves. The heat from the pipe would bring the water in the kettle to a boil. Within three weeks, the children slowly regained their strength, although some of the symptoms lingered. "We were still very weak, dizzy," Motl would write. "My head was spinning. I would try to get up, and I would instantly fall. And slowly, we got back to our old selves."

Through the ordeal, Soybil and Idel managed to avoid becoming infected themselves. Motl and Etel later came to believe that the samovar had saved them—the first of many small miracles behind their improbable story of survival. Other child survivors who overcame typhus found their own miracles to credit. For child survivor Raisa Chernova, it was a pair of pickled apples that she ate while in the throes of the illness, which her mother had received in exchange for an elegant shawl.[58]

During his travels, nineteenth-century Belarusian artist, pianist, and composer
Napoleon Orda captured this view of the former Potocki palace from across
the Southern Buh River. It was published in his Podolia portfolio, dated 1871–74.
The palace would be destroyed in the winter of 1917–18 and later replaced
by a Soviet tuberculosis sanitorium. The property then become the site
of the Pechera death camp. Courtesy Laboratory Stock, National
Museum in Kraków, Inv. No. MNK III-r.a.-3015.

A photo depicts Tulchyn's School No. 1, where the town's Jewish residents were first brought before being herded to the Pechera camp. What appears to be barbed wire, possibly from the town's Jewish ghetto, appears on the right side. "1948" was scrawled on the back of this photograph.
Courtesy Vladislav Vigurzhinsky.

At age twenty, Motl joined the Red Army and was stationed in Brest.
This was one of Motl's most prized photos.

Etel (*left*), Motl (*center*), and Manya (*right*) pose for a photo in early postwar Tulchyn.

Fate would bring (*from left to right*) Eva Poliak, Eva's daughter Svetlana, Anna, Motl, and Lova to the banks of the Southern Buh in Pechera in 1957. They stood at what would have been the base of the former death camp. On the cliff behind them is an eighteenth-century wooden church.

My uncle Igor, born in 1958, was Soybil's first grandchild. Soybil (*left*) is seated with Etel (*middle*) and her new daughter-in-law, Anna (*right*).

A Braverman family photo from the late 1960s. *From left to right:*
Anna, Svetlana, Igor, and Motl.

This memorial, a stone obelisk overlooking Pechera's mass graves, was installed by donor Mikhail Malin in 1976. Courtesy Yad Vashem Photo Archive, Jerusalem. 8199/2.

This photo was taken at my family's Chernivtsi, Ukraine, apartment. Pictured (*from left to right*) are my grandmother Anna, me at three years old, my six-year-old sister, Yuliya, and my grandfather Motl.

Motl and Anna at their beloved Kerry Park, an iconic viewpoint in Seattle's Upper Queen Anne neighborhood, where they lived for a time.

A picture of me and my grandparents, Motl and Anna, at a restaurant lunch celebrating a birthday. I was in my freshman or sophomore year at the University of Washington when this photo was taken.

A research team with the French organization Yahad-In Unum recently captured this aerial of Pechera Park and a rehabilitation hospital, the site of a death camp between December 1941 and March 1944. Courtesy Aleksey Kasyanov/Yahad-In Unum.

The first prisoners to be sent to the Pechera camp passed through these gates in December 1941. The words "Death Camp" were displayed on a wooden board above it. Courtesy Aleksey Kasyanov/Yahad-In Unum.

A view of the former camp building in Pechera, Ukraine, now a hospital
and clinic for adults with musculoskeletal disorders and injuries.
Courtesy Aleksey Kasyanov/Yahad-In Unum.

One hundred and sixty steps separated the former death camp's main grounds from the banks of the Southern Buh below. Today, the stairs bring visitors to the river for leisure. Courtesy Kristina Federovich.

CHAPTER FIVE

Into the Night

O NE NIGHT IN JANUARY 1942, Motl's grandfather died in his sleep. Idel and Soybil lowered him to the ground from the lockers the next morning. A group of Jewish men whose faces Motl and Etel would come to recognize were soon dispatched. After searching their grandfather for valuables, they swung his body onto a sled already stacked with naked corpses. As Motl and Etel would learn, the dead were bound for a pit that had been dug on a hill just east of the village, in what had been the community's prewar Jewish cemetery.

Once again, the Romanians abdicated all responsibility for burying their Jewish victims. In Pechera and across northern Transnistria's camps and ghettos, prisoners organized Jewish committees, or groups of self-governing leaders, to handle such matters while also carrying out Romanian directives. One of the first tasks was usually to organize a burial team.[1] Pechera's Jewish leaders, led by a man named Motel Zilberman, had also formed one.[2] Its ranks included the two men who had taken Motl's grandfather's body. Several times each day, they piled the dead onto their sled—the tangled, skeletal bodies stripped of all clothes—and ferried them away.

"It was frightening to watch the frozen corpses," remembered Mikhail Bartik. "How they threw them on the sled absolutely naked, like firewood, and equally how, the stronger [prisoners] were harnessed together instead of horses and dragged them to the Jewish cemetery."[3]

When the ground froze and burials were no longer possible, the men stacked the corpses in the camp's stables, and eventually, across the courtyard. To Motl, they resembled matchsticks. Similar horrors could be witnessed in the ghettos of northern Transnistria, including Mohyliv-Podilskyi, where one could observe "piles of corpses stacked like cordwood [awaiting] burial in the frozen earth."[4] In Sharhorod, a "black sled" carrying a mound of bodies with a "black cloth . . . tossed unceremoniously over the pile" could not keep pace with the mounting number of victims. Come February, when the ground at Sharhorod's cemetery froze solid—temperatures had fallen to −40°F—gravediggers thawed the earth with bonfires that burned all day and night. In the Bershad ghetto, a "big wagon" transported the dead to the cemetery.[5] One Bershad survivor and deportee from northern Bukovyna described how the wagon was outfitted "with two high poles at each side to increase capacity," between which "lay the naked skeletal corpses of men, women, and children, their limbs dangling through the spaces between the poles. The macabre scene was a daily occurrence."[6]

As the ground thawed that spring, haycarts were used to transport bodies to the mass graves. To ensure that Pechera's imprisoned Jews were dying at an acceptable rate, the dreaded policeman Stoyanov would often accompany Dr. Beletsky into the camp to receive updates on the daily death tolls. "Why are so few of you dying?" Dr. Beletsky would often lament aloud to the prisoners if the number fell below one hundred.[7]

In Pechera, the specter of death was ever present. Across the grounds, desperate prisoners scavenged for grass, leaves, and plant roots. One day, Boris Sandler saw a man walking up and down the corridors of the former sanitarium building with a pan full of potato peels. "Hot pancakes! Premium!" he was shouting. Fellow prisoners rushed in to pay twenty kopeks for a helping.

It became clear to Etel and Motl that their family's time was running out. One of them remembered how Motl and his father had buried an assortment of things under their home in Tulchyn. They decided that they would somehow find their way back to retrieve them—an idea that incensed Soybil, their mother, upon hearing it. "Mama screamed, she cried," Etel recalled. They screamed back, telling Soybil that they were hungry and that if she expected little Manya and Lova to survive, they would need more belongings to trade. There was already talk across the camp of prisoners, mostly women and children, who had managed to flee and beg in Pechera and other nearby villages. They were seen stealing back into the camp with sacks of food for their families. But there were already stories of prisoners who never returned, having been beaten to death and robbed by shepherd boys and peasants,[8] or after being shot by the gendarmes, who were authorized to kill the Jews they caught.[9]

Motl and Etel felt they had to take their chances. By this point, the children had watched the *polizei* settle into a predictable routine: patrolling the camp by day, drinking into the early evening, and retreating to the warmth of their huts near the front gate to sleep. This left much of the camp unguarded overnight. Early one February morning, as Manya and Lova slept, they bundled rags around their heads and feet and kissed their parents goodbye. Near the courtyard, they met Motl's friend Naum, who had agreed to accompany them in hopes of finding something of value for his own family. Under cover of a predawn sky, the trio set off on what would be the first of many escapes. "Some heroes we were," Motl recalled decades later. "I was the leader, and here was Etel and Naum behind me. Big heroes—all of us. Not only did we smell bad, but we were filthy. The lice were all over us."

Near the stairs leading down to the Buh, they found a shorter section of the wall that was about seven or eight feet high. It was well-known to other prisoners, too. Motl squatted down so that Etel could climb onto his shoulders and make her way over the wall. Once they heard her feet touch down, Motl and Naum each gripped the stone ledge and swung their legs over it. After a few minutes of searching, they managed to find a road. It was a clear night and bitterly cold. Compacted snow and ice crackled underfoot.

The journey to Pechera, now two months behind them, had been a blur, and no one could remember the roads that the *polizei* and gendarmes had used. Motl took responsibility for their safe passage to Tulchyn and chose a direction at random. As they walked, the children felt their legs grow heavy. Pain shot across their ankles, knees, and hips as their feet churned through pockets of snow. Their muscles had atrophied from near starvation, and their joints had stiffened after their bouts with typhus and entire weeks spent on the freezing floors of the barracks. The rags they had wrapped around their ankles were already soaked. "I was young," Motl said of his determination to reach Tulchyn. "All I wanted was to eat."

After several hours, a few homes came into view. The sun was just rising over of Bortnyky, a village they encountered six miles into their journey. The travelers picked one house at random—a hovel, really—and knocked on the front door. A young Ukrainian woman answered. On her steps were three children, gaunt, unwashed, and dressed in dirty rags. The escapees explained where they had been and how exhausted they were. They asked if she might help. Their story moved her to tears. The woman, who would introduce herself as Sophia, rushed them inside. For the next two hours, she tended to the children as if they were her own, serving them buttermilk and potatoes and drying their rags over her brick oven, a *pechka*. They met her young son, Grisha, and her daughter, Katya, whose father had been conscripted the previous summer. Sophia assured Motl that by passing south through Bortnyky, he had in fact picked the most direct route to Tulchyn. Unbeknownst to Motl, Etel, and Naum, it was also where many Jewish children would be killed after encountering a heinous group of Romanians.[10]

For Sophia, the very presence of three escapees in her home would be enough to warrant a jail sentence or a large fine, the punishment for anyone found to be harboring Jews.[11] Yet for the next two years, she would welcome Motl and Etel inside whenever they appeared. At the end of this first visit, she packed them food and provided the directions they would need to reach Tulchyn.

After journeying another nine miles along snow-covered plains, they arrived in Tarasivka, and in another four miles, they reached Nestervarka, a village just across the Silnytsya River from Tulchyn. In time, Nestervarka, which was home to a collective farm and vast peat fields, would soon become the site of a forced labor camp. For now, the children found that they could walk undetected, even in the late afternoon, as long as they avoided the main roads. All that stood between them and Tulchyn was the frozen Silnytsya. Rather than taking the bridge into town, which Romanians were likely patrolling, they slid down an embankment farther downriver and crossed the Silnytsya at its narrowest point. They approached Tulchyn from the east.

Their once-vibrant Jewish neighborhood was nearly silent. Most of the homes that had once lined the streets they knew were now stripped down to their foundations. The framing, they would later learn, had evidently been used for firewood. Just as they were about to turn onto Voikova Street, they saw a young child, four or five years of age at most, who was watching them from a street corner. "*Zhidy!*" he suddenly screamed, gesturing wildly to a group of teenage boys in the vicinity, hoping they would do something about the runaway Jews.[12]

Motl, Etel, and Naum broke into a slow trot, about the quickest pace they could muster. Two of the boys pursued them. The third split off in the opposite direction, maybe to get the police. When Motl looked over his shoulder again, he saw that someone had stopped the boys.

"And just where do you think you're going?" an older man screamed at them in Ukrainian while holding them back by their shirt collars. Motl steered Etel and Naum around a corner, where they passed vacant Jewish homes that were in varying states of ruin. They tried a few doors before finding one that had already been kicked in. They climbed to the attic and pulled the ladder up with them. Teary-eyed and out of breath, they watched through a slit in an outer wall for signs of the boys and any *polizei*. As they scanned the area for signs of their pursuers, a distressing scene unfolded below them—every home in view was being dismembered by Ukrainians, some breaking apart the walls, others pulling away wooden floorboards.

The children remained in hiding until sundown, at which point the winds sent a biting chill through the air. Etel reminded Motl that one of his close friends and former neighbors, a half-Jewish boy named Shunya Schwab, lived nearby. His parents had concealed the family's identity after the Germans first occupied Tulchyn, changing their last name to Malin. His mother was an ethnic German, and his father, who was Jewish, had been drafted into the Red Army. Motl agreed to leave the attic. When he knocked on Shunya's door, he expected to see his friend. After a few tries, Shunya's mother, Zhenya, opened it instead.[13]

"Motya, how did you get here?" she asked.

"Ms. Zhenya, please, I need some place to sleep."

"You're alive. I can't believe it. Oh, what am I going to do with you?"

"Ms. Zhenya, I'm not alone. My sister and our friend are with me. We just need a place to rest."

She remained in the doorway for a moment to compose herself. She told Motl to get Naum and Etel and bring them inside. She then locked the door behind them and went to confer with her neighbors, the Wolf family. They agreed to let Naum spend the night with them. Zhenya told Motl and Etel that they could sleep under her daybed on the condition that they leave early the next morning.[14] "Oh, I'm playing with fire," Etel heard Zhenya murmur to herself. She then served them dinner in the kitchen. Shunya sat nearby.

"We talked like a couple of buddies, Shunya and I," Motl said. "I told him everything, except for what we were doing in Tulchyn." Shunya had something to confess to Motl. At some point that winter, he had wandered into the Braverman home and taken Motl's skis.

At six o'clock the next morning, Zhenya woke the children. "Go now," she told them. "You have to go." It was still dark when they met Naum on the street. In a few minutes' time, they crossed the threshold of Motl and Etel's childhood home, among the few on Voikova Street that were still standing. The front door had been left open. Once inside, they found that it had been ransacked. Goose feathers covered the floor. Many pieces of furniture had been stolen; others were gutted by townspeople looking for values sealed inside. Idel's sewing machine, hidden above the boards in the ceiling, had also been taken. Even the few potatoes left behind in the cellar were gone. Worst of all, the attic had collapsed onto their hiding place, perhaps under the weight of one too many eager Ukrainians. Motl realized that this was a godsend; it had deterred the thieves from venturing under the floorboards. Slowly, the three children swept aside the rubble and began to dig. The things that Motl had helped his father stow away were still intact under the plywood lid, including the fabric rolls and a dress, enough items to net them several weeks' worth of food. Motl and Etel packed them in the potato sacks they had brought.

Feeling triumphant, the young escapees began retracing the route they had taken two days earlier, this time without issue. They departed Tulchyn mid-morning and crossed into Nestervarka. From Tarasivka, they found their way to Bortnyky, where Sophia happily received them again. After drying their rags and serving more potatoes and buttermilk, she packed salt for them to take back to the camp. Etel handed her some of the cheesecloth they had found in their cellar to show her gratitude. Grisha accompanied them for part of their walk to the camp before turning back.

Early that evening, they saw smoke rising from the hut near the camp's gate, suggesting that the guards were already asleep. They climbed back over the wall and trotted to their barracks. Manya and Lova were overjoyed when they saw their older brother and sister. Soybil and Idel were in tears. For the first time in months, there was cause for celebration. Yet the thirty-five miles they had traveled that week had taken its toll. For the next few days, they could do little but lie on the floor and sleep. That month, Lova turned three years old, and Motl quietly marked his thirteenth birthday.

The family's fortunes took another series of drastic turns as the winter slowly ceded to spring. A Ukrainian woman from Pechera had hired Idel to sew clothes at her home. Idel would leave for several days at a time, with the woman paying off the guards to overlook the matter. He was paid in food and sometimes money. Boris Sandler's mother, a seamstress, also received permission to work outside the camp for stretches of a week or more. A woman in Bortnyky paid her in beans, potatoes, beets, and on occasion, chicken. The same woman had become one of Stratulat's romantic partners, Boris's mother told him, and she made certain that Stratulat tell the guards not to give Boris's mother trouble.

Inside the camp, a new power dynamic had emerged. The camp's Jewish leadership had become only more emboldened. "They seized control of the camp and established their own order," Motl would write. A well-known physician from Tulchyn, a Dr. Vishnevsky, was remembered as being one of these privileged Jews and for being allotted his own living quarters. He frequently tormented inmates in much the same way the Ukrainian *polizei* did. Wearing a bowler hat and an overcoat with a fur collar, he would kick their boiling soups over while chiding his fellow townspeople for breaking the rules.[15]

One day, a pair of Jewish men, Trudman and Krasnevski, apparently now part of the Jewish administration, stormed into the Bravermans' barracks. They explained that a group of new prisoners had paid them to evict the Bravermans in order to claim the changing room for themselves. Within minutes, they were outside in the cold with nowhere to go and with their few belongings at their feet. Trudman and Krasnevski suggested that they take shelter in the basement of the sanitorium building. There, the Bravermans soon discovered what others already knew: this was where the dying were sequestered, often while in the throes of typhus.[16] "There was no way we would have survived in there," Etel said, estimating the number of prisoners in the basement at fifty. "One day, maybe two days at most."

Soybil found a *polizei* standing guard near the wall and presented him with either a cut of batiste fabric or with an entire roll that had been salvaged from Tulchyn (Motl's and Etel's recollections diverged when it came to this detail). He accepted the bribe and led them to the third floor and then through the doorway of room 37. He flashed his baton at the forty or so prisoners pinned against one another on the concrete floor, forcing them to clear space. "The air was heavy," Motl said. "Many of the people now lying next to us were on the verge of death." With nearly every inch of the floor occupied, it was almost impossible to leave—to go and relieve oneself outside under a tree, for instance—without stepping on someone. The simple act of changing positions at night would set off a chain reaction beginning with one's neighbor, which in turn forced the next-closest person to shift, and so on.

Laying closest to the Bravermans was a former neighbor from Tulchyn, an elderly woman whose husband had once been the director of the Kunis garment factory. The Shpak family also lay nearby. Motl recognized the oldest of the three Shpak children, a teenage girl who was a schoolmate of his before the occupation. To save her loved ones, she would regularly cross the Buh to beg for bread in Sokilets. One day, from the steps leading down to the Buh, Motl saw what appeared to be the girl's body on the frozen river below, her blood staining the ice around her. She had been shot dead by Germans lying in wait on the opposite riverbank. He watched as the team of appointed gravediggers was summoned and as they loaded her onto a makeshift stretcher. Within two weeks of her disappearance, the girl's mother and siblings died of starvation. The elderly woman in their room also died a short time later. Etel last saw her searching the camp's grounds for potato peels. When she looked up and saw Etel, she only asked that Etel find her son and tell him what became of his mother.

Another of their roommates was a young mother, whose final moments would forever haunt Etel. "The woman had two children in her arms," Etel said. "It was clear she had sold everything and didn't have anything left, and now they were going to die. Either she smothered them, or . . . I don't know. She hugged both of her children and they rocked together on the floor. I looked over again and all three of them were dead. It was frightening to watch all of this. Frightening." Standing outside in the courtyard one day, Motl saw an elderly couple lower themselves to the ground under a soft rain. They closed their eyes and never returned to their feet, as if pledging to live out their final hours in one another's embrace.

In the Refrigerator, Mikhail Bartik's little brother lay dying with his family at his side. In prewar Tulchyn, Mikhail's mother would often ply the boy, her youngest son, with *lekach*, or honey cake, to fatten him up. Now, near death, he asked his mother for another bite.

"Mama, maybe here you can give me some *lekach* too? I'm so hungry."

"Yashinka—"

"Oh, I understand. I understand you don't have any. The Germans have eaten it."

Bartik's father and eight male cousins would also die of disease and starvation. His aunt, a woman in her thirties named Elka, spent her final days wandering the camp, singing, "I once was a mother to eight children. And now I'm the mother to not a single one." Soon, she too was found dead.[17]

Every time Boris Sandler's mother prepared a pot of soup, a neighbor from Tulchyn, once the head of a regional treasury department, would come and open the door to their room in the sanitorium building. "Here is the condition she is in," Boris described. "Naked. Barefoot. With a bag wrapped around her. Completely covered in lice. They would give her two spoonfulls. And this is how she subsisted until she died. There were hundreds like her."

Some dying prisoners and their loved ones sought medical help from Dr. Vishnevsky, who figured prominently in postwar survivor testimony, as a last resort. "You're sick? So die then," he would often reply.[18] Survivor Shelia Vaisman's tearful father once turned to him to help save Shelia's ailing brother but was rebuffed. After Shelia's mother was badly beaten by some *polizei*, Shelia's father once again pleaded with Dr. Vishnevsky for help, only to be kicked in return.[19] Boris Sandler's sister Manya saw him "finish off helpless people" with a whip, behavior he would justify with the rhyme, "*Ya ne vrach, ya palach*" (I'm not a doctor, I'm an executioner).[20]

From time to time, new transports of prisoners entered Pechera and replaced those who had perished. In this way, the camp's population was constantly in flux. One of the women now sharing the room with the Bravermans, a deportee from Bukovyna, one day announced to Etel and others in the vicinity that she had just sold her last coat to villagers at the gate. "Now, I'm going to die," she said soberly. Generally, survivors remember the Romanian-speaking Jews as faring the worst of any group brought to Pechera. They were better dressed and were considered far wealthier than the local Jews, and they often had jewels and coins at their disposal, which many had sewn into their clothing before being forced to cross the Dnister. But their advantages ended the moment they ran out of items to trade. Not only had they endured months of torment before ever stepping foot in the camp—in Romanian transit camps, other ghettos, and then during their harrowing marches to the Buh—but the Ukrainian peasants were less likely to sympathize with them when they came pleading for food and respite from the cold.

As historian Dalia Ofer wrote of the Jews exiled to Transnistria, "They were deported to an alien, unknown environment, did not speak the local language, and many did not know Russian. They had no connections with the local population and the physical and cultural environment was foreign to them." While Bessarabian Jews often spoke both Russian and Ukrainian and had a familiarity with the local culture—prior to 1919, Bessarabia had been part of the Russian empire—those from Bukovyna often did not.[21] On the other hand, Bessarabian Jews tended to be sent to eastern and southern Transnistria, where survival rates were much lower.[22]

One of these Romanian-speaking Jews had been a doctor. Fellow prisoners remembered him for being tall and handsome, with a prominent gold crown on one of his teeth. During his final days, he was seen running around the camp naked. He would burst into various rooms, hungry and shivering, before being shoved out.[23] One day, Etel recalled, he was outside somewhere, shouting indiscriminately, when a guard shot him in the head for all to see.

Like the doctor, survivors recalled examples of other prisoners, and sometimes loved ones, whose mental states were more visibly deteriorating. One day, Shelia Vaisman's mother set her, her older brother, and her younger sister down in the camp's "morgue" and left them there. Their father scolded her after the incident. Later, she found the resolve to disguise herself as a peasant woman and walk from village to village asking for food to bring back to her husband and three children. "Outwardly, she did not differ from the Ukrainians much, and this helped her stay undetected," Shelia would recount. The villagers rarely refused her. Sometimes the *polizei* would intercept her mother, beat her, and claim her food. But when she did manage to return with something to eat, Shelia knew to savor it as long as she could. "Even now, as I tell you all of this," she described to her interviewer more than fifty years later, "an image floats up in front of my eyes: how my sister and I would sit down, take this treasure, the piece of bread, mince it up into a thousand tiny pieces, then put them into our mouths and chew for a long, long time."[24]

That spring, the number of people sharing room 37 with the Bravermans began to dwindle. It was not unusual for a person laying an inch or two away to be alive one evening and dead the next morning. Each day, corpses were dragged into the hallways and stairwells for removal by the burial team. In the same hallways, many prisoners also relieved themselves, no longer having the strength to go outside. Most mornings, the burial teams would also visit each room with their gurneys, which were nothing more than two wooden posts attached with ropes. "How many dead today?" they would ask. As payment for their services, they seized all items belonging to the deceased. They were especially interested in hearing which prisoners were on the cusp of death so that they would know to return for their bodies—and most importantly, their gold teeth—the next day. As Mikhail Bartik would recall, the camp's Jewish administration and team of gravediggers were not formally appointed or recruited. It happened that certain character traits brought the men together. The more physically able the men were, the more brazen. "They were lowlifes, miscreants," Bartik said. "Respectable people didn't join them."[25] Ester Bartik, Mikhail's future wife, would always remember how the men treated her young aunt after she died. They slung her body onto the gurney and allowed her head to hit every stair from the third floor of the former sanitorium building to the ground level.[26]

Every other week, Motl and Etel would leave the camp together to search for food. In time, Etel would develop nyctalopia, or night blindness, the result of chronic malnutrition. On warm nights, while passing through fields, Motl would venture ahead to gather potatoes while Etel remained behind, hiding under straw until Motl's return. On occasion, they would take turns escaping from the camp. Etel would travel with other children her age, including Motl's friend Arkadii. Once, while caught between villages and with nowhere to sleep, she and Arkadii broke into a cowshed and stayed there overnight. "I woke up at one point, and suddenly, a cow was standing over us," she remembered. "I could see her breath. How she didn't trample us, I don't know." The next morning, they approached another home and asked the family living there for something to eat. A Ukrainian woman pointed to a pail filled with small, boiled potatoes, used as feed for their pigs.

"Lady, may we take some?" Etel asked.

"Take some, take some, children," the woman replied, after which she offered Etel and Arkadii some frozen potatoes to take with them.

"Oh, when the war ends, we won't need anything, just a *pechka*," Etel said while placing the potatoes in her sack.

By now, Manya and Lova had stopped asking their mother for food. Most days, they said little. "They were such silent, poor children," Etel remembered. To amuse herself and brighten their moods, she and Lova would play a game each afternoon.

"Lovachka, what shall we eat today?" she would ask.

"Oh, I suppose some beans, some soup," he might say.

"And what do you wish for tomorrow?"

"For us to live long and be strong!" he would say, invoking a saying that someone had taught him.

During an especially cold week, Motl and Soybil left the camp together, leaving Etel behind to watch Manya and Lova. One afternoon, Etel glanced at them and could not help but weep. She knew they were hungry. She asked a woman sharing their room if she could borrow a crust of bread for the children to eat, promising to repay her in kind. Etel ripped the bread in two and gave some to each child, taking nothing for herself. When Motl and Soybil walked in the next day carrying bundles of food, Etel ran from the room and kept running until she was in the courtyard, convinced that more could be done for her young brother and sister. After stacking rocks near the camp wall and climbing over it, she felt a strong pulse of wind at her back that propelled her nearly all the way to Bortnyky, where heavy snowfall nearly overtook her. A villager in Bortnyky named Maria—whom Etel had come to know and who had been especially generous during their previous encounters—opened her door to allow a frightened Etel inside. Storms raged for the next three days, stranding Etel inside with Maria and her husband and two sons. They ate meals from the same pot, each extending a spoon into the soups and boiled cornmeal that Maria would prepare.

In Pechera, Motl and Soybil knew that something was wrong. Etel never left the camp alone. Even if she had, there was no need to stray farther than the neighboring Bortnyky, less than a day's walk roundtrip. Fortunately, Motl knew where to find her. While making their way back together from Maria's, Motl and Etel made a grisly discovery: a frozen body. They encountered eight or nine more on the walk, each assuming a different position. One of the victims, a mother, was still cradling her child as she lay on the roadside. They had all been caught outside the camp during the storm.

By April 1942, Romanian records showed that nearly 4,400 of the prisoners in Pechera, as well as those being held in the nearby ghettos, had died.

Another 83,699 Jews remained alive in Transnistria, or as one document put it, the surviving Jews "not yet evacuated from Transnistria."[27] Villagers who had once frequented the camp gates to barter with the prisoners or to hand them scraps of food had all but disappeared. Many were busy sowing their fields. Visits by the woman who occasionally hired Motl's father were growing sporadic. Like the Bravermans, Pechera's surviving prisoners had few options left.

"In the yard of the camp, men dug a hole and secretly stoked a fire," recalled Svetlana Kogan-Rabinovich. "We would boil acacia leaves; sometimes, we would find some frozen cabbage, chestnuts, nettles, sorrel, saltbush. . . . We sucked our blood from our fingers to somewhat satisfy the hunger."[28]

One day that spring, while returning to the camp after begging in the villages, twelve-year-old orphan Ester Bartik was spotted by Smetansky, a *polizei*. Although Ester was walking with a pack of Ukrainian girls who were willing to help conceal her, Smetansky deduced that there was a prisoner in their midst. He gave Ester a beating. She then hobbled to the third floor of the main camp building. It was the lowest point in her imprisonment, she later said. One of her sisters had been missing for nearly three weeks while searching for food. Her other sister and her family were dying in the camp. Ester recalled this during an interview with the USC Shoah Foundation in 1997:

> I don't know how to explain this to you, and maybe you won't believe me. Maybe it's something I should be ashamed to say. That we went around finding grass to eat is one thing—and where did this remaining grass grow? Only near the stables where the bodies were discarded. Otherwise there was no grass. We even went where people defecated. We scavenged for cherry pits there. We washed these pits in the Buh and later sat breaking them open with stones to at least eat the seeds.[29]

Survivors would later report frightening encounters with fellow inmates who had resorted to cannibalism. In one such incident, a man was discovered eating a dead woman's breasts in the sanitorium building's basement.[30] In a recent documentary, survivor Lev Muchnik recalled a similar episode. "I can see before my eyes a young man that I gave hot water to a day or two before," he said. "And he thanked me, took the water with trembling hands and drank. Two or three days after I met him, I saw him lying dead by the front door, outside. He held a woman's breast by his mouth just as if he was suckling from it."[31] Another well-known story that circulated among prisoners was that of a woman who severed one of her breasts in order to feed her starving sister.[32]

Eva Poliak, a first cousin of Motl's future wife, who had belonged to Pechera's small Jewish community before the occupying forces uprooted her family, wrote in a recent memoir that some of the men on the burial squad would periodically bring the children meat from dead animals: "We rushed to this carrion and ate. Sometimes they managed to bring us frozen potatoes."[33]

Word of these incidents traveled to the town of Mohyliv-Podilskyi in northwest Transnistria, the site of one of the largest ghettos. A report from the former president of the ghetto's Jewish committee referenced prisoners in Pechera who "fed themselves with human corpses,"[34] which would later lead historian Radu Ioanid to conclude that Pechera "was the most horrific site of Jewish internment in all of Transnistria."[35] Detainees in the Mohyliv-Podilskyi ghetto were said to have hidden in "cellars and holes under the ground; they escaped to meadows in the rain in order to hide in cornfields and ditches" to avoid being deported to Pechera after the orders were given beginning in the late summer of 1942. Police dogs sniffed them out anyway.[36]

The responsibility of determining which Jews should be expelled from Mohyliv-Podilskyi to Pechera—a virtual death sentence—and which should stay fell on the ghetto's Jewish leaders, who were required to produce a list for the Romanians. After the Mohyliv-Podilskyi ghetto was established, the Jewish committee's initial goal was to save as many Jews as possible. Its leaders used the avenues available to them, including bribery, to angle for concessions that might keep fellow detainees alive.[37] When conditions worsened and it became clear that not everyone could survive, they decided to protect those who belonged to the same communities as they once had.

In northern Transnistria's ghettos, the Jewish leadership almost always comprised affluent, educated, and organized deportees from southern Bukovyna. Having been sent by train to Transnistria months after those from northern Bukovyna had been sent by foot, they were often able to bring valuables with them. Many of the south Bukovyna Jews were born when the whole of Bukovyna belonged to the Austro-Hungarian Empire, before its annexation to Romania in 1918, and had grown up speaking German. They tended to identify strongly with the Romanian language and culture and their hometowns, often more so than with other Jews. Unlike those from northern Bukovyna or Bessarabia, they had never been under Soviet rule and were not suspected of being communists. Many had been prominent figures back home. The result was that 70 percent of the deportees from south Bukovyna would survive life in the Mohyliv-Podilskyi ghetto and other ghettos in the same district.[38] Another favored group of Romanian Jews were those from the Dorohoi district of southern Bukovyna, who were exiled to Transnistria in December 1941. Yet there was no one to advocate for the local Ukrainian Jews. They were outnumbered by arrivals from beyond the Dnister, who tended to look down at them and who viewed their entire way of life as primitive.[39]

There was no shortage of controversy around the decisions made by the Jewish committee's members in Mohyliv-Podilskyi, who were granted the autonomy to lead as they pleased. Fellow ghetto prisoners rightly criticized them for favoring deportees from the same social strata at the expense of less favored groups. Ukrainian Jews were chosen first for expulsion to Pechera and to the nearby starvation camp in the village of Skazyntsi; those from Bessarabia and northern Bukovyna followed. The term employed for these expulsions in particular was *descongestionarea*, meaning to "thin out." Only in spring 1942 did the Romanians make the connection between the awful conditions they had created in Mohyliv-Podilskyi and the proliferation of disease, which began spreading to the gendarmes.[40] While the Romanian authorities could have arbitrarily picked which Jews to bring to Pechera to alleviate crowding in the ghetto, they preferred singling out the poorest and those who they believed maintained Soviet allegiances. The Romanian Jews earned the designation of being mere "trash." Jews from northern Bukovyna and Bessarabia—territories the Soviet Union controlled for a single year in the leadup to war—and local Ukrainian Jews were considered "scum." Still, the Romanians needed the Jewish committee and its Jewish police to help distinguish between the groups.[41]

It came as no surprise then, when Romanian general Mihail Iliescu called for banishing the poorest from the Mohyliv-Podilskyi ghetto to Pechera a few hundred at a time because "they will perish anyway, and the camp in [Pechera] was created exclusively for this reason."[42] After the first convoys reached Pechera in the summer of 1942, another wave followed weeks later. Single mothers—whose husbands had died or were in the Red Army—and their young children were chosen first for deportation. Because they were occupied with caretaking, they were unable to work and were thus considered expendable.[43] The deportations to the starvation camps were so unpopular that the Jewish leaders who negotiated them with Romanian authorities resigned from their posts afterward.[44]

Before the evacuations, many parents decided to leave their children behind, believing that they were more likely to survive in the ghetto as orphans, where a few ounces of bread was provided each day.[45] Those bound for Pechera were packed into freight cars, where doors and windows remained shut until the train stopped in a village nine miles shy of Pechera. Some had died of suffocation along the way. From there, they journeyed the remaining distance by foot, all while enduring abuse from Romanian gendarmes.[46] Of the three thousand Mohyliv-Podilskyi Jews taken to Pechera, just twenty-eight were still alive a year later.[47] After the war, a Romanian public prosecutor who had been assigned to a war crimes tribunal concluded that Pechera "will remain blackened forever" and that like Skazyntsi, it was the "predominant stain on Antonescu's government."[48]

In their testimonies, the new prisoners who were brought to Pechera remembered the horror of entering the camp and witnessing the conditions that its first victims—from Tulchyn, Bratslav, and Trostyanets—had been subjected to. It served as a window into their own fate.

"Here stood living skeletons, in rags, hungry. They were exhausted," said survivor Abram Kaplan, then eight years old, also of Mohyliv-Podilskyi. "They begged practically every new convoy for something to eat. Many of the arrivals did offer them something. They would pounce on scraps of food. Altercations would always break out. These were frightening people to watch."[49]

"There was a group of people, maybe two hundred or three hundred of them," described child survivor Arkadii Glinets upon arriving from Mohyliv-Podilskyi with his family. "It was frightening to watch. They were skeletons. . . . They were naked, wearing rags. They were screaming, asking for food. Some of us still had some bread. They fought over it, choking one another."[50] Arkadii's family then found shelter in one of the former stables, to the left of the main alley. There were no doors or windows and only half of the structure was covered.

In October 1942, the authorities requested the transfer to Pechera of another 3,300 Jews from the ghettos of Sharhorod, Dzhuryn, and Murafa. Only the venality of a Romanian official prevented the order from being carried out. He withdrew his decree after receiving what he had been pin-ing for: a 1.5-carat diamond ring.[51]

When there was no longer enough room in the cemetery for Pechera's vic-tims, the burial team began taking the deceased to a clearing deep in the woods just west of the villages, where three trenches had appeared months earlier. The mass graves were serving their intended purpose after all.

Many prisoners, including Eva Poliak and her loved ones, were under no illusions about surviving the Pechera camp. As she would write in her postwar memoir, they had lost all hope. But occasionally, fellow prisoners lifted her spirits with song. "I remember on one of the outer staircases of one of the barracks, on the stairs there were 'artists' who sang Jewish songs, and we stood below and wept bitterly. But it gave us strength," she wrote.[52]

A handful of children passed the time by composing their own song lyrics—whether on paper or by committing them to memory—to express their despair. Occasionally, a glimmer of humanity shone through the darkness. Once, a couple wed. The bride and groom belonged to affluent families, he from Bratslav and she from Dzhuryn.[53] Others maintained their religious beliefs and customs, particularly the deportees from Bukovyna.[54] Abram Kaplan's mother and father frequently joined a hand-ful of fellow prisoners on the second floor of the former sanitorium build-ing for prayer. His father had brought his tallit prayer shawl from Mohyliv-Podilskyi and wore it beneath his clothes until it was in tatters.[55]

CHAPTER SIX

Life on the Run

I N D E C E M B E R 1941, Heinrich Himmler, the head of the Schutzstaffel, or SS, as well as the German police, became intimately acquainted with what he would later call the "magnificent roads of the Soviet paradise." While on an inspection tour across southern Ukraine, miserable road conditions dogged the all-terrain vehicle he had been riding in. It was said that Himmler himself once got out to help extract it from the mud and that he was later forced to complete his inspections from the air.[1] The experience moved Himmler to accelerate plans for building a road network through the territory, essential for the German advance on Stalingrad (Volgograd). The project would become known as Thoroughfare IV (Durchgangsstrasse IV), or DG IV. Himmler intended to widen, pave, and connect decrepit Soviet roads and highways that began in Lviv (then in occupied Poland, now Ukraine) and extended more than 1,300 miles through southern Ukraine to Stalino (today, Donetsk) and then to Taganrog and Rostov-on-Don in Russia, creating an important supply corridor.[2]

Yet by spring 1942, there were no longer enough living Jews left in Reichskommissariat Ukraine to exploit.[3] Hitler, who was now aware of the shortage of intended slave laborers—surviving Jews as well as Soviet POWs—approved the DG IV plan anyway, with the caveat that the road be built as primitively as possible and that it have a lifespan of only several years. Even a lesser DG IV in the short term could play a role in his fantasy of German colonization and expansion in the East, known as lebensraum (living space), a pretext for the invasion of the Soviet Union and one of the ideas that would lead to the Holocaust. He continued to cling to the notion

of eventually settling the areas around the DG IV with ethnic Germans—
as many as ten million within two decades.[4]

In August, local German SS units began raiding camps and ghettos on
the Romanian side of the Buh in search of workers, an idea that had apparently been proposed by an SS officer who managed a construction zone in
Haisyn.[5] Each transfer across the Buh needed Romanian authorization.
This included a request for five thousand Jews in the district now encom-
passing Pechera. Gheorghe Alexianu, Transnistria's governor, ultimately
signed off, deciding that he had no use for a large Jewish labor force.[6]

Had the war ended in September 1942, after the camp commander, Stratulat, had defied the SS and saved the prisoners of the Pechera camp from
being sent to their deaths, history might have judged him differently. Yet
his subsequent dealings would make him an accessory to the senseless
murder, sexual violence, and endless privations of the Jews under his watch.
In the months ahead, the SS began returning to Pechera with increasing
regularity. Time and time again, Stratulat permitted them to leave with
prisoners who would be deported to DG IV labor camps or who would be
murdered before ever having reached one. Stratulat, the enigmatic commander, was hardly alone in bowing to their demands. All ranks of the
Romanian administration were complicit, the result of "anti-Semitic delirium, and, especially, the inferiority complex of the Rumanian authorities,"
wrote researcher Matatias Carp.[7] As with all Jewish slave laborers, the Germans intended to work them to death. Their daily food rations sometimes
consisted of little more than one serving of pea soup and some bread.[8]
When they were no longer needed, they were shot.

On October 16, 1942, about a month after the first large-scale selection
in Pechera, a German sergeant named Hans Rucker arrived in the camp.
Rucker, who controlled another camp across the Buh, personally appealed
to Stratulat for permission to remove all girls and women ages fourteen to
twenty. He claimed that German hospitals near Vinnytsia needed more
nurses. Stratulat accommodated Rucker's request, allowing him to leave
with 150 child prisoners. The transport, however, never made it to Vinnytsia. "The girls were undressed, beaten and abused by the sadist killers,"
Carp's research showed. "Afterwards they were shot dead. A single girl,
named Frida Koffler escaped thanks to a German soldier who had been a
prisoner in Dachau before."[9] In November 1942, five hundred Pechera prisoners were trucked across the Buh.[10] The same SS unit would return for an

additional six hundred men, women, and girls.[11] On arrival, they would be forced into improvised shelters: schools, warehouses, and barns.[12] At least one more group of prisoners—one hundred in all—would also be sent to slave labor.[13] After their transfers, most were never heard from again.

Nearly all non-Jewish Ukrainian civilians living within thirty miles of the supply line were required to join Jews and Soviet POWs in extracting sand and gravel from quarries, transporting it to construction sites, and building the roads. Of the three categories of workers, it was far more advantageous to be a local laborer than a Jew or a POW. Above all, laborers could remain in their villages. This meant that they could continue tending to their own crops and to barter the yields for other goods.[14] Jews and POWs, however, were confined to the camps and subjected to the cruelty of the guards. Those deemed unfit to work after being "used up" physically and psychologically and from exposure and deprivation were shot. The Germans and their local policemen eagerly carried out the killings, which were done routinely and often arbitrarily, sometimes simply because a construction zone had been completed. The Germans accounted for the killings of "used up" laborers in advance for planning purposes.[15]

On February 1, 1943, a Jewish pharmacist named Rakhil Fradis-Milner observed conditions in the village of Zarudyntsi, the site of a German slave labor camp fifteen miles east of Pechera, where an unknown number of the camp's prisoners had been brought to toil. For protection against the bitter cold, they wrapped blankets around their heads and straw-filled sacks around their shoes. Among them were mothers who had been torn away from their infants, men and women from their spouses, and children from their parents.[16]

Before the war, Fradis-Milner and her family had lived in the city of Chernivtsi, in northern Bukovyna. One night in July 1941, Romanian gendarmes came to deport them. Her three-year-old son, Shura, clutched a teddy bear as they were taken from the city's large ghetto to the Cariera de Piatră transit camp in northeast Transnistria and subsequently shuffled from one labor camp to the next. After learning of Fradis-Milner's profession, the Germans appointed her to be a medical aide. "Cure them with the whip," they told her.[17]

In a letter she would write after returning to Chernivtsi in late 1944, Fradis-Milner described Pechera's ailing prisoners in Zarudyntsi and the fate that would befall them:

People with dull faces that had lost all human expression, who were covered by rags, barefoot, with bodies tormented by scabies and with the most varied kinds of sores that medicine never meets with in normal times, who were sitting on the floor in some tatters or other, anxiously picking off lice. They were so occupied with this work that they barely paid attention to my arrival; only those who were in particular need of my help got to their feet. And suddenly, there was a rush, there were shouts, people were running, their eyes gleaming, some were crying. What was going on? They [the Germans] had brought some bread. Just picture it, they were giving a whole loaf to each person. This was something new; salvation is probably near, the unfortunates thought. It turned out that our good-hearted, efficient Germans, knowing that the Aktion [massacre] would take place on February 5, and that in a few days it would be impossible to know the precise quantity of bread that was needed, and that since it would be necessary to make the calculation, had given an advance on the total amount of bread.[18]

After the September 1942 selection, Motl's father, Idel, and Boris Sandler's sister Manya were sent to a DG IV labor camp in the village of Krasnopilka, sixty miles east of Pechera. By the time they arrived, many of those in their transport no longer had the strength to so much as carry a pickaxe, Manya would recount.[19] The camp's fanatical commandant, Karl Klenk, tortured and murdered Jews both imprisoned within the camp and in the towns and villages surrounding it.[20] In December, the first mass executions were carried out. On Christmas, three children who had managed to escape were caught and killed. They were buried by their uncle. In January 1943, the Germans planned to massacre one hundred people, but doubled that total when ten young Jews escaped.[21] To maintain order in the warehouse housing Jews, the Germans murdered three infants and a couple.[22]

On another occasion, a young boy escaped the camp to search for his mother and sisters. The Germans pursued the child and eventually tracked him down. They then forced the camp's slave laborers, Manya included, to watch as they tied his legs to two different trucks. One of them ordered the trucks to drive off in opposite directions, tearing the child apart. Periodic mass executions were carried out in the weeks that followed. Often, the dead were buried in graves alongside prisoners who had only been wounded. Ukrainian villagers sometimes helped pull these still-living Jews from the graves after hearing their groans. They would then conceal them in their homes.[23]

In February 1943, Idel developed an infection in his heel and could no longer work. Manya would later tell Motl that she had seen his father's (my great-grandfather's) execution.[24] He was among the fifteen thousand Jewish slave laborers murdered in German-occupied Soviet Ukraine after being handed over by the Romanians.[25] As with other DG IV sites, ailing Jewish workers were summarily killed in Krasnopilka by both the SS and Lithuanian collaborationist policemen.[26] Manya would survive Krasnopilka and was later transferred to neighboring DG IV slave labor camps in Mykhailivka and Talalaivka, where she and a few dozen prisoners escaped a final liquidation after learning of the Germans' intentions. Of those who fled with her, many were captured and shot, and others were buried alive. Local villagers helped Manya join a partisan detachment, with whom she stayed until Soviet Ukraine's liberation.[27]

At some point in 1943, Pechera prisoners Rul Shahovna Brondman and her brother Pinya (short for Pinkale), among the last surviving members of their family, were deported back to their hometown of Bratslav as slave laborers. They were assigned to a segment of the DG IV that also passed through the villages and towns of Semenky, Nemyriv, and Haisyn. The Germans had hand-picked a now-emaciated Rul for work in Pechera even as she struggled to stand. She owed her survival to Pinya.[28]

"This was a brawny, strong guy, persistent, who even in frightening times didn't lose his composure," she described in written testimony that would later be housed at the State Archive of Vinnytsia Province. "When the order was passed to transfer us to the Bratslav camp, he carried me, like a log, wrapped in his overcoat, and threw me in the bed of the truck [in Pechera] nearly lifeless."

Before the outbreak of war, Rul had fond memories of her childhood in Bratslav, a town that had once been home to Hasidic sect leader Rebbe Nachman, the great-grandson of Rebbe Yisrael ben Eliezer (also known as the Ba'al Shem Ṭov), the Hasidic movement's founder. Summer evenings in Bratslav had an air of magic to them. Most days, from dawn to dusk, her parents were consumed by their work in the leather trade. When Rul's father was not minding a small leather store attached to a military post, he was toiling away in foul-smelling pits where the animal skins were tanned. But at night, the family's home was filled with friends, neighbors, and music. Her father played the fiddle, and his children often accompanied him. Rul's younger brother, Fima, drummed on little bottles, and her older brother Pinya played the mandolin. The Brondmans were known not only in Bratslav but throughout the neighboring villages and hamlets. That all ended on July 22, 1941, with the start of the occupation.[29]

Rul recalled that the first Bratslav slave labor camp had been established within a school on Lenin Street. It was surrounded by barbed wire. Germans and Ukrainian police guarded the camp. On occasion, some of the locals lobbed food over the fence to the starving workers. "This was our only droplet of salvation," Rul said. Seemingly every day, the same sequence would repeat itself: workers who had become ill or too weak to work were sorted and then trucked away and shot. Then, a group of replacements would arrive. The commander, a German named Goft, whom Rul called "a frightening person, a monster," routinely deceived the camp population about the workers who disappeared each day, claiming they were being sent "to a good camp." Many Jewish girls and women were forced into the Germans' personal quarters, never to return.

Most days, Rul worked in a stone quarry wearing rags and wooden boots. She managed to return to good health while subsisting on a single daily serving of horse-meat stew. But like most other slave laborers, she endured beatings at the hands of a German guard named Arthur, whose blows scarred her body. "Often in my dreams," she described decades later, "I'm under German and police escort, with a yellow star on my right arm and back. And it is always so bright, this star."[30]

In time, Rul noticed a change in her older brother, Pinya. He fixated on taking revenge against the German oppressors and talked of little else. "Thoughts of escaping the bondage and engaging in warfare with the fascists made a monster of my brother," Rul said. "He couldn't give up on it for a minute." Pinya raised the idea of staging an armed revolt with fellow prisoners and recruited ten others to help him carry out the plan. They found an ally in a deaf villager who lived just outside the camp, a partisan. The group used his home to store purloined German weapons, which were sometimes left unattended while the camp's guards supervised the camp's work details. One day, the local inhabitant's role in the scheme was discovered. The identities of his collaborators, who were on their way to see him, were also revealed. They were all captured and detained in a basement once used by the NKVD, Stalin's secret police. "They twisted their arms, knocked out their teeth, stabbed their bodies, beat them unconscious," Rul said. "People reported to us that on the street they heard the screams."[31] Another Bratslav laborer, teenager Evgeniia Tsirulnikova, a friend of Rul's, recalled that during their absence, camp leadership threatened to kill every tenth Jew until Pinya and the others returned.[32] Matatias Carp's research also points to a March 29, 1943, event in which six people were discovered missing from the camp. The camp commander announced that sixty people would be murdered if the "fugitives" remained missing.[33]

When they were eventually discovered, the Germans chained them to one another and paraded them through the streets of Bratslav. Along the way, Pinya pleaded with onlookers not to report what they were seeing to his sister. "Do not say anything to Rul, do not. She will not survive it." Before murdering them in a forest near Hrynenky, the Germans ordered the Jews to kneel, to which Pinya replied, "Soviet knees do not bend to fascist bastards." They responded by stabbing him with a bayonet and throwing him into the pit.[34] By December 1943, the DG IV camps were closed and most of the remaining prisoners shot.

Only after Bratslav's liberation in 1944 did a witness tell Rul the bitter truth about her brother. The villager led Rul to the site of the killings. A small group helped Rul exhume the bodies. She arranged for them to be transported and interred in the local cemetery.[35]

Conditions within the Pechera camp continued to deteriorate. In late 1942, the Jewish administration appealed to Romania authorities for clothing and medicine, a request that was approved, but only if the shipments came from the Jewish Autonomous Assistance Committee, an organization formed by Romanian-Jewish leaders in Romania who along with Jews abroad sought to help deportees in Transnistria. Some survivors later accused the Pechera camp's Jewish committee of hoarding the food shipment they received without ever distributing it.[36]

By early 1943, the conditions inside the camp were so ghastly that a pair of Romanian officials—including the new head of the local gendarmes legion—refused to enter the buildings.[37] Around this same time, Rul Brondman's friend Evgeniia Tsirulnikova was transferred back to Pechera after also being deported to Bratslav. The starvation rations and back-breaking labor in Bratslav paled in comparison to what she now had to endure again.

"In the yard, only shadows were roaming," she said of the skeletal prisoners she encountered, whose eyes were sunken and who wore rags. When Evgeniia approached the entrance to the main three-story building, she discovered a dead mother with an infant still in her arms. Worms were crawling over them. The mother's name was Tina, and they had known one another in their native Bratslav.[38]

By now, many of the camp's children had long recognized the telltale signs of prolonged starvation in one another and themselves, the symptoms of hunger edema: swollen feet, legs, and bellies. Intense mood swings were common, as were bouts of listlessness and depression. Death was usually at hand when the protein-starved bodies began to use their own organs for fuel. Desperate to eat and to feed their families, many prisoners continued risking their lives outside the camp walls. For every child or woman who managed to return unharmed with food or money, another staggered home after being beaten. Some never recovered from their injuries. Others were jailed or murdered and never heard from again. Once, while survivor Ana Rozenberg and her mother were traveling between villages to beg for food, they hid in a haystack to evade Ukrainian policemen, who found her mother and raped her as Ana remained hiding just feet away.[39]

Etel remembered being caught by the *polizei* several times while wandering the countryside with Motl. On one such occasion, two shepherds helped detain them before turning them over to the local *polizei*. They were held in a cell and later released and allowed to return to the camp on their own. Another time, a pair of *polizei* chased after them in a violent rage. "Did they ever hit us," she recalled. "I ran away. Meanwhile, I realize they caught Motya. I'm screaming and looking back, and they're beating him with clubs. As he's running behind me, the blood is pouring down his head. The poor thing."

Boris Sandler recalled that his mother tried to shelter him as much as she could and that he was never forced to leave the camp. "I was a mama's boy," he explained. Other parents were forced to weigh the risks of letting their children beg for food against the certainty of their entire families dying of hunger. The issue became a point of contention for Mikhail Bartik. He begged his mother to let him join his friend Yasha on his trips to the villages.[40] One day, a shouting match ensued.

"Do you want to get shot, like my brother, Moishe?" Mikhail's mother countered.

"What's the difference whether we die here or out there? There is no difference whether they kill me here or out there. Let me go!"

"I won't let you."

"If you don't let me go, I'll drown myself in the River Buh. I can't bear this starvation anymore. I can't stand the hunger."

"I can't let go."

Mikhail's mother went to Mikhail's grandfather for advice.

"Mischa wants to go into the villages with some other kids, to get a hold of a bit of bread or a few potatoes," she told him.

"Listen here, my daughter," he said. "What difference does it make whether he dies here or gets killed out there? We're all going to die anyway. Let him go."[41]

In late 1942, after his eighth birthday, Arkadii Plotitskii, a prisoner from Shpykiv, came to the same realization, that only he could save himself. His mother could no longer walk (some Ukrainian children had stolen her shoes somewhere outside the camp, forcing her to walk back barefoot in the snow). His grandmother, a seamstress, had died, as had one of his two aunts. The other aunt was usually away in the villages finding food, leaving Arkadii and his mother alone and hungry in their room. The first time he escaped the camp, he found his way out near the stairs to the Southern Buh. He returned later with a piece of bread and two potatoes. It was the first taste of food he and his mother had had in eight days. He succeeded the next few times as well. And then, in the squalor of a death camp, Arkadii discovered his singing voice. In the same blue woolen suit that he had come to Pechera wearing—it had been shipped to him from one of his grandmother's sisters, who fled to the United States after the civil war—he began leaving Pechera more regularly. He learned to stand outside villagers' houses and perform songs, both upbeat and melancholy. They often rewarded him with light bundles full of onions, white bread, garlic, and thread. He had learned one of the songs from the adults in the camp, their version of the famous prison folksong "The Sun Rises and Sets":

> The sun rises and sets, but the camp is dark.
> Day and night, sentries guard our window.
> Guard us how you wish, I myself won't leave.

> Although I want freedom, the chains I cannot break.
> Oh, you, my chains, my chains.
> You iron watchmen.
> I cannot break you, and I cannot cut through you,
>   without a sharp knife.[42]

Newly fourteen and beginning to think that his father might never return, Motl also felt that he had no choice but wander the countryside to beg. Sometimes, Etel and Soybil escaped with their friends, stacking rocks at the base of the wall in order to reach the top. But now, the responsibility of feeding the family was mostly his. Pechera and other villages in the vicinity had been overwhelmed by Jewish escapees. The locals—who were struggling to feed their families and to care for livestock during wartime—had grown reluctant to help runaways. The answer was to venture to more distant places.

Early one morning, he and his next-door neighbor from Tulchyn, a boy named Arkadii, scaled the camp wall and headed for the village of Hrynenky. On the way, they passed through the village of Yastrubykha and received a warm meal. In Hrynenky, they went house to house. Some residents were willing to fill their bags with food, but no one would agree to let them stay the night. It was getting dark, and the winds began to kick up. The boys found a barn and broke in, burrowing under mounds of straw and leaving small openings near the top for air. They continued to beg in Hrynenky that week and returned to the barn each night. The barn's owner, who lived in a house next door, stormed in early one morning to find the boys. He showered them with obscenities, and while wielding a broom or some other stick, he chased them outside. He swung wildly and landed blows on their heads, necks, backs, and shoulders. As the boys ran, gripping their rucksacks, Motl felt one of his galoshes slip off.

"So what am I to do but keep going? He might kill me," Motl said. "He was possessed."

The boys ran side by side until they reached a frozen creek. Arkadii continued on. After a moment's hesitation, Motl followed. Not even halfway across, his unshod foot slipped through the ice. After pulling himself out, he pulled even with Arkadii, who was running toward the chimney smoke. Motl could feel his foot going numb. "We knock on doors and a woman sees I'm wet, barefoot," Motl said. "She lets us inside. We told her everything. She unrolled our rags by the oven. While they were drying, we started eating. She warmed us up and gave me extra rags for the foot missing a galosh."

The return trip proved disastrous. Late that afternoon, the policeman Mishka Odessit spotted them near the camp's back wall. "Come here please, boys," he said. They did as instructed. "Now drop your bags and march!" he commanded.

"How can I march?" Motl blurted out. Tears welled up in his eyes.

"These are our things," he continued. "You're taking them away from our family. They're relying on us. Mama, our kids."

"If I hear one more thing, I'm going to beat you to a pulp."

When the boys stood their ground, Odessit charged at them with his carrying pole. Arkadii ran ahead and jumped a fence, leaving Motl to fend for himself. "He caught up to me and beat me half to death," Motl said. "I lay in the snow for a long time. I couldn't move. I couldn't bend down, I couldn't straighten up." A few minutes later, Arkadii helped Motl to his feet. Each boy was incensed. That night, Motl talked Arkadii into helping him confront Odessit. As it turned out, they wouldn't have to. Odessit had hired a Jewish tailor living in the camp to sew him some clothes. He sent his daughters to collect his payment the next day. When Motl and Arkadii saw the girls carrying their rucksacks, which Odessit had apparently given them in lieu of money, they ran up and snatched them away. Most of the food they had collected was still untouched.

By late winter, Motl's flights from the camp were becoming more frequent. His absences stretched to two weeks or more as he covered ever greater distances. He now traveled mostly alone. In between escapes, he stayed in his room resting. "What did we do all day? We just laid there," Motl said. "You want to go outside? Go ahead. Come and go as you please. No one counted us. There was no order, we didn't have any numbers."

One afternoon, he found himself in the pastoral village of Silnytsya, half a day's walk south of Pechera. The weather had been mild all week, but Motl was shivering. His knees and back ached and his head throbbed. He knew he had spiked a fever. He knocked on doors hoping to find a place to rest, if only for an hour or two. Finally, a woman invited him in, telling him she was surprised to see someone from Pechera. She lived with her husband and their four children. It was clear to Motl from the look of things that the family was poor. The woman explained to him that she could not feed him that night, as her own children had not eaten, but that he could rest in one of their bedrooms. That night, the family slept together on the *pechka* while he laid in the corner of another room on some straw, using his coat as a blanket.

He awoke to a full bladder several hours later. Overcome by chills and drenched in sweat, he worried he might collapse if he tried to relieve himself outside in the cold. Instead, he used one of his galoshes and opened the front door to pour out the contents. He managed to sleep another two hours before leaving again to find food. One woman treated him to bread and borscht. Others filled his bags. That evening, he returned to the same family and offered them all the food he had gathered. His stay in Silnytsya lasted another week while he regained his strength. Some of the locals who had been willing to feed him began asking about the camp.

"You know," one Ukrainian woman told him, "fifteen kilometers from here, they say there's a ghetto in Horyshkivka. There are a few families. There are shoemakers, tailors, craftspeople. They're in a ghetto but life isn't so bad. Maybe they'll help you."

She suggested he wait until the following Thursday to leave. If he could find his way to the village of Shura-Kopiivska, he would be able to follow the peasants streaming into Horyshkivka for its market day. She warned him about standing out, as he had done in Silnytsya. There was, after all, a heavy Romanian presence at the train station nearby. The route she suggested that day would take him across fields, through a forest, and over dirt roads. He knew he had reached Shura-Kopiivska when he saw a street full of market-goers. Some were carting the goods they intended to trade, while others carried sacks they'd need for purchases. He mixed with the locals as best he could on the way to Horyshkivka, hoping not to attract any attention. When he finally he saw the village, he stood slack jawed. It had been home to 1,200 residents and 181 families. The men and women were artisans, and some worked at the collective farms nearby. The Jewish population had been confined to a ghetto, but most continued to live in their own homes.[43]

"Something happened inside me. My god. I saw a bazaar. I saw people. Civilization seemed to keep functioning here," he remembered. "Jews were living their lives and no one was bothering them. One sews, another makes hats."

A Jewish woman living there recognized Motl, having been acquainted with the Bravermans before the war. She welcomed him into her home. After he had eaten, she invited her neighbors to hear from the boy claiming to be from Pechera. It was a spectacle. "They all received me well and they asked me all sorts of questions," Motl remembered. "What was happening in the camp? How do people live there? People would come by to see me, as if some alien had descended on them. You can imagine the sight."

Come late afternoon, however, their interest in him waned when he asked if someone might have a spare room. Explaining that the Romanians were liable to appear anytime to count the residents and to check for partisans, they agreed that he should walk another ten miles south to Tomashpil. He was told that its Jews were more likely to help someone like him; that is, someone from the camps. Motl left Horyshkivka's marketplace as it was emptying, knowing he needed to hurry to reach Tomashpil before sundown. He found the town on a plateau, with a river running south of it and a stream flowing to the west. The Jewish neighborhood, which emanated from a square built near the river, comprised three streets. They had once held four synagogues (all destroyed during the war) and a Jewish bathhouse.[44] Like many towns in the vicinity, prewar Tomashpil was once home to a Jewish majority, and it had already seen tragedy.

In early August 1941, after the arrival of Germans in Tomashpil, a group of local Ukrainians gathered at the behest of a German commandant to decide the fate of their Jewish neighbors. They agreed unanimously that the Jews should die. One of the more prominent residents shouted that "the Jews should be exterminated like rotten meat, because they have always lived at the expense of Ukrainians."[45] A priest from an Orthodox church attempted to defuse the crowd, saying that "the [Jewish] people was innocent, that God gives life even to a worm."[46] An hour later, a woman ran into the street and urged the town's Jews to flee: "Dear people, hide! They want to kill you!" But it was of little use.[47]

One hundred and fifty of them were soon rounded up by the occupiers and shot at the edge of a ravine, one of the only massacres to befall the Jewish communities of northern Transnistria.[48] After the bodies of the lifeless victims collapsed into the mass grave, witnesses recalled hearing moaning and screaming, and "for a long time the earth was heaving above the murder victims." A few managed to crawl out, three of them children.[49] Days later, other Jewish residents were forced to bury the dead.[50] A ghetto was then established along a few streets, with a high barbed-wire fence strung around them. The town's Jews were crowded into the boundary, with as many as twelve people forced into each home. A small number of Jewish residents held jobs inside the ghetto's workshops, while the rest were used for forced labor. They received a daily allowance of soup and stale bread. Tomashpil was home to an usually large number of gendarmes relative to its size, given that their jurisdiction extended far beyond the town's limits.[51]

The fence and the substantial number of Romanians based there, as well as *polizei* in the vicinity, failed to deter a growing number of Pechera escapees from seeking temporary refuge in the ghetto. As they would soon discover, the crowded conditions of surrounding ghettos like the one in Tomashpil were appalling, but they were far better than what they had grown accustomed to in Pechera.

Motl crossed into the ghetto just before dark, cold and hungry, and now thirty miles from his family, farther away from them than he had ever been. The first group of people he approached refused to help, as did the next. "People were questioning me, they were suspicious," Motl remembered. One resident explained that he had no food to offer but that he knew of a house where the most destitute of Jews were fed and that he should try going there. When Motl walked inside, he found a line of people waiting to receive their rations of bread and boiled cornmeal. Those ahead of him exchanged furtive glances when they noticed Motl. "Please, please," two of them finally said, motioning for him to step ahead of them in line. After he had received a warm meal and a sack of food, he was left to wander the ghetto's empty streets just before dusk, with nowhere to go. Had he come all this way and endured so much, he remembered thinking, only to freeze to death?

"You are that boy from Pechera, yes?" a woman suddenly called out to him.

They had never met. Yet there was something in Motl that she had recognized—his labored gait maybe, or the way his rags drooped from shoulders. Her son had arrived in Tomashpil in the same state after being rescued from Pechera. His name was Shunya. He was tall, handsome, and a year or two older than Motl. Motl remembered that he had also lived in the camp's three-story building for a time. The boy's mother had hired a villager with a wagon to bring him to Tomashpil, likely bribing the *polizei* for the right to extract him from the camp.

"Of course, I will take you in if I need to," she told Motl. "But listen to me carefully."

She explained that a middle-aged couple living across the street had recently invited a young tailor to live with them. His last name was Voskoboynik. He was drafted into the Red Army and was then captured by the Germans. After escaping a POW camp, he found his way to Tomashpil and fell in love with the couple's daughter. This tailor would learn that his father and younger brother had been brought to Pechera while he was away. The woman led Motl to this home and asked to see the tailor. The tailor took an immediate interest in Motl's story. He then offered him dinner and four chairs to sleep on. The next morning, he asked Motl whether he would be returning to Pechera anytime soon.

"Maybe in a few days. I'll go back when I gather enough food," Motl said.

"You find me my brother. You find me my father. And you say hello to them. And if you can bring my brother back, I will pay you handsomely."

The tailor's younger brother was named Zhenya. Motl agreed, not knowing whether it could really be done or whether this little boy was still alive.

"I said, 'Alright, I'll save him.' I gave him my word," Motl recalled. "What he'd give me, I didn't ask. And he didn't promise me anything. I gave him my word that I would try."

Motl left Tomashpil a week later. In Bortnyky, he stopped for the night at Sophia's home and handed her a few packs of matches he had gathered during his travels, no small gesture. He reached Pechera early one evening, hurled his bundles into the camp, and slowly climbed back over the wall. After a few days' rest, he left his room to find Zhenya and his father. The search brought Motl to annexes and cellars he had not yet seen. He checked the three-story building last, moving from room to room and asking those inside whether anyone knew of a Voskoboynik.

"All I see is the dead and dying," Motl remembered. "You open the door to a ward and oh, the screams. People are laying on the ground looking for crumbs. They're looking for water." Finally, he wandered into a room and heard a reply. The voice belonged to a man who looked to be about fifty years old. Next to him was a young boy, pale and frail. They were lying side by side under a torn red blanket.

"Who are you?" Zhenya's father asked, straining to lift his head off the floor.

"Your son, he says hello," Motl told him.

"My son? Where did you see him?"

"He's in Tomashpil, your older son. I talked with him. He wants me to take Zhenya there."

"Please God. If you could, I would be forever grateful. Please save him. I'm not worth the trouble. But please take him. Save him."

"Fine. Have him ready in two days. We'll head out then."

As promised, Motl came for Zhenya later that week. Joining him was a girl named Sophia, who had either shared a room with the Bravermans or lived down the hall from them. She heard he was planning to lead a boy to Tomashpil and asked Motl if he might bring her there, too. The three of them departed before dawn. Zhenya had only brought a light coat and struggled to keep pace from the very start. Motl put his arm around the smaller boy to help keep him moving. It took the better part of a day for them to reach the village of Silnytsya, about fifteen miles away. Motl had already met several residents there, including a veteran of the Great War who had been maimed in combat more than twenty years earlier. He agreed to feed Motl and Zhenya and put them up for the night. Sophia slept in the house next door. The next day, they reached Shura-Kopiivska, and then Horyshkivka, where Motl turned to the families he had met for help. The longer they walked, the worse Zhenya felt. By the third day, he had trouble speaking and his knees were buckling. He collapsed just five miles shy of Tomashpil. Motl and Sophia comforted him on the side of the road, hoping he might feel better after a bit of rest; they had no water or food to offer him. When a wagon appeared later that afternoon, the driver, a Ukrainian, offered to take them to within a half-mile of the Tomashpil ghetto, but no closer. As they arrived, Sophia jumped off the wagon and ran off. Motl would never see her again. Zhenya was left solely in his care. Slowly, he walked the boy to his brother's house.

"Oh, how happy they were," Motl said, describing how the boy's family received him that afternoon. "They filled a barrel with water and bathed him. They made a big fuss, cooing at him even. No one offered to wash me.

The feeling was, 'You've done your part.'" Zhenya's brother gave Motl the same four chairs to sleep on. This time, he invited him to stay for as long as he liked. During the next three days, Motl wandered the ghetto to beg, much as he had before. He now prized bread and grain above all else; they were, after all, the lightest foods to carry. Zhenya's brother also handed him some money, enough to buy five loaves of bread at the market. It didn't occur to Motl to ask for more or for what he really needed: a pair of new pants or new shoes to replace his crumbling galoshes for the walk home.

One day, while still in Tomashpil, a man named Zalmal Bronfman introduced himself to Motl, adding that Motl had made quite an impression on the ghetto's residents. Bronfman explained that he was the head of the Jewish committee,[52] the significance of which was lost on Motl. Like many committee leaders in northern Transnistria's ghettos, Bronfman was required to report infiltrators to the authorities. Ghetto presidents generally viewed these unwanted guests with disdain.[53]

In Mohyliv-Podilskyi, fifty-six-year-old Jewish leader Siegfried Jagendorf, who had been a Siemens executive before his deportation to Transnistria from southern Bukovyna and who distinguished himself with a clean suit, polished shoes, and gloves, warned fellow deportees about offering "shelter to those infiltrating from the camps," which the Romanians prohibited, and reminded them to report "such illegal person" to the committee's Jewish police. "The police have orders to apprehend these persons and to turn them in to the gendarmes. Anyone found sheltering such persons will be severely punished. The supervisor for each street section will investigate whether such people are hiding in their area. We ask the Jewish population to pay attention to this order because of the serious consequences."[54]

Yet by 1943, the Romanians had reconsidered both their alliance with Hitler and their plans for Transnistria's Jews. In the Tomashpil ghetto, some of the restrictions that had been in place were relaxed. On Sundays, Jews were now allowed to leave the confines of the ghetto to barter their goods for food.[55] Under Bronfman's leadership, Tomashpil's Jewish leaders created a canteen for the poorest and sickest residents where one warm meal was served each day (and which Motl had visited). And a group of women visited homes across the ghetto to collect food and other items for the most destitute.[56]

Rather than having Motl arrested during his second stay in Tomashpil, Bronfman, responsible for the welfare of about a thousand surviving ghetto residents, invited Motl to his home to talk about a personal matter. After presenting a plate of baked beans, he asked Motl for a favor: to find a family he knew in Pechera and to deliver them to Tomashpil. Motl agreed. While packing to leave for Pechera with as much food as he could carry, a few residents approached him with letters. They were addressed to loved ones in Pechera and in the ghettos he had just passed. They offered to pay him for their delivery.

"And in this manner," Motl would later write, "I became both a guide and a mail carrier. I began leading people to Tomashpil by night."

CHAPTER SEVEN

Dzhuryn

M OTL SCANNED THE HORIZON, cupping his eyes. All he could see was white. The light snow flurries that had followed his party out of Pechera that morning had become a raging blizzard. It enveloped the escapees and now obscured the road ahead. Motl came to a stop. He had been here before, in Shpykiv, ten miles southwest of Pechera, under power lines that ran along the edge of a prairie. He knew to follow them until the sweep of beech trees to his left ended at a clearing. From there, he would look for shrubs, which marked the beginning of a path that would bring them to Silnytsya. The trouble was deciphering much of anything in the driving snow and wind.

Waiting behind him was Dina, a fellow prisoner, and behind her were the two women she had paid to carry her young sons, ages four and six, on their backs. Also traveling with them was Dina's ten-year-old daughter, Clara. Dina had entrusted Motl to lead them out of the camp and to safety in Tomashpil. Through word of mouth that winter, she learned of a boy in the Pechera camp who claimed to know the way, could avoid detection, and who had established ties with locals willing to shelter him. After finding Motl, she asked if she could pay him to make the trip again, this time while leading her family out of the camp. Motl assured her that he could but only if she would agree to find someone to carry her young children. He also warned her that the journey would be treacherous and the weather unpredictable.

"I of course risked my life to take them, but there was no alternative," Motl recalled. "I had to think of my sisters and brother."

Rather than risk leading the group past the turnoff, he offered to press on alone until he could reorient himself. Fifteen minutes later, he returned to say he had found the shrubs. They were a quarter mile up to the road, buried under a foot a snow. Just before sunrise, as the group plodded through a field, Dina's boys began to cry, begging to be brought back to the camp. The women carrying them were also in tears. Motl agreed that they should stop at the next house. When they found one, he led his fellow travelers to the barn next door, hoping not to disturb the sleeping owners. The group sat slumped against haybales in their wet rags, waiting for the storm to pass. Although they had been quiet, someone had left the door ajar. Later that morning, a Ukrainian woman walked in to find them all sleeping inside.

"It's nothing," the woman assured Motl as he awoke with a start. "Please, come to the house. Everyone is welcome."

Over bowls of soup, she and her husband listened to Dina's story. They said little in return. Motl then asked if it would be safe for the seven of them to be seen traveling to Silnytsya together.

"No son. Don't try it," the man said.

"Isn't there another way?" Motl asked.

"In deep snow. Untouched snow. More than a foot. You'll have to go through the woods to avoid the villages."

Dina asked Motl to listen to the man and to take them on the unfamiliar route. It was just as the man had described: a punishing slog across rolling, wooded terrain. "We went up and down. I led the way and flattened the snow with my steps," Motl said. "The others followed."

The trail brought them to a field outside of Silnytsya. They continued along the edge of town until Motl spotted the house where his acquaintance, the veteran, lived. On his doorstep, Motl reached into his bags and pulled out boxes of salt and matches. The man accepted the offering and motioned them inside. The next morning, they set out for Horyshkivka and arrived in time for the weekly bazaar. Motl's return drew good-natured taunts from a pair of Jews who had evidently seen him before.

"Ah, welcome back, *g'vir*," one man said, calling him a rich man in Yiddish.

"It's good to see you again, *bogach*," another man echoed in Russian. "Business is good I see."

Now that he had brought women and children with him, most of the locals he encountered no longer viewed him as the vagabond they once thought him to be. "They treated us as equals," he said. "Before, they had kicked me out like a dog." That night, they all received an invitation to sleep in the ghetto's pharmacy. The next day, they walked the remaining ten miles to Tomashpil, where Dina left her boys with relatives. The other two women also chose to remain in the ghetto. Now that Dina knew the roads, she hoped to bring her oldest son here, who was waiting for her in the camp. Motl made the rounds one final time, collecting food and letters.

Early one morning, Motl and Dina left for Pechera with their bundles, their spirits lifted by food, rest, and, for a change, mild weather. As the morning wore on, they quickened their pace. Their fortunes, however, changed when two Ukrainian *polizei* converged on them. Dina launched into a story about how she and Motl had been to the market and were on their way home. The *polizei* were unconvinced. They instructed Motl and Dina to follow them. There was no hiding who they were.

"If the four-year-old child in Tulchyn could recognize runaway Jews," Motl explained, "It would be obvious to these police."

While following the men, Motl fumbled through his bag to find the papers he had hidden in the grain. He allowed them to fall to the dirt.[1] The policemen brought them to the local gendarmerie station. After a lengthy wait, the Ukrainians presented the captives to a Romanian commander. Sitting across a table from the escapees, he asked Motl and Dina who they were and where they were headed.

"We are Jews from the camp in Pechera," Dina said. "Maybe you've heard of it."

He turned to the Ukrainians and asked whether they had bothered to search these Jews and whether they might be partisans. This struck Motl as absurd. How could two pitiful camp prisoners—a boy just sprouting a beard and a mother of four—pass for resistance fighters? What could explain such paranoia?

"I'm not a partisan. I'm trying to bring bread to my family. See here?" Motl said, tilting his bag toward the Romanian. "Grain and bread."

"Home to Pechera! Go!" he screamed.

And they did, without so much as a gendarme to see them out of town or to ensure that they were heading in the direction of the camp. Motl, who expected a beating, was surprised by their indifference. On the one hand, the Romanians were right to fear potential partisan activity, which was beginning to proliferate in Transnistria—and especially in northwest

Transnistria—as the locals grew increasingly hostile and willing to support underground activity.[2] But to Motl, their lax treatment suggested that there was some truth to the rumors circulating in the ghettos and villages: that the Red Army was on the offensive and that the Romanians knew they were in for a reckoning.

Relations between Antonescu's Romania and the Germans were growing fraught. By August 1942, Antonescu and his men "were no longer at the peak of their enthusiasm," writes Raul Hilberg, a pioneering Holocaust historian. "They had just about exhausted their exuberance and were in turn exhausted by it. The Romanian receptivity to German demands for destructive action was at an end."[3] Though Romania and Germany were close allies, disagreements between the regimes around the fate of the Jews under Antonescu's rule were becoming more common. Antonescu was an unabashed anti-Semite, but he was also an opportunist. Sensing that the tides of war were turning in favor of the Soviets—the all-important Battle of Stalingrad, waged shortly before the planned massacre in Pechera, was lost in February 1943—he kept Jews within Romania proper (the Regat, or Old Romania), out of Hitler's camps, because of his "extreme nervousness as to his own fate."[4] Attempts by Hitler's Foreign Ministry to convince him otherwise only agitated Romania's leadership in late 1942 and 1943.[5] There was also the matter of Antonescu's temperament. He bristled at the notion of being told what to do on land he controlled. It was once said that he "did not like receiving orders; he liked giving them."[6]

The Romanians sensed a growing domestic and international backlash and seemed to grasp the enormity of the crimes they had committed and the very real possibility that they might someday be held to account for them. In October 1942, deportations to Transnistria were halted. Mihai Antonescu, in an exchange with a Nazi official on November 11, 1942, shifted the blame for the "barbarism against the Jews" to "peripheral agencies" and not the Romanian government. He claimed that he had tried to intervene on behalf of Jews and seemed to express concerns about "the Jews who have suffered severe circumstances . . . along the [Buh]."[7] This marked quite a reversal from a man who just a year earlier had advocated for gunning Jews down.

Other grievances led to the growing rift between Germany and, arguably, its most vital ally.[8] For one, Romania's military was suffering disproportionately. Of the 350,000 troops deployed to Stalingrad, nearly one in three was killed or captured. Despite the Romanians' pleas, the Germans were reluctant to arm them with better weapons. Germans also repeatedly made derogatory references to the "Romanian race."[9] The biggest point of contention of all emerged after Mihai Antonescu's September 1942 meeting with Hitler in Vinnytsia, where his request for the guaranteed return of northern Transylvania from Hungary—one of the key motivators for allying with the Germans in the first place—was refused.[10]

By mid-1943, Ukrainian villagers had learned that Soviet forces had gained the upper hand.[11] In Pechera, Eva Poliak's former classmates, now apparently part of the underground, occasionally flagged her down from across the camp's gate and assured her that the Red Army was advancing and that her liberation was close at hand. Some of Pechera's prisoners became privy to the news of mounting Soviet victories while traveling between ghettos. In northern Transnistria, other Jews forged ties with local partisans, who relayed what they had heard on radio broadcasts. In the Mohyliv-Podilskyi ghetto, where radios and newspapers were forbidden, Jewish leaders arranged to hear summaries of the 8 P.M. broadcasts airing from New York, London, Moscow, and Berlin.[12] Prisoners in the nearby Vapnyarka camp had smuggled in a radio to hear the news for themselves.[13] In Tulchyn's ghetto, which had been repopulated with deportees, a top partisan asked a Jewish leader to translate German-language BBC programs for him (he was correct in assuming that the reports coming out of Moscow were far from objective). During a June 1943 broadcast, the names Pantelleria and Lampedusa were mentioned over the air, in reference to the pair of Mediterranean islands that had been bombarded and captured by Allied forces during Operation Corkscrew, setting the stage for the invasion of Sicily.[14] July and August brought perhaps the most decisive development to date. Soviet forces repelled a desperate assault near the Russian city of Kursk, the site of history's largest tank battle, and permanently shifted the balance of power.

Meanwhile, in Mohyliv-Podilskyi, the Romanians rescinded an order to send Jews to work in the peat bogs of Tulchyn. They also ordered Jewish leaders to dismantle facilities that were being relocated to Romania. Their anxiety was palpable. "One could feel the tension among the military officials in [Mohyliv]," wrote Siegfried Jagendorf.[15] There were other indications that the momentum was on the side of the Soviets. Earlier that year, a

German military hospital moved westward to Tulchyn.[16] Hearing these rumors, even if true, was of little comfort to Motl. At most, they provided a momentary reprieve. Whether or not a Soviet victory was on the horizon, there was no escape from the weight of being his family's main provider.

Motl's continued appearances in Tomashpil in the winter of 1943 tested the patience of the ghetto's Jewish committee. As he was slipping out through the barbed wire one day while returning to Pechera, his bags filled with bread, flour, and grain, he heard a familiar voice call to him. "I fed you and I asked you to help me," an irate Zalmal Bronfman said. "And this is how you repay me? Don't ever show your face here. I will have you arrested."

By now, Motl was far from the only Pechera escapee fleeing to Tomashpil. In 1943, many surviving prisoners abandoned the camp for the safer ghettos they had heard about or for ghettos that had been established in their hometowns. Travel between the villages had become less dangerous, as the locals were becoming less inclined to attack Jewish escapees. They feared the Soviets would hold them accountable.[17] Many Ukrainians were deeply religious and felt that they had to help suffering Jews; if anything, Ukrainians were now becoming more sympathetic to their plight.[18] After some had initially welcomed the Romanian occupation and were alarmed by the turn of events at Stalingrad, the majority would grow to resent the occupiers. Transnistria's farmers, for instance, were outraged when the Romanians confiscated most of the produce harvested in 1941 and 1942 and shipped it to Romania. All the while, their own communities went hungry. Young Ukrainians in particular were buoyed by news from the Eastern Front.[19]

Like Motl, other older boys were now guiding fellow prisoners out of Pechera and to the relative safety of the ghettos, having learned the roads and developed networks of trusted villagers. One of the boys, an eighteen-year-old named Monia Roizman, helped lead Arkadii Glinets and his family—his father, mother, aunt, sister Hanna, and nephew Leonid—back to their native Mohyliv-Podilskyi. Their return began after sundown one day in March 1943. They followed Monia out through a side gate and walked west toward Shpykiv, where they stopped at daybreak. They tried to stay out of sight, going outside only to quench their thirst, which involved puncturing frozen roadside puddles and licking the ice. The next night, they continued in the direction of Sharhorod, passing through the village of Rakhny-Lisovi. "And then, while on our way, our little Leonichka [Leonid] died," a tearful Arkadii told an interviewer, describing how the little boy was buried near the road. "My sister ripped some leaves off a tree, and ripped the sleeve off her shirt, and placed it on him. She thought she could come back for him." After Monia delivered them to the Mohyliv-Podilskyi ghetto, he and Arkadii's family parted ways. Within two weeks' time, everyone but Arkadii would fall ill and die, leaving him an orphan at the age of fifteen.[20]

In Mohyliv-Podilskyi and the other ghettos of northern Transnistria, there was a growing sense that the massacres and deportations that once felt imminent no longer were and that it just might be possible to outlast the war. Jewish exiles from the reclaimed territories, as well as those from southern Bukovyna, were hopeful that they might be repatriated. They received parcels and money from relatives in Romania. In many of the ghettos, their family units had remained mostly intact, giving the prisoners something to live for until their eventual rescue.[21]

In the winter of 1942–43, Tulchyn's ghetto was repopulated with Jews deported from northern Bukovyna. The experience in Tulchyn of these newcomers during the coming months stood in stark contrast with the lives lived by the ghetto's original inhabitants, an indicator of just how much Romanian policy had shifted and how Romanian and German-speaking Jews were received. Many of the gendarmes were now willing to relax the rules.[22]

Among the new arrivals was fourteen-year-old Gerhard Schreiber, a boy just eight months older than Motl, who had grown up in Chernivtsi before the war. His family had spent the preceding months in a barren transit camp on the Buh called Cariera de Piatră, a former stone quarry that had also once been a Soviet penal colony. Among the prisoners held there were German-language poet Paul Celan's parents, also of Chernivtsi. Per Schreiber, Tulchyn's ghetto was considered "the most coveted" place among their rumored destinations, and for good reason. Some of the prisoners, including the Celans, would later be transferred east of the Buh to the notorious Mykhailivka slave labor camp, which few would survive. For Schreiber, who had had several brushes with death, seeing a town like Tulchyn after all this time was an "enormous" shock, an experience he would describe in his memoir.

> It was a city [alright], paved streets, houses, we couldn't believe our eyes. And, to our great surprise, there were a few local Jewish families who received us. The Jewish ghetto, as it was called, comprised one street with small individual houses, about 250 to 300 yards long. Our group, about 100–120 people, found shelter in either empty houses, which had windows and doors, or with the local Jewish families. These were the few remnants of a larger Jewish community, who had survived the mass killings, which occurred when the Germans occupied the city. They were retained by the Romanian authorities, because of their skills, since most skilled craftsmen had left with the retreating Soviet troops.[23] There was a dentist, a dyer, a watchmaker, a capmaker and a few others. The dyer, was the most prosperous of them, his business extended over two houses, one could see the colored fabric being hanged out to dry from afar.[24]

The Schreibers soon found themselves living with another family in a two-room apartment. There was a woodburning stove and an outhouse attached to the rear of the home, a vast improvement over the communal ditch used in Cariera de Piatră. Schreiber slept on a wooden platform with five others, while his grandfather and great-aunt slept on cots in the other room. "We also had a table and chairs, it was almost unbelievable," he wrote. The food they ate, provided in part by a committee of Jewish leaders in Bucharest, amounted to "slightly above subsistence."[25] In time, Schreiber's father became deputy head of the newly-formed Jewish committee, while Schreiber volunteered for work at the German military hospital that had been relocated to a high school in Tulchyn. A German warehouse keeper who opposed the war and hated Hitler encouraged him to pilfer boots, clothing, and blankets. The blankets were repurposed into overcoats. One day, Schreiber was assigned to work in the kitchen.

"Aside from the fact that I could eat things, of which we could only dream, like chocolate, sardines, all kind of cold cuts and other delicacies, I had the satisfaction of having Waffen-SS officers trying (and succeeding) to bribe me to get second helpings," he wrote. "This was the beginning of my smoking habit, since they never offered me money, only cigarettes."[26]

Nearly two years into the occupation, Motl had grown to resent the expectations his mother had placed on him and resentful of her decision to keep the children in Pechera rather than resettling in a ghetto. He was tired of the endless walks, the solitude, the beatings, and being treated like a vagrant everywhere he went. In Pechera, the guards were more ambivalent than ever. Sometimes they were absent from their posts. It seemed to Motl that this was his family's chance to leave the camp for good. "How was it that other Jews could have it so much better? And why shouldn't I?" he remembered thinking.

Shaken by the harsh encounter with Zalmal Bronfman, the head of the Tomashpil ghetto's Jewish committee, Motl vowed never to return. Motl's friends and former classmates in the camp had been talking more and more about the ghettos of Krasne and Dzhuryn and about the foreign Jews who lived there. Compared to the horrors of camp life, the ghettos seemed bearable. And best of all, his friends had claimed, everyone ate.

Motl began pleading with Soybil to let him bring her and the children to one of these places. If not, he threatened to go alone and to never come back. And yet his mother was unmoved. She scolded him for having suggested such a thing and told him to think about his siblings instead. Only a few months earlier, Soybil's sister Haika, who was also imprisoned in Pechera, had attempted to reach the town of Dzhuryn alone. Members of the Jewish police reported her to the gendarmes within a week of her arrival there, leading to her arrest and months-long detainment. Though they would be reunited before the war's end, Soybil assumed she had been killed.

"I was sick of asking to go," Motl recalled. "I told my mom, 'I'm going to leave forever to Krasne!' She never thought I would actually follow through."

"I don't want to hear it," she would tell him.

One morning in mid-March 1943, he left Pechera alone and went in an altogether new direction. It was the last he would ever see of the camp. The roads had once again become a slurry of dirt and snowmelt, made all the worse by the region's cresting rivers. The sixteen miles to Krasne would ordinarily have taken Motl a few hours to cover. Instead, his journey had already taken the better part of a day. The sun was setting by the time he arrived in the Krasne ghetto, which was home to about a thousand Jews, most of them deportees from across the Dnister.[27] There were now twice as many Jews from Bessarabia and Bukovyna living in Krasne as there were local Jews.[28] Given the extreme crowding in each home, no one was interested in hosting Motl for the night. While wandering the streets, he stopped at the ghetto's workshop, where he found a carpenter working late into the evening. The carpenter told Motl that he was welcome to sleep on some wooden planks. The next morning, the ghetto's Jewish police discovered him and ordered him out, before he had even had a chance to eat at the new cafeteria. Krasne's Jewish committee, led by a man named Berger, had gained a reputation for turning escapees away.[29]

Refusing to return to Pechera, he asked them for directions to Dzhuryn. The nineteen-mile walk was just as grueling as the previous day's. "The mud seeped into my shoes," Motl remembered. "My feet were wet." Come early evening, the world around had grown faint. His eyesight, like Etel's and his mother's, was beginning to fail him. He was still a few miles north of Dzhuryn, somewhere near Derebchyn, when he was forced to stop for the night. A woman in one of the few houses he encountered offered him a meal and her brick *pechka* to sleep on. He left for Dzhuryn the next morning. He found the town atop two hills, with a shallow stream running between them. The ghetto was established on the sloped and unpaved streets of the Jewish quarter, on the eastern hill. The Ukrainians lived on the western hill.[30]

Before the German occupation of Dzhuryn began in July 1941, air raids destroyed a well-known sugar factory and damaged a small synagogue. Later that summer, the Germans joined the local *polizei* and gendarmes in beating Jewish worshippers found in the town's "big" synagogue. The attack coincided with one of the Jewish High Holidays, either Rosh Hashanah or Yom Kippur. A thousand or so local Jews were soon joined in the ghetto by 3,500 from Bukovyna and Bessarabia. At the behest of a local rabbi, Dzhuryn's Jews welcomed these newcomers and opened their homes to them. A thousand of the Jewish deportees who could not find housing were instead put up in the synagogue, as well as in barns and warehouses.[31] The local Jews, many of them elderly women or impoverished mothers, provided deportees with blankets, clothes, and food.[32] The new arrivals, in turn, provided critical social services. By early 1943, a prominent rabbi from Siret, Bukovyna, named Barukh Hager organized a kitchen for the poor, serving a thousand daily meals that consisted of soup, lentils, a potato, and bread.[33] Jewish doctors managed to contain a typhus outbreak in their new fifty-six-bed hospital, limiting the death toll to four hundred people,[34] resulting in one of the lowest mortality rates of Transnistria's ghettos.[35]

By the time Motl first appeared in March 1943, a clear social hierarchy had been established. The more affluent and educated Romanian Jews from southern Bukovyna were among the most privileged. The seven-member Jewish committee was led by the attorney Max Rosenstrauch and his deputy Moshe Katz, deportees from southern Bukovyna who had been appointed by local Romanian leaders. The committee did not form right away but in spring 1942, after the arrivals had weathered the "shock" of their deportation and first winter in Transnistria.[36] They also formed a twenty-person Jewish police force. Around 120 of the Romanian-speaking deportees bribed the gendarmes for the right to inhabit homes outside the ghetto to avoid the crowded hovels that their coreligionists were forced to share, some of which had been partially destroyed.[37] The wealthier Jews introduced new varieties of goods to the market square—suits, furs, gold watches, linens—as barter for meals or sacks of potatoes from the Ukrainians.[38] For a suit, one could receive fifty pounds of flour; for a pair of socks, some bread.[39]

One of the best-known chroniclers among the new arrivals was forty-year-old Lipman Kunstadt, who kept a diary and wrote daily in Yiddish. Kunstadt had been a journalist, writing for newspapers in both Romanian and German, and was the general secretary of the Jewish community in Rădăuți, his hometown in southern Bukovyna. His family's deportation began on the last day of the Jewish holiday of Sukkot in October 1941. After the last two legs of the journey—crossing the Dnister by raft and being trucked to Dzhuryn—he began working as the ghetto committee's secretary. For his services, he received a loaf of bread each morning.[40]

In his diary, Kunstadt frequently denounced the ghetto's Jewish leadership. Rosenstrauch, in particular, was a frequent target of his sardonic rants. His entries depict a man who fraternized with the Romanians, readily bowed to their demands for slave laborers without receiving concessions in return, and turned a blind eye to the abuses carried out by the Jewish police, all to retain his post.[41] In the social order that Kunstadt described, local Ukrainian Jews and those from northern Bukovyna and Bessarabia occupied one of the lowest rungs. They were, as he put it, *treif*—a derogatory Yiddish word meaning unkosher—and "the sacrificial roosters for Kaparoth," an atonement ritual practiced ahead of the Yom Kippur holiday.[42] The lowliest of all were the Ukrainian Jews who escaped the camps of the Buh only to become the primary targets for labor roundups, which were orchestrated by the Jewish police to fulfill the Romanians' quotas. They were, according to Kunstadt, the "treif of treif."[43] By virtue of entering the ghetto to begin with—which was forbidden—and without being registered to the Jewish committee's roster, their presence was in fact illegal.[44]

In one entry, dated October 24, 1942, Kunstadt recounted Max Rosenstrauch's reaction when camp escapees from the Buh sought shelter in Dzhuryn:

> The Colonial Chieftain [Rosenstrauch] in particular really enjoys himself when he is fated to address the new arrivals in High German: "Who called you here?" he shrieks. "What is [Dzhuryn], a city of refuge? Here you won't even spend one night." The sobs and wails of the exhausted babies and women (few men escape) would move stones but not the hardened hearts of the closed heavens. The doctor's [Rosenstrauch] servants make sure that [Dzhuryn] will not become a city of refuge. They take the "deserters" to the soup kitchen, where they receive a double portion of soup and a loaf of bread, and by night they send them out of the ghetto, trusting them to the divine providence.[45]

Like many of the more affluent newcomers, Kunstadt was appalled by the primitive living standards imposed on him in Dzhuryn. The first thing he had noticed about Dzhuryn was the ever-present mud, which he described on May 6, 1942.

> As soon as the gates of the [Dzhuryn] paradise opened before me, on October 29, 1941, at ten at night, this mire clung to me in all its grace. We have only just climbed down from the German truck that had dragged us to this corner, and already I was introduced to the mud. It was a dark, wet evening and I slid and found myself lying face down in a revolting, thick, ice-cold mess. . . . My sole consolation was not being alone in this, as I was not the only one sporting this fine appearance. The stubborn mud kept swelling to this very day, in May, so much so that I had no choice but to surrender to it.[46]

Kunstadt also took issue with the village's lack of sanitation and out-houses, an indictment on the local Jews. The ghetto's lone water well and its inconvenient location—more than a kilometer uphill from the ghetto in heavy mud—also drew Kunstadt's ire:

The place has a single water well, an ancient facility, which can be reached with difficulty equal to the parting of the Red Sea. During mud season one drowns, and in the winter one drags oneself at great peril up the mountain—over a kilometer on flooded, slippery soil. People armed with cans, jugs and pails stand in a long line by the pump and wait, sometimes for hours, until they can get a little water. There are always fights, with people often coming to blows over who gets a pail of water sooner, and who sacrifices their health to gain a little rusty water as old as Methuselah. . . . The inhabitants of [Dzhuryn] never saw fit to dig a few more wells. Yet if you talk to them, you will hear the claim that they alone are truly civilized, while the newcomers from [Bukovyna] have never had even a taste of civilization.[47]

Another Dzhuryn diarist, eighteen-year-old Miriam Korber, also of southern Bukovyna, wrote about the shock of her first Transnistrian winter—of being "frozen to the marrow"—and how the "wind of the steppe bites with a fury unknown to us who lived in the mountains."[48] Like Kunstadt, she bemoaned the absence of sanitation and placed some of the blame on the local Jews. "You can tell the degree of civilization by the status of the toilets. Well, until the present day I still have not found a decent toilet in the Ukraine. People relieve themselves wherever they can. Filth everywhere."[49]

Korber's family ate regularly by trading their belongings for food, sub-sisting mainly on potatoes, beans, and boiled cornmeal. Despite the misery that pervaded daily life, she recognized that her family was more fortunate than many others. The sight of beggars scared her, because she feared that she too might soon become one of them. She was forbidden from going anywhere near the synagogue, which was thought to be a source of disease. When her father, a devout Jew, became ill with typhus, many assumed that he had contracted it there.[50]

Unlike the Ukrainian Jews, those from southern Bukovyna began to receive money from relatives who had remained in Romania and the majority of the relief aid that began to flow into Transnistria.[51] One shipment in particular, containing shoes and suits, was addressed to southern Bukovyna's Jews, and the majority of it was certain to be allotted to them. Despite his misgivings about the locals, Kunstadt was critical of the Jewish committee's callousness, particularly when so many of the Ukrainian Jews and camp escapees came wearing nothing but rags.[52] Writing in January 1943, Kunstadt noted that they were not entitled to eat at the public kitchen, "because their names are not on the lists, and maybe no one wants to know they exist. They are chased away with sticks."[53]

After finding his way to the town's "big" synagogue, Motl joined a thousand people packed into the 2,500-square-foot space.[54] He spent the next three days resting. Those wedged beside him included an ever-growing number of Pechera runaways, including forty who had arrived in November 1942 alone.[55] To remain there, they needed to evade the notice of the ghetto's Jewish committee and the Jewish police in charge of rounding up slave laborers at the Romanians' behest. Jewish deportees from Bukovyna, on the other hand, stood a chance of securing a permanent stay.[56] Motl's immediate neighbors suggested that he visit the public kitchen, where the poor could now eat once a day. They were right. He was soon slurping soup and *mamaliga*, the Romanian variant of boiled cornmeal porridge. He was now certain he could make his case to Soybil, and he intended to return to Pechera to convince her.

His departure came sooner than he expected. A fellow prisoner from Pechera, who had also escaped to Dzhuryn, told Motl that he had just seen Soybil and his siblings. They had apparently bribed their way out and traveled to Krasne by cart to look for him, only to have the ghetto's Jewish police throw them out a day later. Soybil, Manya, Etel, and Lova were said to be stranded somewhere outside of Krasne with nowhere to go. That same afternoon, Motl rushed to find them but got only as far as Derebchyn, where a Ukrainian family took him in. Motl quickly discovered that he was not the only escapee to be spending the night there. A Jewish girl was also staying with the family. She was twelve and an orphan. She told Motl she had no place to go and that she did not care what would become of her. Motl told her he was walking to Krasne the next day, and the two agreed that she should come along. They left together the next morning. Motl did not know it then, but his family was only a few miles away and walking in his direction.

Soybil had spent the morning imploring her youngest two children to muster the strength to continue along the road so they could see their big brother. Manya, who had been in poor health in Pechera, begged to sit down and rest instead.

"Mama, I can't. Leave me here," she said.

"Manichka, look there, do you see those railroad workers in their booths?" asked Soybil. "You do? Let's see if we can just reach them."

"Mama, I can't," Manya said, but she managed to stay upright, clinging to her mother's arm.

This went on for some time, until Etel spotted something in the distance: a carriage. Etel waved the coachman down and asked if he might bring them to Dzhuryn.

"I said, 'Oh sir, please help us.'" Etel recalled. "He took one look at us, with compassion in his eyes, and there we soon sat in his cart. We maybe went two kilometers, and no more, and we see two people walking. And it's Motya and some girl."

Of all the emotions his mother was feeling in that moment, Motl believed that she was mostly relieved—relieved that she and Etel now had help managing Lova, now four, and Manya, six. Motl clambered on while his companion stayed behind and watched them pull away. "I still feel guilty to this day," Motl would later say. "Where did she go? What happened with her?"

On the ride to Dzhuryn, Etel recounted the week's events—how she and Soybil had first realized Motl was gone for good, how Soybil had asked a peasant woman for help (the same woman who had hired her father and paid him for his tailoring), and how the woman had arranged for a cart to take them all to Krasne. Soybil explained that they had spent a single night in the Krasne synagogue before the Jewish police forced them out. They had been staying with other families ever since.

"One day, we found ourselves inside some Ukrainian woman's house with an earthen floor," Etel added. "Lova, he wanted to pee and to poop. He wanted this and that. The ground in our room was dark, dirty. Me and Mom, we couldn't see."

The driver, who was eavesdropping, had either heard enough or realized that he had unwittingly been transporting camp prisoners. He brought his horses to a stop and forced his passengers off the cart. They were now stranded on a forest road and still miles from Dzhuryn. Motl turned to his brother, thinking he would put him on his shoulders. But Lova, screaming and flailing, wanted no part of it. He carried Manya instead while Soybil tended to her youngest. Manya collapsed as soon as they reached the house in Derebchyn where Motl had slept the night before. Soybil and the Ukrainian woman laid Manya on a wooden platform and began rubbing her body with snow until she regained consciousness. The woman lit her *pechka* and prepared a kettle of soup for them. Soybil paid her for the help.

As they sat down to eat, the Ukrainian woman told them about the goings-on in Dzhuryn. She had heard that a day earlier, the Jewish police warned the beggars that they were about to be deported. Around thirty of them were forced from the synagogue and locked out. When these Jews began screaming in protest—loud enough for the entire ghetto to hear—the committee reconsidered. They were told that they could stay and that their names would be written into the roster within a week. Soybil took this to mean that if they hurried, she too could secure a permanent place for them in the ghetto.

"I'm not eating with these spoons," Lova then cried out, interrupting the conversation. "I don't want a metal one!"

The next morning, they set off for Dzhuryn.

"We walked, but there were no roads," Motl would write. "Snow melted under our feet. We sank in the mud. My mother carried my brother and I walked with Manya on my shoulders."

After reaching the ghetto, Soybil began asking where she might find the Jewish administration. The children waited outside while she sought them out. She was back an hour later, but in tears. Although she had been successful and they had permission to stay, the Jewish police would allow it only if she cut her waist-length hair. The dark braid they had inspected, now streaked with gray, was full of lice. They were allotted a small space on the first floor of the synagogue. "All of this reminded us of life in the death camp," Motl would recall. "But life in the ghetto was entirely different." The most immediate difference was the availability of food. And they would no longer have to live with scabies and other skin conditions that had tormented them. A doctor examined Soybil and each of the children and arranged for the ghetto's pharmacy to provide ointment. The lesions in the skin between Motl's fingers healed in less than two weeks. The

Bravermans soon made a name for themselves in the synagogue. Soybil became known simply as "the woman with four kids."

To supplement the little that they ate in the kitchen, Motl sought work from some of the villagers. His first job was to mill grain in someone's cellar, which he would do for hours on end. Benevolent Jews living in the ghetto also helped poorer families. Each day, a new house would be marked to let residents know where they might find some slices of bread.[57] Occasionally, Motl would leave the camp to beg for food, much as he had earlier.

In summer 1943, the synagogue's residents were relocated to the second level, so that the first floor could be returned to a place of worship. Around the same time, some of the Jewish boys and men ages seventeen to fifty-five were transported to Tulchyn's peat bogs. Motl was fortunate: he was still considered too young for the back-breaking work.[58] That fall, Motl and some of the boys his age began leaving the ghetto to work at nearby farms for some food and money. Once, while returning to Dzhuryn after a day's work, Motl and his older friend Boris—who would one day marry Etel and become the father of her only child—were stopped by a Romanian officer driving a chaise. He reeked of alcohol. Seated next to him was a young Ukrainian woman.

"*Jidani*," he said, "Come here."

He then loaded a rifle and took aim. His companion screamed and lunged at the weapon, nearly pulling it away. After being pushed aside, she started kissing his hands, begging him not to shoot. With the entire village now watching, the man relented. He stepped off the cart and snatched Motl's and Boris's bags. He then took them by the shoulders and stood them in front of the horses. If he couldn't shoot them, he would settle for trampling them. When he returned to his seat, he seized the reins and gave them a violent jerk. The boys had already turned to run. They followed the road up a winding dirt slope. They could hear the horses struggle on the incline, their hooves skating on ground slicked with mud. As they rounded the bend, Motl and Boris ducked into someone's garden and out of view. They crouched against the base of a fence and watched the Romanian ride past them. That evening, during their walk back to Dzhuryn, they saw the same cart outside a tavern. It was left unattended. They grabbed their food from the seat and turned toward the ghetto.

In time, Motl and other boys he knew volunteered for some of the nearby road projects. "We would move rocks with wheelbarrows. We would assist other laborers. Whatever was needed. We would dig. We would flatten," he said. He also volunteered to be taken to Tulchyn's peat bogs, where he helped dig drainage ditches used to divert some of the water. In the weeks that followed, Motl noticed that the gendarmes patrolling Dzhuryn and the surrounding communities were becoming more visible. They were rumored to be searching for partisan units who were known to communicate with Jews. Partisans were becoming more active in Dzhuryn and the nearby Murafa, part of a growing underground movement that began in spring 1943.[59] Some of the ghetto's Jewish children, who often snuck out in search of crops that had been left in the fields, as well as kindling, encountered them in the woods. They gave the children money to be used for buying them cigarettes and rolling paper. Some of the partisans also had relatives living in the ghetto. One of their ghetto contacts, a tailor, made clothing for them out of the fabric and sewing supplies they had smuggled in.[60] Near the end of 1943, Motl heard a gunfight erupt between a partisan unit and some gendarmes. One member of the underground shot two of his Romanian foes dead. The Romanians' bodies remained in the open for some time because their countrymen feared retrieving them. An elaborate funeral followed.

In late 1943 or early 1944, nearby bombardments put the Romanians on high alert. Motl saw them digging trenches to prepare for the coming onslaught. Yet by March 1944, the Romanians were nowhere to be found. They were supplanted by Nazi soldiers in retreat. The Germans took over an old post office, where they established a temporary command post and kitchen. Jewish children studied their sullen faces from afar, including young Etty Zigler and Fima Bronshteyn, whose two families shared a home across the street from their temporary headquarters. To Etty, who would watch them through cracks in her boarded-up windows, these Germans hardly resembled the robust young men who had upended her family's life nearly three years earlier. "The soldiers sat on the doorsteps and on the muddy ground looking tired, haggard, and dirty. Still, we were afraid of them. We sat inside, huddled together, cold and hungry, not daring to go for water or firewood," she would recall.[61]

Fima Bronshteyn, whose family belonged to Dzhuryn's local Jewish community, was nine years old when the Germans first occupied his hometown. He would always remember the day he left his family's hiding place in the summer of 1941 and witnessed the humiliation that these foreign soldiers inflicted on old Jewish men, forcing the elders, whose beards they had sheared, to sing in Yiddish while walking in a circle holding brooms and brushes as their German tormenters looked on and laughed. Now, more than two-and-a-half years later, Fima observed the panicked Germans and how they "feverishly packed their equipment, rolled up cables, wires, etc."[62]

"They were wet and were desperately trying to warm up," remembered Raisa Vorobeva, then thirteen. "We sat there like flies worried one might turn around [and kill us]. None of us trusted them."[63]

Soon, warplanes were spotted in the skies above Dzhuryn. Etel began to wave to the airmen, who she assumed had been deployed by the Soviet air force. After they flew overhead, banked sideways, and began to shower the countryside with bombs, Etel realized that she had been mistaken; these were German planes. Ghetto residents who were not already in hiding scattered to find cover. Motl, who was standing outside the synagogue, grabbed Manya and ran for the fields as windows shattered around him. The force of one of the next blasts sent Raisa Vorobeva careening into one of the open pits that had been used as a public latrine. Motl later heard others speculate that the Germans were targeting bridges but missed.

For the next two days, most of Dzhuryn's residents remained in hiding. From Etel's vantage point on the hillside, she could see the Germans trudging westward on the road leading to Mohyliv-Podilskyi and the Dnister. On the third day, March 19, a Sunday, a partisan unit entered Dzhuryn ("They were just young boys," Etel said). Fima Bronshteyn remembered seeing the first fighter arrive on horseback. "I still remember his face, as I saw him up close," he said. "It was still quite cold, but he had on black britches and a shirt, with a jacket on top, a *kubanka* hat on his head . . . and a machine gun hanging across his chest. He started asking people if there are any Germans or Romanians around." The remaining Germans shot the man dead in a gunfight.[64]

Several hours later, the Red Army followed the partisans into Dzhuryn. Even so, Raisa Vorobeva and her siblings refused to leave their cellar until their father, who had been scouting the roads leading into town, splayed open the doors from the outside.

"The Russian forces are here!" he shouted. "The Soviet Army!"

He had just greeted one of the first soldiers, who poured him a shot of vodka. They toasted to the liberation. Raisa's father was so overjoyed that he broke into song. "There was such happiness," Raisa said. "To realize no one was guarding us anymore was to exhale. The partisans were dancing and playing their accordions. A new life began."[65]

Another of the first Red Army soldiers to have entered Dzhuryn's ghetto, a Jewish captain, had added reason to celebrate: he had just helped liberate his father.[66]

Most of the Jews who would survive their initial imprisonments in Pechera had long ago left for the ghettos of Tomashpil, Dzhuryn, Krasne, Bershad, and elsewhere. But between three hundred and four hundred stayed behind in the camp.[67] By now, corpses were simply left to rot around the camp's grounds, many of them covered in worms.[68] Eva Poliak and what remained of her family were among the camp's still-living prisoners. The final weeks of their imprisonment was a perilous time. They, too, feared that the Germans would return to finish what the Romanians had started. Earlier that month, the same partisans who had provided Eva with periodic updates had returned with good news. "The boys told us that ours were advancing and that the distant cannonade was already heard," she wrote in her memoir. "They asked us to suffer a little more. But our strength was running out."[69]

By March, local Romanians were nowhere to be found. But as many prisoners feared, retreating Germans reoccupied Pechera and surrounded the camp, perhaps to destroy it and finish off the still-living Jews. Prisoners who were still mobile had already left their rooms and were hiding wherever they could, cowering in the basement of the main camp building, in the cellars, and under planks. Night seemed to blend with day.[70] As the battlefront drew closer and as the cannonade grew louder, survivor Arkadii Plotitskii, now nine, overheard one of the Germans say to another, "Hitler *kaput*."[71] Another survivor recalled seeing Germans with machine guns move in from their posts along the outer wall to surround the sanitorium building.[72]

On March 16, 1944, the day before Pechera's liberation, eleven-year-old survivor Lev Muchnik and his mother wandered across the Buh to Sokilets. "No cats, no dogs, no people were visible," he recalled. They walked into a barn and stayed the night. The next morning, Lev heard a din. He and his mother stepped outside and saw a mass of people and several vehicles heading straight for them. He assumed that the men could not be Germans; maybe they were partisans, or perhaps even Russian soldiers. He remained on the roadside to find out. One of their trucks pulled up beside him.

"Who are you? What are you?" a soldier demanded in Russian.

"I escaped a death camp," Lev said.

"A death camp? Here?"

"Well, not far from here."

"Please, have a seat in the truck."

Lev and his mother joined a Red Army captain and two soldiers and showed them the way to Pechera. When they arrived at the camp, Lev shouted out the window in Russian, urging fellow prisoners not to panic and to step out of their rooms.[73] Arkadii Plotitskii, who had emerged from his hiding place, watched the trucks enter through the gate. Soldiers wearing fur hats, with epaulets on their uniforms, were seated inside. Arkadii ran back toward the main building's basement, where he had been hiding.

"They are ours! They are ours!" he shouted.

"Shut up, snotty!" someone snapped.[74]

As it turned out, the Red Army captain now in their midst—Boris Neyman—was no ordinary soldier. He was also a Jew. Neyman and his reconnaissance battalion had apparently been on orders to travel through Shpykiv when someone alerted him to the perilous situation in Pechera. If he didn't hurry, the informant told him, there wouldn't be anyone left to save.[75] As he and the men in his command surrounded the camp and approached the former sanitarium building, Arkadii suggested that Neyman announce his presence in Yiddish.[76] After hearing assurances from the boyish captain with almond-shaped eyes who had come to liberate them, a woman cried out in Yiddish, "He's a Jew! He's a Jew!" Another dropped to her knees to kiss his boots.[77]

Lev brought Neyman and his men to the places where he knew the prisoners would be hiding. Some survivors were able to walk out on their own. Others had to be helped out. An hour later, on Neyman's orders, a field kitchen was delivered. By mid-morning, the able-bodied prisoners were free to return to their hometowns.[78]

Some survivors, like Eva Poliak, found it hard to believe that their ordeal was over, that after "entering through the gates of hell," they were simply free to go after so many months of misery. She half expected to be shot the minute she walked out. Instead, she spent one last night in the camp, as did a large group of fellow survivors. The next morning, two daring women passed through the gates, looked around, and signaled to the others that the street was clear and that it was safe to leave.[79] Most made the journey home by foot, while a handful hitched rides in Red Army tanks. They would soon discover, however, that there was little to return to—not their houses, which had been ransacked and dismantled, and, all too often, not the men from whom they had been separated for so long, the fathers, brothers, and sons who had been drafted into the Red Army, 40 percent of whom died in battle or as prisoners of war.[80]

These prisoners, who had remained in Pechera until the very end, would later describe the story of their liberation for survivors who had waited out the Romanian occupation in the ghettos. "They told how [Soviet] soldiers and officers, having liberated the camp, knelt down in front of them and cried, being shocked since these were the first living Jews they had met during the war," remembered Regina Leshchinskaya, who made a run for the stone wall in Pechera with her mother and two sisters during the camp's final hours, as German soldiers fired away at them with their machine guns.[81]

Ion Antonescu's undoing came in August 1944. For months, he had refused to agree to an armistice being brokered with the Allies, even after allowing his representatives to negotiate one. Hitler had caught wind of these discussions and was preparing to invade Romania. Hungary, once a close ally, had already paid a steep price for its treachery, and the Germans invaded the country in March 1944. Later, they would help deport hundreds of thousands of Hungarian Jews to Auschwitz-Birkenau, including those from northern Transylvania. When confronted by Hitler in March 1944, Antonescu once again pledged his loyalty and continued to oppose any agreement with the Allies. In doing so, he left Romania increasingly vulnerable to the surging Red Army. By April 10, 1944, the Soviets had reclaimed Odesa, Romania's administrative headquarters in Transnistria. Still, Antonescu continued to oppose the conditions of the armistice, which among other things called for the Romanians to turn on the Germans, recognize Bessarabia and northern Bukovyna as belonging to the Soviets, and allow Soviet forces to pass through Romania without occupying it.[82]

In August 1944, Romania's twenty-two-year-old King Michael organized a coup with the backing of the country's four opposition parties. The king had played a mostly ceremonial role during the war but recognized the grave threat of a Soviet occupation. On August 23, he invited the marshal to his royal palace. After giving him one last opportunity to side with the

Allies, Antonescu replied that he would agree to a peace but only if he could warn Hitler ahead of time. Unwilling to risk further delays, King Michael asked Antonescu whether he would agree to step down so that another leader could make the deal, but Antonescu refused. The king had heard enough. He summoned four armed guards to arrest both Ion and Mihai Antonescu, who was also on the premises. They were led upstairs and locked in a vault before being taken to a safe house. A week later, they were handed over to the Soviets, who had just arrived in Bucharest.[83]

Romania would soon declare war against Germany. The about-face, which deprived Germans of the vast oil reserves they had relied on to fuel the war effort, was thought to have shortened the course of the war by months.[84] In May 1945, the Red Army surrounded Berlin and, along with the Western allies, forced Germany's unconditional surrender. Antonescu never did give up the remaining Jews still living in Old Romania, who had been used as bargaining chips until the very end.[85] In October 1942, he had halted plans to deport them to the Belzec killing center in Poland two thousand at a time.[86] As a result, the odds of a Jew surviving the war within Old Romania was far higher than in almost any other Axis-held land in Europe, notwithstanding the deaths of hundreds of thousands in the reclaimed territories and Transnistria.[87]

In May 1946, Ion Antonescu and three of his close associates, including Mihai Antonescu, were sentenced to death by the People's Tribunal in Bucharest. The following month, they were executed by a Romanian firing squad. It would be another fifty-eight years before a Romanian head of state would admit to the country's complicity in the Holocaust, which led to the deaths of at least 220,000 Romanian Jews and 180,000 Ukrainian Jews.[88] The vast majority of surviving Romanian Jews—375,000 in all, including those who had been deported[89]—would make their way to Israel. Most local Jewish survivors remained inside the Soviet Union, where for decades, their stories were largely silenced.[90]

After the war, two Romanian war crimes tribunals investigated 2,700 cases but sentenced less than one-quarter of the country's suspected war criminals, many of whom were tried in absentia.[91] Unlike the Nuremberg trials, which gained international attention, records of the oral testimonies gathered from suspected perpetrators were kept out of view. The proceedings and the findings were highly politicized by Romanian nationalists within Soviet-controlled Romania, preventing the evidence of crimes committed

against Jews and Roma from becoming part of the national consciousness. Most sentences were eventually commuted.[92] The fate of the Pechera commander Stratulat remains unclear.[93]

Jewish leaders in Transnistria were not immune from prosecution. After
the war, a Soviet military tribunal convicted Motel Zilberman—a victim
of the Romanians himself—for his conduct in Pechera as the head of the
Jewish administration. Zilberman was accused of beating fellow prisoners
to death and accepting bribes. He was released from a forced labor camp
in 1957, several years early, for good behavior.[94] Max Rosenstrauch, the head
of Dzhuryn's Jewish committee, was convicted of collaboration and spent
three years behind bars.[95]

In 1945, a Romanian war crimes tribunal sentenced Mihail Danilof, one
of Mohyliv-Podilskyi's ghetto leaders, to twenty-five years in prison for,
among other things, negotiating with the Romanians over which prisoners to send to Pechera as the head of the ghetto's Jewish police. Danilof,
who had also led the Jewish committee for a short time, had been among
a small contingent of Jews deported to Transnistria from Romania's Dorohoi district. His minority faction challenged Siegfried Jagendorf and the
ghetto's Rădăuți Jews for control; both chose overwhelmingly to protect
south Bukovyna Jews above all others.[96] "It was crucial that we sacrifice
some people to save the other 17,000 who remained in [Mohyliv]. Without
our intervention the entire ghetto was under risk of evacuation," Danilof
would write during his trial.[97] Although the Mohyliv-Podilskyi ghetto
leader Jagendorf was asked to "answer charges brought by survivors," his
emigration to the United States with his wife in 1946 precluded the possibility of a trial.[98]

CHAPTER EIGHT

Silence

From 1941 to 1945, famed Soviet Jewish writer Vasily Grossman covered the Eastern Front as a reporter for the *Red Star*, the Red Army's newspaper. He wore glasses, suffered from asthma, and lived with a variety of phobias—hardly the archetype for a war correspondent. Yet he summoned the courage to report from the front lines, venturing where few others were willing to go, even as many of his counterparts relied on information fed to them by army officials. While embedded with combat units, he witnessed the war's most decisive battles and was among the first to document the Holocaust's aftermath. Following the German Army's defeat in Kursk, Russia, in August 1943, and with the German forces in retreat, Grossman traveled westward with the Red Army as it began to liberate towns and villages where Jewish life once flourished.[1] As his travels brought him to eastern Ukraine, Grossman came to a startling realization: except for a single Jewish lieutenant who had been in hiding since the early days of the war, he had encountered no other living Jews.[2]

The reality weighed heavily on Grossman, a native of the city of Berdychiv, who learned that his own mother had been among the victims of mass murder.[3] The deafening silence led to an article called "Ukraine without Jews," which he submitted for publication in fall 1943: "You will not see the black, tear-filled eyes of a little girl, you will not hear the sorrowful drawling voice of an old woman, you will not glimpse the swarthy face of a hungry child in a single city or a single one of hundreds of thousands of shtetls. Stillness. Silence. A people has been murdered."[4]

Of the Jews living in prewar Ukraine, comprising the largest Jewish population in Europe, at least 1.6 million were killed between the years of 1941 and 1945. By far, the highest death tolls were in German-controlled territory. The few who remained alive did so by fleeing ahead of the German advance, being mobilized by the Red Army, or by going into hiding. Others survived German labor camps and eventually escaped into Transnistria. Across Transnistria, survival rates were higher.[5]

On March 20, 1944, the day after Dzhuryn's liberation, a snowstorm blanketed the town and the roads leading out of it, leaving the Bravermans stranded inside the synagogue for one last week. It took another three days for them to walk thirty miles to Tulchyn. When they reached their hometown's former Jewish quarter, they found Voikova Street in ruins.

"We saw only rubble," Etel remembered. "Only stones remained. We had nowhere to stay. So Mama stops a city official and says, 'Where do I go? My husband died. I have four children.'"

"Just take an empty one and live there," he replied.

While wandering central Tulchyn, they spotted a small hut on Lenin Street, just east of the Cathedral of Christ's Nativity, not far from the old market. It had whitewashed clay walls and a hipped roof made of thatch. They peered in through the front windows and saw no one inside. Motl went to the rear of the house and tore off a lock. He reemerged at the front door and showed his family in. The entryway led to a single room and to a small kitchen and a second room, though it may well have been called a closet. There was no furniture, no running water, and no outhouse. They spread their belongings across the wooden floors, marveling at their own good fortune. "What a room this is!" Motl remembered thinking. Unaccustomed to having so much space for only themselves, they invited another family of four—fellow Pechera survivors with nowhere to go—to sleep beside them that first night, huddling together under potato sacks that Soybil had found. Mice scampered by as they tried to sleep.[6]

The next morning, Soybil and the children went looking for the Ukrainian woman who had once offered to store their things. When she saw the Bravermans appear unannounced at her doorstep, she launched into an explanation about how everything of theirs had rotted away in her cellar. "My dear Sonya," she told a weeping Soybil. "Don't worry." She went back inside and then returned to the porch holding a hundred rubles and a quilt.

"Oh, how good it felt to sleep under it on the second night," Etel remembered. "You can imagine for yourself what it was like, after so many years."

Later that week, Soybil asked her new neighbors whether they knew of a home remedy for night blindness. She then bought chicken livers at the market and boiled them in a kettle she had found. As instructed, the children stood over the kettle and peered down into the steam. Their vision gradually returned to normal (though eating the nutrient-rich liver more than likely helped). Another neighbor told Soybil to visit the local army garrison, where she could purchase cheap old uniforms and boots for her eldest children to wear. Etel remembered walking about town for the next few months in outfits made of someone's old military overcoat. There were also dormitories in the same army complex where one could find heaps of feathers. The pillowcases were long gone by the time Soybil had come looking for them, so she hauled the feathers home in sacks, which would become pillows. She came back a third time to claim some old bed frames.

Many of Soybil's old acquaintances were overjoyed to see her and the children in Tulchyn again. They provided what help they could. Eventually, local officials determined that the Bravermans were entitled to live in the small house they had broken into. Other returning Jewish survivors had a more mixed experience. Many returned to find their homes still standing but with strangers now living inside. The problem was widespread, but there was little legal recourse. A 1937 Soviet law stipulated that anyone absent from a home for six months or more could lose their claim to it.[7] Still, it would be years before Tulchyn and the surrounding towns could even begin to adequately meet the housing needs of its returning Jewish survivors.

In Tulchyn and across much of the now liberated Soviet Union, non-Jews often found it hard to believe that their neighbors had really disappeared to the camps and ghettos only to return. They assumed that most Jews had simply lived out the war in the Soviet interior, when in fact, only a small percentage had.[8] Some believed that hatred of the Jews was what brought the Germans to Ukraine and that the Jews were to blame for the misfortune that followed. They accused Jewish men and boys of dodging military service and fleeing to Uzbekistan instead. "The Jews, they contended, had abandoned the town during the occupation when the going got tough," writes Jeffrey Veidlinger.[9]

Once home to the region's largest Jewish community, only a fraction of the town's prewar Jewish population came back alive. After spring 1944, just 1,303 Jews were believed to be residing in Tulchyn and the surrounding communities.[10] Now that they were vastly outnumbered by Ukrainians, many grew self-conscious about their Jewish identities and their speech, choosing to speak Yiddish only in private. Some renounced their names.[11] Veidlinger, a scholar of the postwar shtetls of Ukraine's Vinnytsia Province, writes that "the Yiddish speech that had echoed through market squares for generations was silenced overnight. When sound returned, it was overwhelmingly in Ukrainian, forever transforming the aural landscape."[12]

As 1944 wore on, Motl still clung to the hope that his father was alive somewhere and that he might one day return, though he kept these thoughts mostly to himself. He would sometimes go looking for his boyhood friends from Voikova Street, and at first, he refused to believe that only Arkadii had survived. He later heard that just two others had been accounted for. Both were killed while looking for food somewhere outside the camp. Motl, now fifteen, and Etel, seventeen, would each take night classes, but neither completed their formal schooling. With Soybil minding the household and watching Manya and Lova, Etel began working at a small canteen, or dining hall. Motl found a job at a large shoe factory. Soybil constantly worried that her eldest children would miss their shifts, so she would wake up before dawn to ask their neighbors if they knew the time. "I remember how overjoyed we were when we bought a clock," Etel remembered.

Their new home on Lenin Street was soon bustling with activity, not only with Manya and Lova flitting in and out of the house but also with the new friends that Motl and Etel had made. Their company was a source of comfort. "Friends visited Motl, girlfriends visited me," Etel said. "How joyous it was in our one room. We would dance. We were young." For fun, Motl and his friends would walk to the peat fields and swim in the drainage ditches where they once worked.

During the lowest moments of their imprisonment in Pechera, many inmates worried that there would be no one left to tell their story. Throughout the war, developments in Transnistria had largely been ignored by Soviet media.[13] Beginning after their liberation, it appeared for a time that the whole of the Soviet Union—and perhaps the world—would come to learn what they had endured. Yet they soon discovered that they could do little more than grieve privately for all they had lost.

Between August and September of 1945, in the first months after Germany's surrender, Soviet ethnomusicologist Moisei Beregovski and his top colleagues traveled to Vinnytsia Province to collect musical folklore. His team stopped in Tulchyn and Bratslav, as well as in Bershad and Zhabokrych. Using a phonograph, they recorded songs recited to them by local Jews, including the young survivors of the Pechera camp.[14] A ten-year-old boy from Bratslav performed one of them. He wondered who was going to wake him up in the morning and tuck him in at night now that his mother had died. "I never saw my mother again," he sang. "I never saw my mother again. They drove her to her death, to the other side." A sixteen-year-old boy named Yosef Braverman (no relation to my family, as far I know), who had returned to Tulchyn, recited a song he had written in 1942 about longing for the childhood that had been stolen from him. "Our suffering [and] our sorrows will soon be known to the whole world," he sang.[15]

Privately, Beregovski marveled at what had been etched into his waxen cylinders. "The more we learned of the horrific and inhumane conditions of life in the camps and ghettos, the more difficult it was to imagine the possibility of the existence of song in this reality," he wrote in his journal. "[Nevertheless], . . . songs, as well as art in general, occupied a prominent place in the life of the camps and ghettos."[16] Beregovski and his team recorded several dozen songs during their Vinnytsia expedition. They intended to compile the written lyrics into a larger anthology of wartime songs.

Beginning in spring 1944, Pechera survivors were also interviewed by officials with the Soviet Extraordinary State Commission for the Determination and Investigation of Nazi and their Collaborators' Atrocities in the USSR (ChGK).[17] Stalin had formed the commission a year earlier to capture the full extent of the carnage wrought by the Axis invasion. ChGK investigators had already learned that the victims of German atrocities were Jewish and that the crimes were often also perpetrated by local collaborators. With the approval of the Soviet authorities, another group, the Soviet Jewish Anti-Fascist Committee, and its literary group, headed by famed writer Ilya Ehrenburg and subsequently by Vasily Grossman, began compiling evidence. Ehrenburg and Grossman hoped to publish their findings in a project that would become known as *The Black Book*. Stalin supported this endeavor, believing it would encourage Jews abroad to help fund the war effort.[18] Some of the material they gathered related to the Pechera camp.

At some point, Stalin's position changed. Although nearly half the Holocaust's victims were Soviet Jews, Soviet authorities began denying the specificity of the Jewish wartime experience and instead equated it with what Soviet citizens of all stripes endured during the Great Patriotic War, the name for the part of World War II waged on Soviet soil. This new policy of universalizing the Holocaust would ignore, downplay, or deny that Jews were specifically targeted for annihilation.[19] The Communist Party embraced suppression and began to rally all nationalities and ethnicities around the collective triumph over fascism without "giving the war to the Jews."[20]

In early 1944, ChGK officials received new directives: omit the identities of murdered Jews in their reports and use the euphemism "peaceful Soviet citizen" instead. They were also instructed to shield Ukrainian collaborators. These accomplices would now become merely known as the *politsiya*, and each policeman as a *politsai*, with no nationality attached to them. Stalin opposed identifying local Ukrainians as the collaborators, in part to avoid raising uncomfortable questions. He gave some thought to deporting these traitors, and were it not for the sheer number of them, he may well have tried. He also feared that Russian soldiers, the predominant demographic in the Red Army, would be less motivated to finish off the Germans if they felt they were fighting to save only Jews from extermination. "Thus, as a result of Stalin's policies," wrote scholar John Garrard, "we are left with a macabre situation in which neither the victims nor the perpetrators of a genocide were properly identified by the country in which that genocide had taken place." [21]

Making this policy of forgetting even more egregious was the fact that most Soviet Holocaust victims were killed openly, in broad daylight, and if not in plain view of their non-Jewish neighbors, then within earshot. This occurred mainly in the Soviet Union, and especially in Ukraine. In much the same way, Transnistria's camps and ghettos operated in the open, within or close to the communities where local Jews had once lived.[22] Researchers from Yad Vashem were first granted access to the reports—evidence of the first stage of the Holocaust—nearly five decades later, just before the Soviet Union's collapse.

One ChGK report, dated May 9, 1944, written not long after the new policy was put into effect, included testimony by Pechera survivors Liusia Sukharevich and Mania Ribalova, who were originally from Shpykiv. They had since returned to their hometown and were now working at a state bank. Their testimony mentions that Jews like them were the ones initially forced into Shpykiv's ghetto, later deported to Rohizna, and finally taken to Pechera in September 1942, where a death camp held Jews from various locales. They also named two members of Pechera's Jewish leadership, Motel Zilberman and Dr. Vishnevsky. While Romanians and Germans are referenced numerous times, the local policemen they would encounter in Pechera—"M. [Smetansky], Iasha Simirenko, and others"—are merely called policemen, with no indication of their nationality.[23]

Beregovski's materials from the Vinnytsia expedition, including some of the earliest accounts of life in Transnistria's camps and ghettos, would never reach Soviet audiences during his lifetime. In 1950, authorities arrested him during Stalin's anti-Jewish campaign, when prominent Jews were branded as "rootless cosmopolitans" and accused of disloyalty. After his release in 1956, his collection was confiscated and thought to be lost forever. Vasily Grossman's "Ukraine without Jews" was never published by the *Red Star*, and the Russian-language version was suppressed by Soviet censors in 1943. In 1947, Grossman's *The Black Book* was banned, and copies of the manuscript were destroyed, but not before some had been shipped abroad. A Russian-language version was first released in Israel in 1980 (though a chapter on Lithuania was missing).

In the years following the Pechera camp's liberation, its grounds were restored and the former sanitorium began operating as a hospital again. Its verdant surroundings and the serene Southern Buh all belied the village's wartime history. After coming of age, communities of child survivors began returning to Pechera's mass graves to honor their loved ones. In accordance with local Jewish customs, some visited during the last month of the Jewish calendar, Elul, which falls between August and September and leads up to the High Holidays. At first, the groups made the trip by foot. Later, they hired taxis and vans to ferry them to the cemetery and to the woods that held the trenches. They came with bouquets of flowers and pebbles to lay near the shallow graves. At the Jewish cemetery where her parents were buried, on a hill outside of Pechera, Riza Roitman would find little bones protruding from the mounds.[24] At the site of the unmarked trenches west of the village—accessible only by a gravel road that few knew how to find—villagers would tell mourners that they had seen the earth "breathe" after the frequent burials between 1942 and the end of 1943, a sign that not every Jew being covered by dirt was already dead.[25]

Motl, however, felt no inclination to return to Pechera. At twenty, he began his compulsory military service and was sent to Brest, where he was assigned to an antitank regiment and later promoted to sergeant. He returned to Tulchyn three years later and found work at a small shoe workshop, designing, stitching, and assembling the outer shells of boots while colleagues adhered the bottoms. One summer evening, he met his future wife, Anyuta (Anna) Kernasovskaya, at a dance club. He was twenty-eight and thought himself a good dancer; she was nineteen and wearing a freshly pressed dress that her older sister had sewn for her, one of only two that she owned. "I was healthy and beautiful, and more beautiful than today's young ladies," Anna said.

Anna's roots were not in Tulchyn, but in Pechera. On weekdays, she attended classes at a technical college not far from where Motl lived, and on weekends, she would take a truck to her family's home. As Motl would later learn, Anna was descended from one of Pechera's last Jewish families, a family with ties to none other than the Potockis.

In the mid-1840s, members of the Potocki family moved their court to a palace on the Southern Buh. Anna's great-grandfather, Boruch, and his young family, along with other workers and servants, followed the Potockis there from their homes in Kraków, Poland. As a contractor, Boruch supported various construction and engineering projects in and around the estate. He also built an expansive home for his extended family in the village. Boruch's son Chaim—Anna's grandfather—grew up in Pechera and married a woman named Sara, a frail but big-hearted woman who hailed from Bratslav and belonged to the affluent Spector family. They had fifteen children together, only eight of whom—four daughters and four sons—would survive into adulthood. Anna's mother, Freida, was their sixth-eldest living child. They would all live in the home that Chaim had inherited from his father.

While their children were still young, Chaim and Sara built a farm on their property, where horses and cattle grazed and where they raised chickens. The family's cellar was always stocked with milk, sour cream, and butter. Sara would often wake her grandchildren each morning with a glass of warm milk. Ukrainian villagers who fell on hard times knew they could depend on Chaim for his advice and generosity. The village's Jewish population had reached nearly nine hundred (out of 2,455 total) in the late nineteenth century, but in 1919, pogroms carried out by Ukrainian nationalist leader Semyon Petlyura's gangs decimated Pechera's Jewish community amid the Russian Civil War. By 1926, only sixty-two Jewish residents remained.[26] In the aftermath, Chaim became the Jewish community's spiritual leader. He welcomed worshippers into his home for the Friday Sabbath and to form a minyan, or prayer quorum. He owned a Torah scroll and knew Hebrew. Every Jewish wedding, holiday, and circumcision in Pechera was marked at his home. On holidays such as Simchat Torah, he would don his festive white *kittel* robe and dance alongside his guests and young grandchildren with a Torah in his arms. The 1930s brought Stalin's collectivization policies, which stripped Chaim of his farmland. Around this time, Chaim went missing. On the day he returned, his grandchildren saw him with an emaciated face and with a half-frozen beard, suggesting that he had been imprisoned.

In the years following the pogroms, a time of economic turmoil made worse by Stalin's policies, many of the region's Jews fled wherever they could, often to large Soviet cities in the east or abroad, with most never to return. Some would maintain ties with loved ones who remained behind. Sara's family, the Spectors, left Bratslav and found their way to Canada. Canadian parcels soon began to appear at Chaim and Sara's home. At first, they welcomed the help. But when the Soviet government began to brand those communicating with relatives beyond Soviet borders as "enemies of the people,"[27] Chaim insisted that all packages and letters go unanswered.[28]

When they came of age, two of Chaim and Sara's sons went to work at the sanitorium. A few years before the German occupation, Anna's mother Freida moved away to Krasne to live with her husband, Moishele, and his family. They had two daughters, my great-aunt Luba in 1935, and my grandmother Anna in 1937. With German and Romanian forces advancing toward them, Moishele had a decision to make: remain with his wife and daughters or volunteer for the front. As the head of a military warehouse, he had been deployed to Finland, Poland, and Bessarabia in a span of just two years. Given his age and service record, he could have opted to stay home. Instead, he felt that he owed it to his detachment to join them in defending their homeland. Anna would not remember much about the day that she helped see her father off to war, only that he was about to be driven away by cart when he said goodbye. "When it was time for him to go, he hopped off the cart, hugged everyone, and said that he'll return," she said, wiping away her tears many decades later. "That's it. I never saw him again. I don't remember him. Not one bit." Anna was nearly four years old when the occupation of Krasne began. Luba had just turned six.

In fall 1941, Freida and her daughters, along with Anna's paternal grandparents, were imprisoned in the Krasne ghetto with 350 other Jews. They were forced to abandon their large home and move in with a relative already living within the ghetto's confines. All the comforts that Anna and Luba had known as young children under the tender care of their parents evaporated overnight. "The Romanians didn't kill us, they just tortured us," Luba said. "Once they came into our home, took our pillowcases, and left the feathers. These were the kinds of bastards they were." Freida's former neighbors and other Ukrainian villagers helped keep Freida and the girls alive by handing them food through the barbed wire. "Once Mom got some sunflower seeds," Luba remembered. "She divvied up each kernel evenly between the three of us. The scraps [the Ukrainians] gave us, that's what we survived on."

One day, Anna was left unattended while the rest of her family went to sort out some matter. She had just remembered that her favorite dolls were at home and decided that this would be an opportune time to find them. Unlike her older sister, Luba, who had taken after their mother, Anna inherited her father's light brown hair and blue eyes. She was already aware that she could pass for a Ukrainian girl. She wrapped an old kerchief around her head and left the ghetto undetected. Her former neighbors were astonished to see little Anna bounding toward them. They saw to it that she found her dolls, and they packed her a small bag of food. Anna then slipped back into the ghetto, just as she imagined she would. Her mother and sister had not even noticed she was gone.

Before long, the Romanians gathered some of the local Jews and marched the convoy to Tyvriv, a town ten miles northeast of Krasne, where a ghetto had been established. Anna, Luba, Freida, and Anna's paternal grandparents took refuge inside an abandoned courthouse, where they stayed until March 1944. When a Red Army cavalry unit first appeared, Anna, now six and a half, ran up to one of her liberators, who was sitting astride a horse. In Ukrainian, she asked, "Have you seen our daddy?"

"Listen, everyone who heard it burst into tears. She couldn't understand," Luba said.

By 1945, demobilized soldiers began returning home from the front. Those passing through Krasne sometimes preyed on the very populations they had fought to liberate. "They would break into our homes," remembered Anna:

All of these women would hide. One hides in a basement here. One behind a couch there. One in a closet. We children just sat and sat. One of the bandits came into our house, shined a flashlight in, and they broke the doors open and entered. I remember like it was yesterday. I sat on one of the bandit's laps. I cried, and asked if on the front he had seen my papa.

Life became even harder for Freida and the girls when Freida's in-laws, distraught by their son's likely death, moved away to the Crimean Peninsula to live with other relatives. With no one to watch her girls while she worked, Freida hired a young woman named Nina to care for them. In 1946 and 1947, Soviet Ukraine was once again struck by famine. Though Freida struggled to feed her family, she almost always left a glass of milk out for Nina before her arrival each day, knowing that Nina, a poor peasant girl herself, would otherwise be too polite to accept any of her food directly. One day, as Anna and Luba played, they heard a strange noise emanating from one of the bedrooms. They found Nina convulsing on a bed after having vomited. They slammed the door closed and held it shut. They decided to find their mother at work, who in turn rushed to tell Nina's mother what had happened. When no one answered the front door, Freida walked in and found a pot of poisonous mushrooms still boiling on the stovetop. Nina's mother lay on the floor a few feet away. A neighbor of theirs named Andrei, who had a carriage and two horses, brought them both to the hospital. Although Nina's mother recovered, Nina was never the same. For months, Anna and Luba were terrified that their mother would somehow be held responsible for the poisonings. They were, after all, Jews, and Nina was a farmer's daughter. The mere sight of Nina's mother home continued to remind them of the frightening episode. (The experience would also lead to Anna's lifelong aversion to mushrooms.)

One day, Freida's sisters, who had survived the Pechera camp, journeyed to Krasne to visit their nieces. They all wondered why Freida continued to live alone in poverty with no one to help raise her daughters. They asked if she might consider returning to Pechera. Their four brothers had perished, and one of their homes still sat vacant (this brother, Srul, died as a Soviet prisoner of war, and his wife and children were killed after escaping the camp). Freida agreed to move in. The four houses had been built side by side in a grassy glen. In the winter months, the winds tended to blow downslope, trapping in the smoke that poured out of the wood-burning ovens and leaving an acrid haze hanging over them.

"Another perfect chapter started," Anna recalled. "Cold. Hunger. Wind always rushing through this hut. The walls turned into ice. If you were to leave a piece of bread on the table, it would turn to wood—completely frozen."

In 1949, Freida found work as a receptionist at the former camp building. During Freida's first year of employment, it operated as a rehabilitation hospital for wounded veterans. The next year, it received psychiatric patients, one of whom made unwanted advances on Freida during each of her shifts. Each year, a new patient population would cycle in. In the summer months, Pechera began attracting city folk from as far away as Leningrad (now Saint Petersburg) and Moscow, who were drawn to Pechera's bucolic setting, the pristine Buh, and the bounty of the countryside. At night, they would light bonfires on the riverbanks, where only a few years earlier, Germans shot Jews for sport.

In the summertime, Anna ran a small produce stand. Those summering in Pechera would buy her mother's fresh-baked bread, as well as apples, cherries, watermelons, cucumbers, onions, and potatoes. Some of the produce was harvested from her family's gardens, while the rest came from small farms in Sokilets. Anna stored the proceeds in a small round candy box and kept a mental ledger of which farmers she owed what. Each evening, Anna and her mother would walk across the bridge to Sokilets to repay them; invariably, they would leave a few extra kopeks behind. "They fiercely loved me," she said. Growing up, Anna attended the local primary school. Many afternoons, on the way to visit their mother at work, Anna and Luba would stop to pluck small watermelons from the vines growing near the river. They would also frolic in the waters and tan on the boulders below the former sanitorium.

In 1957, twenty-eight-year-old Motl, spindly and well-dressed, traveled to Pechera to meet Anna's family for the first time. After he and Freida, his future mother-in-law, exchanged pleasantries, she reminded Anna that there was still work to be done. Motl helped Anna split logs and draw water from a well. When he offered to carry the buckets of water, she insisted on hanging them from the ends of a carrying pole. On the walk home, Motl tried his hand at balancing the pole on his shoulder, only for the water to keep sloshing out. When it was Anna's turn, she swiveled it from one shoulder to the other without spilling a drop, much to the amusement of her future husband and other passersby.

Between Motl's visits, some of the neighbor kids would run up to Anna and ask, "Is Motl here? Is Motl here? When will he be?" During another weekend in Pechera, Motl walked into Anna's cousin's home to say hello, only to come face to face with a weathered older man with a rifle at his side. It took a few moments for Motl to place him. It was none other than Mishka Odessit, the policeman. As Motl would later learn, Mishka was convicted of collaborating with the Germans and Romanians after the war and had just finished serving his sentence, a decade of hard labor. Forced labor—the most common punishment for the *polizei*—usually lasted between ten and fifteen years. Many of the convicted guards were released by the mid-1950s after having served only part of their sentences.[29] The same was true of Odessit, who now walked free in Pechera and worked as a fur trapper. Anna's cousin's family, all of them Pechera survivors, would reluctantly buy his animal pelts. When Motl saw him, he considered throttling him then and there. If not for the stern look that Anna's uncle shot him, he may well have.

Other *polizei* who had served across northern Transnistria were also rumored to have been tried and jailed for acting as German and Romanian agents. These trials were usually held behind closed doors and almost always without broad public knowledge or press coverage. This was to preserve the myth that all Soviet citizens had resisted the occupying forces. Trials were often staged in the very communities where the criminals had operated, and only in the case of small villages were trials open to the locals. Like Motl, most people who became aware of the proceedings heard about them through word-of-mouth or directly from witnesses who had testified against their tormenters. It was also quite common for vigilantes from the Red Army to kill collaborators.[30] That had apparently been the case for the other Mishka, "Mishka with the Kubanka," who was said to have been shot dead by a Jewish Red Army officer keen on taking justice into his own hands. Survivors had outed this Mishka over his wartime conduct.[31]

In fall 1944, survivor Svetlana Kogan-Rabinovich was brought to Kharkiv and forced to identify former camp guards from a lineup. A Soviet investigator told Svetlana that if she did not comply, she would be treated as a traitor and shot. "They brought in the handcuffed *polizei*, who stood in two rows, unkempt, looking down," she recalled. "It was difficult to identify them, but I did identify Smetansky." She would later testify about him before an NKVD war tribunal.[32] Another infamous Pechera collaborator, Dr. Beletsky, was spotted in Tulchyn after serving his time, his hair now gray. He disappeared only a few weeks after his return.[33] Less than two months after their liberation, two Pechera survivors from Shpykiv told ChGK agents that Dr. Vishnevsky was working again in Tulchyn.[34]

On August 25, 1957, Motl and Anna were married. Anna moved in with Motl's family, hoping it would be a temporary arrangement. A bedsheet separated their side room—all eighty square feet of it—from the slightly larger room where Soybil, Lova, Etel, and her own young son, Mitya, would sleep (Etel had recently divorced her first husband Boris, and Manya had moved away to Lviv for school). The newlyweds had reason to believe that they might be assigned an apartment of their own one day. That summer, Soviet first secretary Nikita Khrushchev had announced a sweeping plan to replenish the country's depleted housing stock within a decade. What they did not expect was to spend nine of those years waiting for the wave of housing construction to reach Tulchyn.

In 1958, Anna gave birth to Igor, the couple's first child. When Igor was old enough to sit up and play on his own, Anna would lay out an old military overcoat and set Igor on it with some toys while she cooked dinner on an old kerosene burner. The coat had belonged to her father, one of the few items of his she still owned. By 1959, amid a baby boom, the Jewish population in Vinnytsia Province, which had been divided into both Romanian and German territory, stood at just 35 percent of what it had been before the war. In Tulchyn, there were 2,500 Jewish residents, less than half the prewar total.[35] During the next two years, Igor watched as one of Tulchyn's first four-story *Khrushchevkas*—the colloquial name for the apartment blocks being erected across the Soviet Union under Khrushchev's decree—rose just steps from the Bravermans' hut next door.

A friend of Anna's who had connections to the town council promised to help put the Bravermans on the priority list for one of the units. There was reason for optimism, and even Igor, now three years old, joined in the excitement, each morning asking to visit the construction site to have a word with the good-natured superintendent. Invariably, Igor would request that the man take a stick and draw plans for the finished building in the dirt. "He would always oblige," Anna said. Before long, the Bravermans received devastating news: a local dignitary had received the apartment they were promised. That same year, Soybil passed away at fifty-seven.

By the age of four, Igor began roaming the neighborhood with his friends and engaging in the same antics his father once had, like chasing horse-drawn carts. He would often watch neighbors patch the walls of their ramshackle houses with a mixture of straw, dirt, and manure, a paste they would combine and mix in buckets. On a memorable summer day in June 1962, his father took him across the street to an annex building on the grounds of the eighteenth-century cathedral where a small crowd had gathered to watch the 1962 World Cup Final between Czechoslovakia and Brazil. Igor, who would become a lifelong soccer player, was transfixed by the little men moving across the ten-inch screen. It was the first time he had ever seen a television.

In 1964, Motl and Anna's daughter Svetlana (my mother) was born. Igor's stroller, tucked into a corner of their room, became her crib for the first twenty months of her life. In the same space, they hung their clothes from the nails that Motl had driven into the walls and stored their produce under a nightstand. On the other side of the room was a bed and a table for Motl's sewing machine. Residents of the new thirty-two-unit building next door took pity on Anna and Motl and their children, whom they adored. They all knew the family's story and tried to reassure the young couple that their time would also come. There was already talk of another *Khrushchevka* coming to Tulchyn, this time on Kirov Street. Like the first, it would stand four stories tall and have a brick façade. When construction finally began, Anna would bundle Igor and Svetlana and bring them to the town council building, an imposing concrete mass near the palace, where she would plead for an apartment. She threatened to keep returning until someone gave her an answer. They would also visit the construction site on Kirov Street, becoming such frequent fixtures that even the builders took notice.

"The workers saw me and these children," Anna recalled, "and they said in Ukrainian, 'That's it. If they don't give this woman a unit, we'll raze the building to the ground ourselves.'"

Finally, in February 1966, they received permission to move into a top-floor apartment. There was a living room, two bedrooms, a bathroom, and a large kitchen. To Igor, the most welcome change was not just the added play space or the indoor plumbing but the cast-iron fins of their radiators, which kept the new flat warm during the dead of winter. He would never forget how difficult it had been to fall asleep in his first home under the intense heat of a wood-burning stove a few feet away, which his parents would light before bed. By morning, with the fire reduced to embers, the house would feel like an icebox again.

During their first two and a half years on Kirov Street, Etel and Mitya also lived in the new apartment. They shared one of the bedrooms while waiting for another apartment to become available. They then moved into another new four-story *Khrushchevka* with a grocery store on the ground floor. It was also built steps from the hut that Motl had first broken into, which had since been leveled to make room for the new buildings.

Motl and Anna used the occasion to furnish their apartment with luxury items that few others could find—a sleeper sofa for their living room, a lacquered-wood writing table for Igor, a vacuum cleaner, a small boiler to heat water for their baths, and later, a piano for Svetlana. "Then we bought a refrigerator that stood in the hallway," Anna said. "No one had anything, and here we were. Such a beautiful home. Everyone who walked in thought so." They acquired almost everything *po blatu*, or through the so-called economy of favors, by which Anna and Motl offered special access to the shoes and clothes they sold at their state-run stores—always in short supply, and rarely available through usual means—in exchange for the items they coveted.

About half the families living in Igor's new apartment building were Jewish. The Jewish children received Slavic names and spoke mostly Russian to their Jewish and Ukrainian peers. Igor's friends learned Yiddish words and jokes and adopted Jewish mannerisms. On the sloped stretch of Kirov Street in front of their building, they played soccer when it was warm and hockey in the winter months. "There was no animosity between our groups—none," Igor recently said. Svetlana recalled walking the full length of Kirov Street until it met the banks of the Silnytsya River, where her parents would take her and Igor to swim and play.

Through the 1960s, Jewish communal life in Tulchyn continued to decline. The town's lone synagogue survived the war but was shuttered by the authorities in 1959.[36] It, too, would be torn down.[37] Jews who still maintained their religious traditions were forced to organize private prayer groups, attending them in secret for fear of being arrested.[38] At home, Motl and Anna spoke only Yiddish. But beyond their use of language, their cultural expression was limited to the occasional meals Anna prepared. My grandparents, born in the late 1920s and 1930s, were part of what scholar Anna Shternshis calls the transition generation—the first children to begin to "disassociate Jewishness from Judaism" in the Soviet Union.[39] Although Soviet authorities denigrated religion, they encouraged national and ethnic minorities to maintain their food traditions, one of the few ways Anna could transmit ancestral memory to her children.[40] Pork dishes, a favorite of Motl's, were also a staple. As a family, they celebrated the occasional holiday, though informally and without the accompanying rituals and prayers. As children, Igor and Svetlana recalled clandestine trips to a family friend's home on the eve of Passover and returning with pillowcases full of freshly baked matzo. Otherwise, they had little interest in religious observance.

For decades, Motl was reluctant to talk about his wartime suffering outside his close circle of friends and family. The Soviet Union was barely two decades removed from Stalin's "anti-cosmopolitan" campaign against Jews—which lasted between 1948 and 1953, and which thawed under Khrushchev beginning in 1961—but whose effects continued to chill Jewish memory and expression. Any attempt to distinguish Jewish suffering during the Great Patriotic War from the suffering of the collective could have serious consequences. Motl and the survivors he knew had resigned themselves to staying quiet. Far from any major metropolis, they were less concerned about their personal safety than they were about losing their jobs or inviting ridicule. They felt there was little to be gained from sharing their stories.[41]

"Did we talk about it? No, we never talked about it," he said. "They might say, 'You were in a camp? Alright, you were in a camp. They [Germans] brought us to work, too. People in Leningrad, they also suffered.'"

Occasionally, Motl would share his memories with Igor, describing a chapter of local history—the Holocaust—that was noticeably absent in his school textbooks.[42] The word "holocaust" never gained popular usage in the Soviet Union. The words "annihilation" and "catastrophe" would become the best approximations. Among Jews, the word "pogrom" was sometimes used, which also described the prewar mob violence that their families had experienced.[43]

It would also be more than three decades before survivors were allowed to install monuments commemorating victims who lay in mass graves near the Southern Buh.[44] Through the 1970s, there was little indication that a death camp had operated in Pechera. When survivors finally asked regional authorities for permission to honor their loved ones with a monument—two miles west of the village, out of sight, and in a remote clearing where trenches had first appeared in the late summer of 1942—they neither approved nor rejected the request and offered little in the way of assistance. "The Germans killed us in the open," said Mikhail Bartik, who would become one of the leaders of Tulchyn's Jewish community. "They [the government] killed us spiritually."[45]

A stone obelisk was installed by donor Mikhail Malin in 1976 and topped with the figure of a mourning mother. She appears to be peering down into the soil. Inscriptions in both Russian and Hebrew are affixed to the monument. The Russian text reads:

> Ponder this! Thousands of these miserable people did not live to see victory. The German-Fascist killers and their police brutally cut short their breath, voice, thoughts, the lives of women, children, and the elderly. Their death words cannot describe. This is your mother, your father, your brothers, and your sisters who were killed and to whom you owe your new happy life. Do not suffer, but internalize the hatred and swear that you will not permit such sacrifice again. Preserve their bright memory through your descendants. Do not forget! This is their bequest.

When Bartik and other survivors first encountered the trenches after the war, they discovered that all but one had been filled with bodies. The last unfilled trench was a reminder, perhaps, of the fate survivors and their descendants had narrowly escaped. To Bartik, apathy on the part of the provincial government to help preserve the site and call attention to the camp was an affront to the victims, yet another method of expunging the Holocaust from public memory.

The most famous example of this policy of forgetting was at Babyn Yar (Babi Yar), a natural ravine on the outskirts of Kyiv where more than thirty-three thousand Jews were shot during a two-day span in September 1941, one of the largest massacres of the Holocaust. Many more Jews would be murdered there before the war's end. Yet for decades, the site remained without a monument. Even Jews who wished to recite the Mourner's Kaddish nearby needed official approval to do so. Eventually, poets, writers, musicians, and activists succeeded in drawing international attention to what had clearly been an attempt at erasure. After the authorities considered building a market and a soccer stadium on the site, they relented and allowed a bronze memorial to be built in 1976, albeit a mile from where the atrocities had taken place. The resulting statue and its plaque failed to distinguish any of the site's victims as Jews (a smaller percentage of non-Jews, including Soviet prisoners of war, communists, Roma, and other civilians were among the hundred thousand killed there). An inscription at the base of the fifty-foot-tall monument reads: "Here, in 1941–43, the German Fascist invaders executed over 100,000 citizens of Kiev and prisoners of war."[46]

Three years later, Kyiv received a ten-person United States presidential commission, sent by Jimmy Carter, which laid a wreath at the monument. The Americans were tasked with making recommendations for a new Holocaust memorial to be established in Washington, DC. They had spent the previous legs of their journey inspecting memorials at Maidanek, Treblinka, and Auschwitz. What they found at Babyn Yar stunned Elie Wiesel, the commission head, who addressed those in attendance:

When I stood here fifteen years ago there was no monument at [Babyn] Yar. But we all knew what [Babyn] Yar meant. Now there is a monument at [Babyn] Yar. But what kind of monument is it? We all had hoped to find a memorial for all the Jews who died as Jews, as well as for all the others who died here. But the Jews are not being remembered.

During the 1979 visit, reporters questioned Wiesel about his criticisms. Since the Germans did not differentiate among those they killed in September 1941—whether Jewish, Ukrainian, or Russian—why, they wondered, did Wiesel object to the monument's omission of Jewish victims specifically?

"That is not what we know from history," he responded. "I say it not with bitterness but with sadness. In those 10 days that I spoke of, only the Jews were killed, not as citizens of [Kyiv] but as Jews. I would like to see here—please, one word about the Jewishness of the Jewish victims."[47]

In the West, the Holocaust was beginning to enter public consciousness as a singular phenomenon, distinct in scale and sheer horror. Striped uniforms, sealed trains, German ghettos and concentration camps—Auschwitz in particular—would become synonymous with the Jewish wartime experience. Yet far more Jews were killed at German killing centers, by bullets over pits and ravines and in gas vans, than would ever die in a concentration camp. Complicating matters was that the Auschwitz complex included multiple subcamps, including a concentration camp, a labor camp, and later, gas chambers and crematoria at Birkenau. The majority of Jews brought to Auschwitz were gassed immediately, having spent no time in the concentration camp. Europe's largest Jewish populations—from occupied Poland and the Soviet Union—were largely murdered elsewhere, often during the early stages of the Holocaust and well before gassing operations began at Auschwitz. "The image of the German concentration camps as the worst element of National Socialism is an illusion, a dark mirage over an unknown desert," concludes scholar Timothy Snyder.[48]

In 1985, French filmmaker Claude Lanzmann debuted his nine-and-a-half-hour Holocaust documentary, *Shoah*, to worldwide audiences. Two years later, PBS aired it across the United States over the course of a week. Trains and railroad tracks were a common motif, interspersed with interview scenes and footage of pastoral landscapes. Lanzmann had gathered more than 350 hours of interviews, but in the final release, only one of the survivors shown on-screen was a Soviet Jew. The Holocaust in the Soviet Union received brief on-screen treatments in the 1978 U.S. miniseries *Holocaust* and the 1988 miniseries *War and Remembrance*, in which dramatized scenes from Babyn Yar were used to represent the Soviet experience.[49] Yet as Jeffrey Veidlinger notes, mass shootings, which would become commonly associated with the Holocaust in Ukraine, were "largely foreign to the experiences of Transnistria's Jews," much like other symbols from German camps and ghettos in Nazi-occupied Europe.[50]

The absence of Soviet Jewish voices, Soviet records, and Romanian documentation—unavailable until the overthrow of communist dictator Nicolae Ceaușescu in 1989—would have an enduring impact on how early Holocaust discourse would be shaped.[51] The Romanian Holocaust was largely omitted, explaining why Transnistria is sometimes called the Forgotten Cemetery.[52] Much of Transnistria's story has been told by Romanian survivors and scholars, and often with a focus on the Romanian deportees and on the southern districts, including the camps in the Kingdom of Death.[53]

Through the late 1990s, Transnistria's overshadowing was reflected at the United States Holocaust Memorial Museum's Hall of Remembrance, a hexagonal space containing an eternal flame and walls bearing the names of famous Holocaust sites. In June 1996, survivor and Florida resident Ruth Glasberg Gold entered the hall and saw that Transnistria was not represented. She noticed the omission after giving an earlier lecture about her book, *Ruth's Journey: A Survivor's Memoir*, an account of her family's deportation from Chernivtsi to the Bershad ghetto. She would spend nearly three years lobbying the museum to incorporate Transnistria into the hall.

"We [cannot] put up the name of every little shtetl," the museum's then-director told Ruth during their initial phone call. "Since Transnistria is not the name of a town, but a region . . . we might want to put up the name Odessa." After a two-year campaign and six-hundred petition signatures, Gold succeeded. At a ceremony held in April 1999, Gold unveiled the engraving "Transnistria" just above "Janowska" and "Bergen-Belsen" and to the left of "Death Marches." As she would tell those in attendance that day, including the museum's new director, Transnistria's inclusion meant that she had succeeded in ways that she could not as a starving child prisoner in Bershad, where in late 1943, she used money that her family had sent her to help pay for a monument dedicated to the ghetto's victims, her parents and brother among them. She returned to Bershad for the first time in 1988, now as an American, only to discover that the monument had not withstood the ravages of time. Her memoir and contribution to the museum, she said in her address at the unveiling ceremony in 1999, would be her "defense against oblivion."[54]

After Mikhail Gorbachev was elected leader of the Soviet Union in 1985, he introduced a program of reforms to restructure Soviet economic and political life. He also heralded a new era of glasnost, or openness, in literature and media, and insisted that there would be "no forgotten names, no blank spots" in Soviet history. In 1988, Mikhail Bartik, then fifty-nine, first pressed Soviet officials to recognize that a camp had existed in Pechera. He also began corresponding with prominent journalists. After he was interviewed on Soviet radio, fellow Pechera survivors from across the Soviet Union began sending him and his wife, Ester, letters. Bartik was also invited to Moscow to speak at a gathering of Holocaust survivors, after which he had a chance encounter with Boris Neyman, who in a subsequent correspondence with Bartik had revealed that he was the young army captain who had liberated the Pechera camp. Fellow Pechera survivors from Soviet Ukraine began raising funds to build new memorials in many of their hometowns. Abram Kaplan and a survivors' group helped create one in central Mohyliv-Podilskyi in what had been the former ghetto. Bartik established a handful of memorials where Pechera's Jews had perished, including one in Torkiv and one in Bortnyky. In Bratslav's Jewish cemetery, the community created a monument dedicated to Rul Brondman's brother Pinya and the other Jews massacred by Germans for their planned uprising. Several communities of survivors added memorials near Pechera's mass graves. Soviet authorities, meanwhile, continued claiming that the Pechera camp never existed, despite documentary evidence to the contrary.[55]

Only in 1989 did Bartik and fellow survivors get their wish when a plaque was affixed next to the front gate of the former camp, which was now a health resort.[56] Survivors and dignitaries gathered to mark the occasion. Musicians were invited to perform. A local newspaper printed a story about the event with Bartik pictured in one of the photos, flanking a speaker.[57] Yet the plaque's inscription obfuscated a crucial detail: the identities of the victims and the local collaborators:

> In the village of Pechera in the district of Tulchyn on the territory of the former Potocki estate during the years of the German-fascist occupation of 1941–1944 there was a fascist death camp in which thousands of peaceful Soviet citizens died.

By this time, the Bravermans had long ago moved to Chernivtsi in the southwest of Soviet Ukraine, where my grandmother Anna's aging mother, Freida, and older sister, Luba, now lived. Like Tulchyn, Chernivtsi had its own dark history. Prior to Romania's annexation of Bukovyna in 1918, the city was called Czernowitz, home to a thriving, assimilated Jewish population that identified strongly with the German language and German culture. Czernowitz was the Austro-Hungarian Empire's easternmost provincial capital—the capital of Bukovyna—and became known as both the "Vienna of the East" and "Jerusalem on the Prut River." To move to Czernowitz from the surrounding Yiddish-speaking communities was to leave the old world behind. A bridge leading them across the Prut River and into Czernowitz served as the portal to modernity.[58] The city then became Cernăuţi under the Romanians for two decades, Chernovtsy under the Soviets—the only name I would grow up hearing—and Chernivtsi in an independent Ukraine.

During the initial weeks of the German-Romanian occupation of northern Bukovyna in the summer of 1941, several thousand of the city's Jewish residents were murdered. A large synagogue was torched. About forty-eight thousand Jews were confined to a ghetto in October 1941 in a boundary meant for perhaps a few thousand. More than twenty-eight thousand of them would be deported to Transnistria.[59] Those who were allowed to remain behind in the ghetto may have owed their survival to the city's mayor, Traian Popovici. It was the mayor who convinced Antonescu and Bukovyna's governor to exempt twenty thousand Jews from deportation. On October 10, 1941, an impassioned Popovici reminded the governor and a handful of the other Romanian officials that history would not be kind to the Romanian people if they followed through with Antonescu's orders to deport everyone. He described his appeals to them sometime before his passing in 1946, writing:

The entire scene that played before us remained in my memory because it was dramatic and I couldn't control my anger. I became aggressive, a behavior which was not usual for a mayor dealing with a governor who was the direct representative of the Marshal. I pointed out to him the responsibility which he personally had and how he would be depicted by history, then I made him aware of the difficulties we would face at the peace conference when Romania would stand before the court of civilized nations. I spared no argument to point out the enormity of the step which he was about to take. I spoke of humanity, the traditional Romanian kindness, barbarity, cruelty, crimes, and shame. I called upon the virtue of our ancestors. . . . I also reminded him of Spain's shame which can't wipe from its history the persecution of the Jews in 1492 under Torquemada. I said to him literally, "Governor, the French Revolution which brought mankind rights and freedom took merely 11,800 victims, while you are on the threshold of sending 50,000 people to their deaths when it is almost winter."[60]

Five days later, Bukovyna's governor spoke to Antonescu by phone. They agreed to spare some of the city's Jews, heeding Popovici's recommendation that they would be more useful if they remained behind. Popovici, who was then branded a "Jew lover" by Romanian officials, would write:

I demanded protection for the highly educated Jews and those who practiced the beautiful arts. I demanded consideration for those who served the people, retirees, officers, wounded veterans. I demanded that the masters of all industrial branches should be kept. I also demanded, in service of humanity, an exception for physicians. I demanded for the purpose of rebuilding, to spare the engineers and architects. I asked that in the name of intelligence and civilization, judges and lawyers be spared.[61]

The Chernivtsi Jews whom Popovici helped spare were the only living Jews in Bessarabia and the whole of Bukovyna not sent to Transnistria.[62] The majority of those who were allowed to remain in the city's ghetto until its 1944 liberation eventually made their way to Romania before immigrating to Palestine and Israel, as would residents who had survived their deportations to Transnistria and crossed back into the city on the bridge over the Prut.[63] In the decades that followed, the city attracted new Jewish arrivals of a different sort, Russian-speaking Jews from across the Soviet Union.[64]

One day in December 1983, while working at her mother's shoe store, my mother Svetlana Braverman, a nineteen-year-old college student, met my father, Grigoriy Goldenshteyn, a twenty-six-year-old architectural draftsman. Their meeting was anything but a chance encounter; it had been arranged ahead of time by relatives. They were engaged to be married a few months later. On their wedding day in August 1984, the private driver hired to bring them from the ceremony in Chernivtsi to their reception never showed up, having had one drink too many. My mother, in her wedding dress and bridal headpiece, and my father, in a slim-cut suit and bowtie, were forced to take a grimy, smoke-filled taxi to the lodge they had reserved in a neighboring suburb, where 150 friends and family were waiting.

Grigoriy's cousin from Kishinev (now Chişinău, the capital of Moldova) managed to book them an extravagant honeymoon cruise around the Black Sea. They made the trip from Odesa to Soviet Georgia in the company of an elderly interloper, who had also booked the same cabin room. At sea, the passengers were treated to entertainment from Odesa's acclaimed theater and opera group. Also featured was the famous singer Iosif Kobzon, the "Soviet Sinatra," who in 1946 had made a name for himself in grade school by winning a contest and performing for Stalin (who applauded afterward).[65] At one point during the trip, my father chanced upon this national icon in the ship's bathroom as he was preening in the mirror and adjusting his toupee.

Like his wife, Grigoriy was also born to a family of Holocaust survivors. At the outbreak of war, his mother, Taisiya Flomen, who was seven at the time, her brother Arkadii, and her parents were evacuated from Taraclia, then a city in Romania's Bessarabia province (now in Moldova). They later found themselves in Serhetabat, Turkmenistan, a town on the Soviet-Afghan border that lay at the southernmost point of the Soviet Union. Taisiya had family in Chernivtsi. Her uncle Isaak Gross and his wife, Liza, had owned three apartment buildings along the city's Kotlyarevskoho Street, not far from the main square. After the Soviet annexation of northern Bukovyna in 1940, most of their property was expropriated by local party officials, leaving them with a single hallway. "We'll happily take the apartments off your hands," Taisiya's future husband, my paternal grandfather Mikhail, liked to imagine them saying. Isaak and Liza, who had no children, spent the war inside the Chernivtsi ghetto.

After their liberation—they had lived only a few blocks away from the nearest ghetto boundary—Isaak and Liza were told by local authorities that they could keep just one of their apartments, which had three rooms and a kitchen.[66] Strangers now occupied the others. One day in late 1944, they received a letter from Taisiya's mother, who had written to them from Serhetabat asking where she and her husband and two children should go. "Come to Chernivtsi and we will share these three rooms," Isaak replied. And they did. In the years that followed, Isaak, who had been a professional artist, painted scenes from ghetto life in his home studio.

Grigoriy's father, Mikhail Goldenshteyn, was born to a wealthy family from Bilhorod-Dnistrovskyi, a city on the Black Sea and also in Bessarabia (in an area that is now part of Ukraine, just southwest of Odesa). The

Goldenshteyns were known for their grocery and hardware stores. Mikhail's father died unexpectedly in 1940 from complications of diabetes after a routine surgery. Mikhail was twelve when his family was evacuated to Azerbaijan in summer 1941. His mother and six-year-old sister, Sara, died of typhus en route. He buried them himself. Between the ages of fourteen and eighteen, he lived in a Baku orphanage, years that were marked by hunger and loneliness. After completing his mandatory military service, he began searching for surviving family members. When he learned that one of his aunts and her children now lived in Chernivtsi, he found her address and wrote to her, telling her about Sara and his mother. She wrote back, inviting him to stay in Chernivtsi. He met Taisiya there in 1954 while working as a machinist at a local factory, where he would eventually rise to chief mechanical engineer. They would raise their two children, Grigoriy (my father) and Rose (my aunt), in Isaak and Liza's apartment. Rose remembered that in addition to the paintings he had produced of the Chernivtsi ghetto, Isaak painted portraits of her and my father Grigoriy as young children. After Isaak died of cancer, Liza moved to Israel with his paintings in tow. It was her dream to open an exhibit dedicated to her late husband's art, a dream that, by all accounts, was never realized.

In the late 1980s, my grandfather Motl heard that the city's Jewish cultural society, named after the late Yiddish writer Eliezer Steinbarg, was soliciting written testimony from local Holocaust survivors. The group hoped to compel Soviet authorities—and later the Ukrainian government—to provide supplemental pensions and restitution during a time of rapidly falling living standards. The news inspired Motl to commit his story to paper for the first time. He asked his daughter Svetlana, a Russian literature major at Chernivtsi State University (now Yuriy Fedkovych Chernivtsi National University), for her help. He spoke uninterrupted for more than an hour, dictating the words that she hurriedly transcribed by hand. He later added his own notes to the submission. Ultimately, the group's efforts had made little difference. For his trouble, he received a free regional bus pass.

One day in the mid-1990s, after having moved to the United States, a small booklet arrived in the mail. The pages were filled with survivor testimonies, including his own abridged account. The booklet, published in 1994, was the third in a five-volume series created by fellow Transnistria survivors who, like him, had settled in Chernivtsi with their families in the decades following the war. Yet the front and back covers bore stripes, evoking an imported experience, that of Jews who had been imprisoned in the German camps to the west. Even the book's subtitle, "People Remain People," was an apparent reference to a passage in Vasily Grossman's astonishing article, "The Hell of Treblinka."[67] These were understandable editorial decisions. In their bid to bring awareness to a little-known chapter of the Holocaust, survivors evoked one of the Holocaust's most widely recognized symbols—that of the striped uniform—and one of the three Operation Reinhard killing centers in Poland. Only now, half a century later, did the experiences of Transnistria's survivors begin to register more broadly as new testimony emerged."[68]

Unbeknown to Motl, a copy of his submittal from years earlier had also found its way to the United States Holocaust Museum, which had acquired 901 Russian-language affidavits from the Chernivtsi Jewish survivors organization in 1993. They were catalogued, put on thirty-five microfiches, and stored in four boxes.[69] Motl's handwritten pages were now among the millions of documents in the museum's Soviet collections, which according to the museum have remained largely untapped by researchers.[70]

CHAPTER NINE

America

IN 1995, AN ARTICLE IN THE *SEATTLE TIMES* trumpeted the arrival of a curious band of foreigners: 3,500 refugees from the former Soviet republics. Clusters of neighborhoods and apartment complexes were said to be filled with Russian speakers, many of whom settled in the Seattle suburb of Bellevue. Seeking the comforts of home in an unfamiliar place, their appetite for pickled herring, rye bread, and imported sweets sustained four new delis. There was even talk of hatching a new Russian-language newspaper. As one recent arrival quipped to the reporter, "Soon it's going to be like Brooklyn."[1]

Each wave of newcomers helped loved ones make the same pilgrimage, which is how my family and I, Jewish refugees from a newly independent Ukraine, found ourselves at Seattle-Tacoma International Airport three years earlier, on the night of July 25, 1992. Making the journey with my sister, my parents, and me were my maternal grandparents, Motl and Anna. My father's side of the family had preceded us in emigrating to the United States. Almost every relative of ours had already left or would soon follow us out, and if not to the United States, then to Israel (my uncle Igor and his family, before they moved to Canada) or to Germany (Lova and his family).

In the weeks leading up to our departure, I would often find my grandfather Motl standing at the TV in our Chernivtsi apartment, staring into the glowing screen in his track pants and sleeveless white undershirt, his hands at his waist, grumbling about a man named Boris Yeltsin. Motl was sixty-three and stocky, with unruly gray hair that ringed the back and sides of his head. Now that our furniture was gone, my sister, parents, and I slept on comforters that had been laid across our great room. My sister, Yuliya, was six, and I was three.

Our journey began on a railway platform near the Prut River. We boarded a sleeper car that would soon bring us to Moscow, our second time in the Russian capital in less than a year. We were summoned to the U.S. embassy the previous winter for immunizations and an interview with the Immigration and Naturalization Service (INS).[2] With the enactment of the Lautenberg Amendment in 1990, Jewish families from the former Soviet Union no longer had to prove a "well-founded fear of persecution" to be granted refugee status and were instead presumed eligible if they could show "a credible basis for concern." After returning home and waiting for the INS to adjudicate our application, we received a letter confirming our eligibility and granting us permission to resettle in the United States in a few months' time.

At the train station, our twelve suitcases were wheeled into one compartment; my grandparents and our family friend Misha, who would help see us to Moscow, crowded into a second; and my parents, sister, and I took a third. I settled in by the window as our train began its slow crawl north to Ivano-Frankivsk. Small towns and vast prairies were soon sweeping past us. Within a few hours, we were skirting the Carpathian foothills near Lviv. Sometime that evening, our train veered east to Kyiv. A full two days would pass before we reached the end of the line in Moscow. We remained in our compartments long after everyone else disembarked, having bribed the attendants to let us off near the train depot instead. An armed security detail we had hired met us there and brought us to the airport on a private bus.

After finding our terminal, my grandmother Anna, fifty-four, offered to watch the suitcases while my parents took my sister to dinner. Meanwhile, my grandfather Motl, Misha, and I wandered the airport. We found a quiet place to sit in what looked to be an empty lounge. The three of us shared cans of tinned meat while Misha and my grandfather sipped vodka. The story would become etched into family lore.

Later that night, after my sister and I fell asleep in our lounge chairs, my grandparents took out the last of their banknotes and turned toward the airport shops, determined to spend every kopek. During the first months of Ukraine's independence, the value of the currency that succeeded the Soviet ruble had plummeted.[3] With the country in economic freefall, my grandparents lost most of their life savings to hyperinflation. What remained, they reasoned, would do them little good in the United States. When my grandparents returned, they had Turkish leather coats draped over their arms and gold watches dangling from their wrists. They also bought silver earrings for my mother and sister to wear to the United States (it had been my father's idea to have them pierce their ears for this very occasion).

A few weeks earlier, my grandparents had also traveled to eastern Poland by train to buy jeans, T-shirts, and sweatshirts in varieties that had never been available to us. Their haul included two two-liter bottles with a caramel-colored liquid bobbing inside, which they mistook for wine. These new items were now tucked into suitcases with the rest of our belongings.

We began our ascent a few hours later. Of the next twenty hours, I would remember only the shock of eating cold airline food, sleeping on my father's shoulder, and a brief layover in New York. After touching down at the airport just outside Seattle, we emerged from the plane to find a small contingent of family and friends waiting to greet us. My mother and grandparents were still wearing their leather jackets, the sweat now streaming from their brows. After our brief reunion, my paternal grandmother, Taisiya, gripped my hand as we walked toward the exit and as someone took our photo. We were now the latest in a growing wave of post-Soviet Jews to arrive in North America, the culmination of a decades-long movement that would reshape entire communities.

In the airport garage, we piled into a few cars and set off for the modest two-bedroom townhouse that the six of us would be renting for only a short time. As my mother stared out into the warm night from the sedan she was riding in—at the ribbons of freeways, the tract housing, and the empty sidewalks—she felt the weight of regret. At twenty-eight, she and my father, Grigoriy, thirty-five, had brought their young children and aging parents to a country they knew little about, whose language they did not speak, where their university educations would not help them find employment, and with only vague assurances, in letters from those who had settled in the United States ahead of them, that their future here would be brighter.

In the former Soviet Union, they had been forced to list "Jewish" as their nationality on internal Soviet passports, a practice that dated back to the 1930s and which became an instrument for discrimination. Jews could be denied entrance to universities—where Jewish enrollment was artificially capped through quota systems—solely on the basis of their identity ("Why should we train specialists only for them to leave for Israel?" seemed to be the sentiment). They faced open discrimination when applying for jobs and were excluded from certain professional fields. Glasnost had finally made it possible for critics of the government to air their grievances, which also allowed anti-Semites to voice theirs. Jews observed a growing chorus of anti-Semitic attacks in the media, and we were once again being scapegoated and cast in familiar roles: Zionists who were disloyal to the Soviet Union and party to a worldwide conspiracy.[4] My father's family, like countless others, believed that the 1988 and 1990 pogroms waged against Armenians living in Azerbaijan were a clear sign that the Soviet government could not and would not protect its citizens from ethnic violence. And still fresh in their memories was a rumored 1988 chemical spill in Chernivtsi that caused respiratory and neurologic symptoms, as well as hair loss, in more than one hundred children. The government obfuscated the accident for weeks.[5]

Yet Chernivtsi was my parents' beloved hometown. Our Viennese-style apartment had been spacious and bright, with parquet floors and French doors that opened to our great room. It was where my grandmother Anna had hosted boisterous dinner parties after my parents were married, the dining table enlivened by Bessarabian dishes from my father's side of the family—including a smoky, roasted eggplant-and-garlic spread, served with tomato wedges—to complement the simple soups and pork-and-potato stews that most appealed to my grandfather Motl.[6] Given the lack of food availability, some of the ingredients had to be collected over a span of weeks, and often *po blatu* (the economy of favors was still alive and well).

Our apartment's windows looked out over a cobblestone boulevard just two blocks from the famous Kobylyanskoi Street, or the Herrengasse, as it was known before World War I (and Strada Iancu Flondor after Bukovyna's annexation to Romania).[7] For my mother, a simple stroll down Kobylyanskoi, a promenade lined by buildings, cafés, and storefronts that originated in the Habsburg era, was occasion enough to dress up, just as it had been for the city's prewar Jews.[8] Yet when she wheeled the first of the suitcases inside her new living room, now standing an ocean away and deep in the heart of suburbia, the room seemed to spin around her.

Early the next morning, sunshine streamed through the blinds in our second-floor bedrooms. My sister and I left our new beds and padded down the carpeted stairs to the living room. The adults were already awake, unpacking suitcases and dressing the cupboards with a faux-wood-grain liner. As I soon discovered, our refrigerator and pantry had already been stocked for us. After a breakfast of macaroni and cheese and hot dogs—a stand-in for the more familiar *sosiski*, or Russian pork sausages—my father's sister (my aunt Rose) arrived to give us a walking tour of our new neighborhood. A visit to the local grocery store that day would leave a lasting impression. My mother discovered flavored yogurt in one of the refrigerated cases, oranges piled high in the produce aisle, and Wonder Bread on one of the shelves. They would each become part of our new rotation. That same first week, we were invited to a family friend's apartment complex, where we encountered an outdoor pool. It was the first time any of us had used one. While the adults were lounging, I decided to have a closer look at the water, gliding the tips of my fingers across the still surface. My grandfather, who sprang from his deck chair, startled me with a primal scream before sweeping me aside to safety.

The abundance of citrus fruit and our new poolside retreat, however, would not solve our biggest problem. The government checks that soon began arriving covered rent but little else. Our airfare had been loaned to us by the International Organization for Migration, leaving us owing several thousand dollars. The first installment would be due in a few weeks. We bought groceries with food stamps, enough for the essentials, plus the occasional indulgence, like the blue tubs of imported boysenberry preserves and round tins of Danish butter cookies. There was also the issue of laundry. We shared a small laundry closet with our next-door neighbors. The washing machine was free to use, but the dryer was coin-operated. We began hanging our wet laundry on a clothesline strung across the patio. A few days later, we received an unexpected letter in the mail. It was explained to us that our landlord and neighbors did not take kindly to our method. It did not take long for my grandfather Motl to give our suburban neighborhood in Bellevue, called Newport Hills, a new moniker—*Newporthillivka*. He was already missing city life.

In September of that year, I turned four. We celebrated with dinner and cake. Afterward, my grandmother retrieved the two bottles of Polish "wine" she had purchased. She set four crystal glasses on the table and filled each to the brim. They toasted to my health and to our new lives in the United States. Then, a look of momentary disgust came over their faces. The content of their glasses was not wine at all, but a thin, carbonated syrup. They had just had their first taste of Pepsi. Years later, I would learn that my birthday had moved my grandmother Anna more than she had let on. She had, after all, turned four during the first year of Krasne's occupation, something she would remind me of when my own firstborn child reached the same age.

That fall, my parents enrolled at a local community college. On weekday mornings while they were away, my grandparents and I would walk my sister to her elementary school classroom. Most afternoons, my grandparents would take me on tricycle rides in the parking lot outside our townhome. I would weave between the parking stalls and stop only at the light posts, where I imagined gas stations to be. My grandmother kept me wellfed with a steady diet of buckwheat and chicken *kotlyeti*, or ground-meat patties. To pass the time, my grandfather Motl and I would sometimes take a bus to the nearby Factoria Mall. I would ask to go to the arcade, where I drifted from game to game with glee, convinced that I was in fact the one manipulating the cars or characters on the screens, even with "Insert Coins" flashing.

At home, the secondhand Zenith television in our living room became one of my family's first portals to American culture and the English language. It was also through our television that we learned about the universal gesture for hitchhiking, which came in handy when the used Dodge Aries sedan my father had just purchased stalled on the highway one night. My grandfather and I took a liking to the CBS series *Highlander*, about a sword-wielding immortal intent on decapitating his foes. That was about all I could gather.

Only a few months after moving into the townhome, we packed up to leave. My parents had found a less expensive apartment in a subsidized housing complex a few miles away, not far from Bellevue Community College, as it was known then. My grandparents made the move with us and continued to live down the hallway from my sister and me, as they always had. Even now, I was still pestering my grandfather to tell me stories. He would usually offer the one about the boy and the wolf. There wasn't much to the plot, beyond a young boy walking in a forest alone until encountering a wolf. The boy would run away, climb a tree, and wait from the safety of the branches until the wolf had gone. At the end of each retelling, I would run to my bedroom and record my own version on an old tape deck before playing it back for him. Once, I told my grandfather that I wanted nothing more than a Power Wheels Jeep Wrangler, the kind I had seen other kids in our apartment complex drive around the playground. My grandfather suggested I close my eyes and pray for one. When the car failed to materialize, I cried. A neighbor named Ludya, a fellow émigré my grandfather's age, tried to console me that afternoon. "Take it from me. It helps to be more prudent with what you ask him," she told me.

Within a year, my grandparents would find a small apartment of their own, moving into a Seattle Housing Authority tower on the south slope of Seattle's Queen Anne neighborhood, near one of the city's toniest residential areas. They furnished the living room with wall-to-wall lacquered-mahogany furniture and hung an area rug on the wall behind their sofa. During our weekend visits, hearty lunches would be followed by walks through Upper Queen Anne, where I stared wide-eyed at the manicured lawns, ornate homes, and vintage brick apartment buildings. My grandmother Anna would usually lead us to a place she called *her* overlook, by which she meant Kerry Park, maybe the city's most famous viewpoint. It was not unusual to see a bride and groom posing for photos near the railing or to see a TV news crew film a weather segment against the backdrop of the downtown skyline, the Space Needle, Elliott Bay, and, weather-permitting, Mount Rainier. Other times, we would walk downhill to the Seattle Center, spending afternoons at an amusement park built for the 1962 World's Fair. My sister and I often joined hordes of other children in running up to tag the International Fountain while dodging water that would jet out from its steel dome.

Before long, other guests began to frequent their Queen Anne apartment—young English-language tutors sent by a local Jewish social services agency. They included a married couple named Ruth and Kevin. When my visits coincided with theirs, I liked to sit at the dining table and observe the lessons. From what I gathered, my grandmother was less interested in learning conversational English than in plying her earnest American guests, and Kevin in particular, with meat dumplings—and to delight in their compliments. My parents also welcomed a language tutor to our home, a kindhearted American named Michael, who would conduct English lessons at our dining-room table over cookies and instant coffee.

From time to time, we would crowd into his two-door Chrysler convertible for day trips just outside our adopted hometown—an early-evening ferry ride from downtown Seattle across the shimmering waters of Elliott Bay, a short hike in the foothills of the Cascade Mountains, a trip to the Skagit Valley Tulip Festival, a drive to the West Seattle waterfront neighborhood where he and his wife, Kathy, made their home and where we were treated to our first salmon dinner. He continued to offer lessons to my parents months after our term had ended. Our paths would cross again at a festival held a year or two later at the Seattle Center. My parents, who now held their first full-time U.S. jobs—my father at an architecture firm, my mother as a teacher at a local Jewish community center's preschool—surprised even themselves with how easily the right English words came to them that day.

Yet even now, to the broader Jewish American community that had so embraced us, we remained an enigma. We did not fit the mold of the big-city intelligentsia class who now embodied Soviet Jewry abroad. We were not dissidents.[9] Nor had we come bearing the traditions of the Jewish immigrants from a century earlier, who would come to represent an idealized past for American Jews.[10] What we and many of our fellow Russian-speaking Jewish émigrés did possess was a direct link to a bygone world.

While we felt a profound connection to our Jewish heritage, we were ambivalent about religious and cultural practices, had little awareness of Jewish dietary laws, and were a people whose culinary traditions were almost indiscernible from Soviet ones. Mostly, we identified with Russian culture. We were far from alone. In one survey of Jews who left Ukraine in 1992, respondents said that being a "genuine Jew" had little to do with Judaism. Less than 1 percent believed that attending synagogue, knowing Jewish traditions, or observing the Sabbath were the most important arbiters of Jewishness. Pride in one's nationality and defending "Jewish honor and dignity" were rated as the most important. Many Jews from Ukraine felt that they were Russian Jews at heart.[11]

In Chernivtsi, my mother and grandmother Anna were afraid to so much as be seen walking outside a synagogue, and never more so than during the High Holiday services of Rosh Hashanah and Yom Kippur, when the congregants' prayers were audible from the street. They set foot in a synagogue for the first time just before our emigration, leaving a donation that they hoped would bring us good luck overseas. My mother's fondest holiday memories were of decorating her family's New Year's trees, called *yolki*. In pre-revolutionary times, *yolki* were a symbol of Christmas. But under the Soviets, trees and other Christmas traditions were appropriated to New Year's. Even Santa Claus took on a new persona, becoming *Ded Moroz*, or Grandpa Frost. In lieu of religious holidays, families like hers would take to the streets for public demonstrations on May 1, the Day of the International Solidarity of Workers (May Day). The other major holidays were May 9, Victory Day, which commemorated Nazi Germany's surrender, and New Year's Day.

Through her first job in the United States as a preschool teacher, my mother began learning Jewish customs from a colleague. She once observed how the woman showed three- and four-year-olds the finer points of lighting a menorah. One Friday evening after work, she came home with a bag of challah dough, part of the same batch that her young students had used to make their own small, braided loaves. She and my father tried their hand at the same activity that evening, the beginning of a new tradition.

With a Slavic first name and a Jewish last name, I struggled to place my identity during my grade-school years. When classmates and teachers would ask about my background—often after roll call on the first day of each school year—I would say that I was Russian or sometimes that I was Ukrainian, though neither label seemed to fit. I asked to simply go by "Max." My father's answer to the question of our nationality was that we were Jewish, which made things all the more mystifying. At grocery stores, cashiers would sometimes ask about the origins of the last name on our checks, exchanges that I would come to dread. "It's German," my father would wryly answer.

In time, I noticed that some of my elementary school classmates wore crosses. One night, I found a pair of popsicle sticks in my bedroom and glued them together, one over the other. I then strutted to the dining table for dinner wearing a ribbon of tape around my neck with my new cross dangling from it. Suffice it to say, my father, who had worn a gold Star of David for as long as I could remember, was less than enthused. He had the same reaction when my mother suggested bringing home a New Year's *yolka*, or even a garland, for fear someone might get the wrong impression about us.

Of all my family members, my father would become the most keen to reclaim our heritage, now that we were free to express it. He began fasting on Yom Kippur, the Jewish Day of Atonement. He installed a mezuzah outside our front door, the small wooden case holding a parchment scroll with passages from the Torah. We began lighting a menorah on Chanukah. On the Jewish holiday of Purim, we would head to my grandmother

Taisiya's apartment and leave for home with a paper bag packed full of freshly baked hamantaschen cookies, their triangular shape meant to evoke the three points of the Purim villain Haman's hat.

It was also his idea to begin bringing us to a small orthodox Jewish temple in Bellevue for weekend services. It was there, in a small, leased space above an optometry clinic, that I had my first taste of cholent—a traditional meat, bean, and potato stew—and later, during Saturday morning children's classes, where I heard stories from the Old Testament, mastered the Hebrew alphabet and learned which blessings to pair with which food groups. In class, my sister and I received Hebrew names: I was now Mordecai, and my sister was Esther. Every now and then, our congregation's rabbi would invite us to his home for Sabbath dinner on Friday evenings. Some of the families that would join us there had similar backgrounds; others belonged to well-established families who had spent generations in America. My sister and I took part in the congregation's children's choir, which performed at the Crossroads Shopping Mall during the week of Chanukah. My grandparents Motl and Anna attended each concert (for several years running, photos of our choir were published in our suburban newspaper).

Despite my newfound Hebrew reading skills and the embrace of our new community, the idea of attending hour-long services, conducted entirely in Hebrew, a language we could never hope to understand, began to wear on me. Attempting to follow along with the English translation in my prayer books felt like an exercise in futility. My father and I looked to our fellow congregants for the cues to sit and stand. Our appearances became more sporadic. Eventually, we stopped attending services altogether. I managed to retain some of what I had learned for the next year or two and brought my knowledge to a Jewish summer camp in Seattle. The biggest adjustment was having to wear a yarmulke on my head each day (I wore mine under a teal-billed Seattle Mariners hat). By summer's end, thanks to my kickball exploits and recall of biblical stories, I was named runner-up Camper of the Year. I narrowly lost the top honor to a boy named Moishe, who had sidelocks and wore a small tallit prayer shawl under his shirt, its fringes (tzitzith) hanging down over his pants. My reward: a new bicycle.

By 1998, after more than five years of living in the United States, my family became eligible for naturalization, the process by which foreign-born residents can become citizens. For months, all four of my grandparents rehearsed for their interviews and oral exams. To pass the civics tests, they would need to answer six of ten questions correctly. I delighted in quizzing them from a bank of possible questions about American history and the various functions of government—Name three of the original thirteen states. Who wrote the Declaration of Independence? Who is the governor of your state? For each of them, passing the test and gaining citizenship was among their proudest accomplishments.

During those early years in the United States, only my grandmother Anna offered me a window into my family's past and the lives we had left behind. Sometimes, she would begin telling me the story of how as a little girl, she donned a kerchief and managed to sneak out of her ghetto. But she would stop short of elaborating. Other times, she volunteered stories about her father, Moishele. Once, before the Great Patriotic War, he was returning home from a previous military deployment when his truck overturned. A toddling Anna appeared before him in a vision as he lay unconscious in the cab, one of his arms broken. Growing up, her mother, Freida, would repeat the story to her as her father had told it, hoping it would bring her comfort in his absence. Her eyes would almost always well up at the mere thought of the war and of hardscrabble decades that had flown by.

One afternoon, while watching TV in my grandparents' apartment, I overheard them ask my mother to help with an application sent by the Claims Conference, an organization that negotiates with the German government to secure modest restitution payments for Holocaust survivors. They seemed to be debating—my grandparents in Yiddish and mother responding in Russian—about whether it was worth mentioning that my grandmother Anna helped her mother, Freida, wash the Germans' uniforms. I knew even less about my paternal grandparents, only that their families had been evacuated far from home and that not everyone returned.

I dismissed these fragments as something altogether different from the stories of the Holocaust that I had encountered in school and in movies. In the fourth grade, our teacher read aloud the book *Number the Stars*, about the rescue of a Danish girl and her family from Nazi-occupied Denmark. In the same classroom, I would thumb through a well-worn copy of *Anne Frank: Life in Hiding*. Later, my father rented the movies *Life is Beautiful* and *The Pianist* for my sister and me. During a college course on the

Holocaust, I was assigned Primo Levi's *Survival in Auschwitz* and Art Spiegelman's *Maus*. In our lecture hall, I learned about the role played by the Einsatzgruppen in decimating Jewish populations in the Soviet Union. I felt a kinship with the victims, which had drawn me to the topic. But it never occurred to me that my own family could have been subjected to the same horrors. I compartmentalized what I had heard from my grandmother Anna as an example of the hardships that all Soviet families had surely faced during the German occupation. I had little reason to think otherwise. As I would later learn, my closest childhood friend and the best man at my wedding, whose family lived in Vinnytsia before their resettlement in Bellevue, was equally in the dark about his family's past. He only knew that his grandmother had spent the war in Mohyliv-Podilskyi.

For much of my childhood, I wondered if what I sometimes observed was a sign that some long-ago trauma, hidden from the rest of us, was still exacting a toll. There were the urgent phone calls from my grandmother Anna, sometimes three or four of them each day. If we picked up the receiver one ring too late or were not home at the time, she assumed the worst. Routine mishaps, like a pair of house keys going missing or the onset of a winter cold, were treated as validating events that would only reinforce her angst. No family vacation plans were ever announced to her until a day or two before our departure, knowing that the news would be met with fear and foreboding until the moment we came home.

On her birthdays, we would bring over boxes of chocolate, only for her to store them in her cupboard for months at a time, refusing to indulge unless she could share the chocolates with us. Clothes and shoes that we gifted my grandfather Motl never made it out of his coat closet, accumulating there for years with the tags still attached. During the final few minutes of any visit to her apartment, my grandmother Anna would begin to frantically bag food that she would insist we take home, in large enough quantities to fill the trunk of our Subaru station wagon. This went on for years, no matter how much we protested and no matter how much we insisted that we had plenty to eat.

One day after school, when I was about ten years old, my grandfather Motl brought me to an outdoor basketball court behind the neighborhood elementary school. Another elderly man and his grandson joined us. As the other boy and I took turns heaving shots at the same hoop, our grandfathers inferred that they were from the same part of the world and struck up a conversation. Happy to have met a new friend, I asked the other boy whether he was Jewish too. He told me he was not. When it was time to go, the four of us crossed the street together and went our separate ways. At home, my grandfather looked concerned. "Why would you ask that question of the boy?" he said. I had no answer and spent the rest of the afternoon replaying his comment. I was convinced that I had jeopardized our newfound friendships.

Growing up, both sets of grandparents and my great-aunts remained a constant presence in our lives. My grandmothers would take turns busing from their apartments in Seattle to our home in Bellevue each weekday, where they fixed lunch for my sister and me after school and watched us until our parents returned from work. By the time high school arrived, all four grandparents moved back to Bellevue to live closer to family. Together, we would celebrate almost every family member's birthday, whether with home-cooked meals or at one of the few restaurants that they found palatable. One of these was Goldberg's Famous Delicatessen. In addition to standard East Coast-style deli fare, the multifold menu included Old-World Jewish cuisine, which Central- and Eastern-European immigrants had brought with them in the nineteenth and early twentieth centuries but which bore little resemblance to the spreads that would later be found on Soviet-Jewish tables (a divergence brought on by Soviet food policies).[12] My family gravitated toward the pickles, potato knishes, latkes, and beef-stuffed cabbage, which reminded them of the variants they themselves sometimes prepared. They tried other Jewish American staples on the menu, like roasted brisket, only to reject them on first taste and to pile their uneaten meat slabs on a single plate.

By the late 1990s, our adopted hometown of Bellevue, best known for its affluent downtown neighborhoods and posh shopping mall, was entering another growth spurt. New office towers were sprouting in the central business district, less than two miles from where Jeff Bezos had founded Amazon in his home garage (then known as Cadabra Inc). Microsoft was continuing its ascent in the neighboring suburb of Redmond, ushering in a new era of prosperity for the region. Yet even then, a patchwork of subsidized apartment complexes, a multicultural mosaic where dozens of languages were spoken, defied Bellevue's reputation as an enclave only for the wealthy. Russian speakers were concentrated in the east end of town, in the

Crossroads and Lake Hills neighborhoods, where most of the ballyhooed Russian delis, bakeries, and piroshky shops had taken root. For the initiated, it was also where one could spot elderly Russian-speaking men with frayed baseball caps observing chess matches at the Crossroads Shopping Center and where couples dressed in one or two layers too many strolled the parks, waited at bus stops, or walked home along busy arterials with bags full of groceries.

While their children and grandchildren were focused on acculturating and building their new lives, members of the older generation kept mostly to themselves. When my grandparents and great-aunts socialized, it was with family and neighbors. In this way, they lived off the radar. For several hundred of them, a local community center called Circle of Friends became a refuge from the solitude of their apartments. Etel spent several days each week there in the company of people with similar backgrounds. They would watch Russian TV programs together, visit with healthcare providers, listen to visiting speakers, and take exercise classes.

Anna and Motl were reluctant to be seen at Circle of Friends, or what they cynically viewed as a daycare for the elderly. They took especial pride in their independence, toting their own grocery bags home, running their own errands, and busing to their old Seattle neighborhood on occasion, if only to walk to Kerry Park and reminisce about the first years in the United States. When my grandfather was in his early eighties, he took up swimming at the local YCMA. Each time I visited, he would update me on his previous week's lap totals. "Ten times like this, then a break, and another ten times like this," he would say from his living room chair, pantomiming each swimming stroke.

One day in 2005, my grandfather Motl took a bus to the Bellevue Library to spend an afternoon perusing Russian-language newspapers and magazines. He climbed the staircase and walked toward the second-floor stacks. As light poured in through the clerestory above, he settled on a copy of the *Novoe Russkoe Slovo* (New Russian word), a New York-based newspaper for Russian readers. He brought it to a nearby table and scanned the first seven pages. The lead photograph on the eighth page, the cover of the opinion section, took him aback. It had been taken on the outskirts of Pechera, at the site of the mass graves. In the foreground was a fence, and beyond it, the unmistakable sight of trenches. Some were full, covered in overgrowth. At least one other lay partly empty, a reminder of a fateful day in September 1942 and the act of defiance to which he owed his life. According to the caption, the photo had been contributed by a Zhenya Voskoboynik, a name Motl had not heard in more than six decades. The author of the accompanying op-ed, citing various memoirs, appealed to readers to help preserve the camp's physical memory with private funding.[13] Motl made a photocopy and brought it home to show his wife Anna. "Can you believe that?" he told her. "Zhenya Voskoboynik exists. He is out there."

That afternoon, he called the phone number listed by the writer's name. When she answered, Motl told her that he had read her article and that he, too, was a survivor of the Pechera camp. He explained that he had saved the man who had taken the photograph. They were both just boys then, he said. He asked if she would provide Zhenya's phone number. The woman said that she could not, as he had died several years earlier. She wondered if he might like to speak to his daughter instead. That same day, my grandparents' phone rang. It was a woman named Svetlana. She asked my grandfather about the villages he and her father had passed through on the way to Tomashpil and about the clothes her father had been wearing. None of the answers seemed to satisfy her. They never spoke again.

He would later mention the conversation to his childhood friend and fellow survivor Arkadii, who now lived in Israel. During one of their lengthy phone calls, Arkadii, hearing the disappointment in my grandfather's voice, suggested another person for him to reach: Clara, the girl whose family my grandfather had also helped lead to Tomashpil. He offered her phone number. Clara was even younger than Zhenya but grew up in Tulchyn after the war and worked in the same general store as my grandmother Anna. One of her brothers also worked at the shoe factory. They all knew one another in adulthood, but my grandfather had never raised the topic of the walk to Tomashpil while in Tulchyn.

"Back then, it wasn't a respectable thing to ask," he said. "In that time, there was no discussion about this. About the camps. To the contrary."

When he phoned Clara in New York, they realized they had not spoken in more than thirty years—not since Motl and Anna and their children had left Tulchyn for Chernivtsi. Yes, she told him, she remembered leaving Pechera and walking to Tomashpil with her mother and brothers. But who guided them there during the winter storm in 1943? She was sorry, she told my grandfather, but she did not know. She had been too young to remember.

In spring 2014, two years after my last interview with my grandfather, I received a text message from my sister. "Are you sitting down?" she wrote. My grandfather had recently noticed a small growth on the side of his neck. His physician didn't think much of it, but my grandfather insisted that he receive a CT scan. In addition to the lump, he was also experiencing lower back pain. A battery of tests revealed the inconceivable, that he had metastatic lung cancer. The tumors had spread throughout his body, and an especially large mass had formed on one of his hips, explaining why his walking had become so labored. I called my mother when I heard the news. We both tried to make sense of it. She wondered, weeping into the receiver, whether it had anything to do with the noxious compounds he had used for shoemaking in Chernivtsi. After his day shifts at a shoe repair store, he would spend evenings holed up in an unventilated room in our apartment, where he assembled materials purchased on the black market into footwear. His wife, Anna, would sometimes sell the shoes from the backroom of the state-run store she managed in lieu of the government-provided merchandise, an illicit operation that carried considerable risk and weighed heavily on their minds. All this allowed us to live a more materially comfortable lifestyle than most other families in our orbit. For the price of a pair of boots, acquaintances and strangers alike would show up proffering cases of butter, rounds of cheese, and meat by the bucket.

Two months after his diagnosis, his oncologists at Bellevue's Overlake Medical Center had an update. The drugs he had been prescribed had slowed the cancer's progression, even shrinking some of the tumors. But the good news was short-lived. Further tests a few weeks later revealed that the tumors were once again growing and multiplying. Pain medication and radiation therapy—to winnow down the largest growths and make him more comfortable—was the only course of action. From then on, the insomnia he had learned to live with only got worse. He would sometimes stay up all night watching the news on his couch.

"Well, Maksik," he told me the next time I saw him, as I slipped off my shoes in the doorway. "Your grandpa is in a bit of trouble."

"No, *dedushka*. Everything will be OK," I offered, not knowing quite what else to say.

On June 30, 2015, thirteen months after his diagnosis, he passed away. He was eighty-six. On the first anniversary of his death, my wife gave birth to our first child, a coincidence that has always held a special meaning for my mother and grandmother.

In September 2020, more than eight years after I first began interviewing my family, I received a phone call that I thought would never come. On the line was a Svetlana Voskoboynik from New Jersey, returning a voice-mail I had left two weeks earlier asking about her father Zhenya. We spoke for half an hour. "Don't take this the wrong way," she told me, "but I don't think your grandfather was the one who led him out." The next morning, she sent me photos of her family, a letter her father had once written describing his plight in Pechera, and a copy of the very picture that had been printed in the *Novoe Russkoe Slovo*.

When we spoke again the next day, Svetlana said she did not remember having a conversation with my grandfather, but for my benefit, was willing to at least entertain the idea that he and her father had crossed paths. There was just one problem. Her father's name was not Zhenya. It was Aleksander. He was born in Tulchyn in January 1931 to Zejlik and Bella Voskoboynik, the youngest of their fifteen children, some of whom had died in childhood. When the war began, Aleksander's oldest siblings were spread across Ukraine, having started their own families. Zejlik and Bella and their three youngest sons—Aleksander, Boris, and Lev—were imprisoned in the Pechera camp in December 1941, where Lev was shot and killed while accepting food at the camp gate. At some point, Aleksander noticed that the swelling in his feet had spread to his abdomen and chest. He was no longer hungry but was overcome with thirst. The more water he drank, the worse the swelling became.

One of Aleksander's relatives from a nearby village offered to pay a Ukrainian man to save Aleksander and Boris and to bring them to Tomashpil, where their brother Ehilyk had lived before being mobilized. After receiving a heavy gold chain in payment, the man first led Boris across the frozen Buh before returning for Aleksander. Zejlik and Bella remained behind and perished. In Tomashpil, Boris married a young Jewish woman before joining up with the Red Army. Their son was born while the war was still raging, a child Boris would never meet. Of the Voskoboyniks sent to Pechera, only Aleksander lived to see the Soviet liberation in spring 1944. When the war was over, his six surviving siblings, most of whom had children of their own to attend to, paid little mind to Aleksander, now fourteen. He had never felt more alone. Aleksander went to live with some of them in Kyiv, where he finished the eighth grade and met his future wife.

He then enrolled in a trade school in Riga, Latvia, and moved in with one of his sisters. After completing the program at sixteen, he proposed to the girl he had met in Kyiv. He would eventually ask for a work assignment that would take him "as far away as possible" from his family. He got his wish. He was sent to the far reaches of eastern Russia, the Kamchatka Peninsula, famous for having the world's highest concentration of active volcanoes. His son Arkadiy was born in 1954, and his daughter Svetlana in 1960. He and his wife later moved to Siberia, where the pay was better and where anti-Semitism was less pronounced, before returning to Kyiv. In 1972, he decided to change his given name, Abram, to Aleksander.

"Can you imagine, being an Abram in Kyiv?" Svetlana said (*Abramchik* was a common epithet used against Jewish men).

In 1973, the summer after his son Arkadiy had completed his first year at university, Aleksander booked the two of them a trip to a health resort in the countryside. As they arrived in the village of Pechera, it dawned on Aleksander that the resort was housed on the former grounds of the death camp in which he had been imprisoned as a boy. He had trouble sleeping and chain smoked throughout their stay. At the time, the first monument had not yet been erected near the mass graves, nor had a memorial plaque been installed near the camp's former gate. It was during this trip that Aleksander took the photograph that appeared in the *Novoe Russkoe Slovo* thirty-two years later. Aleksander decided to bring his son home a week early, surprising his family. "And when they came back to Kyiv, his face was gray from sleepless nights, tears, and worries," Svetlana remembered.

In 1988, Aleksander, his wife, and Svetlana's family—including her three-year-old daughter—emigrated to Boston before moving to New Jersey. Aleksander passed away in 2002 at the age of seventy-one after battling pancreatic cancer. Svetlana, who had earned an engineering degree in the Soviet Union, changed vocations after completing a three-year training program. At sixty, she is now two decades into a career as a nuclear medicine technologist.

Some years ago, Svetlana heard that a synagogue in New York was raising funds for a Holocaust memorial, giving congregants a place to honor
loved ones. Along with her contribution, Svetlana sent the organizers the
names of relatives who had perished—to be engraved in the memorial—
and a photo of the mass graves in Pechera. The materials found their way
to the woman who would author the 2005 *Novoe Russkoe Slovo* article. She
must have misattributed the photo to Svetlana's mother and Aleksander's
wife, Zhenya, a name that is not gender specific.

There are parts of Aleksander's story that bear striking similarities to
the one my grandfather had told. He was roughly the same age as the boy
my grandfather had saved. A Russian or Ukrainian helped deliver him to
Tomashpil's ghetto. At least one ailing parent had been left behind in the
camp. From there, their stories diverge. Aleksander lived with a soap maker
in Tomashpil and not an older brother. The soap maker allowed Aleksander
to sleep in his loft from 1943 to 1945 on the condition that he wake throughout the night to stoke a fire on the main floor, over which cauldrons of lye,
grease, and animal bones quietly simmered (the raw ingredients used in
soap making). Ehilyk returned only after the war and his demobilization.

Svetlana assured me that it was only natural for my grandfather to want
to believe he had found Zhenya in the pages of a newspaper. He was not
the first person to suggest a tenuous connection to her family. While working at a local hospital some years earlier, she was preparing an IV for an
elderly Spanish-speaking patient when the woman looked down at Svetlana's badge.

"Is this your married name?" she asked.

"No, this is my maiden name," Svetlana answered.

The woman explained that Voskoboynik was a family name, and that
she, too, hailed from Tulchyn or somewhere thereabouts. Her family had
fled to Argentina in 1929 or 1930 when she was only a year old. They settled
in Buenos Aires, where she grew up. She and her husband, a Polish Jew,
eventually moved to the United States with their three children. At the
appointment, the woman said she was convinced that she and Svetlana
belonged to the same extended family. She offered to host Svetlana and her
husband for dinner, where the two couples spoke Yiddish. When they met
again at Svetlana's home, they began flipping through photo albums. They
were all struck by the woman's uncanny resemblance to Aleksander's sisters.
In Svetlana's mind, there was now no doubt that she and the woman were

related. Their continued visits marked the beginning of a years-long friendship. Svetlana was willing to bet that I, too, would find my answers.

In between our phone calls and emails, I began to accept that the closure I was after—and the validation I had wanted for my grandfather, if only for saving Zhenya—would prove elusive. I had followed the past as far as it would take me.

Epilogue

April 2020

On a blustery spring morning, librarian Vladislav Vigurzhinsky embarked on what would be his fourth virtual tour of Tulchyn of the past three days. In the video, he stands in an unmarked intersection with his back to a church on Haharina Street, near the town center. In a previous incarnation, this was Stalin Street, and before that, Church Street. Historically, he says, locals viewed this juncture as the unofficial dividing line between the urban Jewish quarter to the north and the country lanes to the south, where Christian residents had lived.[1] On today's guided tour of Pushkin Street, the points of interest include one of the handful of preserved shtetl homes still standing in Tulchyn. The one Vigurzhinsky has selected is maybe the most recognizable of them all, having been photographed in recent years by a handful of visiting scholars from Saint Petersburg and heritage travelers from the West.[2] It is a wonder the residence is even standing. The entire structure is undulating. The five front windows now sit on different planes, and the stairs leading up from the street are quite literally crumbling. Vigurzhinsky points to the street-level storefront, which like the front gallery (a porch) and tiled roof, was typical of Tulchyn's shtetl homes.

Three years ago, Tulchyn's Jewish population stood at just 150.[3] It appears that this house, on its last legs and one of the final vestiges of prewar Jewish Tulchyn, may outlive the very community that it continues to evoke. Someone has affixed a sign to one of the front posts, with the words "Hut for sale" scrawled on it. It is difficult to tell whether the offer is serious or someone's idea of a gag. "I won't buy it," Vigurzhinsky jokes to the unseen camera operator. "Too expensive."

Next up is the old market square, where for centuries, Jews and Christians came together for their weekly market day. After that comes Central Park, where Vigurzhinsky's itinerary ends. Here, the affable Vigurzhinsky strikes a more somber tone. He mentions the civil war pogroms of 1918 and 1919 that were carried out mere blocks from where he is standing, on the opposite end of Pushkin Street, which would color Jewish-Christian relations for decades to come.

Over the next few weeks, his near-daily online tours continued to grow in popularity. Vigurzhinsky, forty-seven, is a Tulchyn native with a thin black mustache and a cherubic face. He has amassed a considerable social media following, not only for his role at Tulchyn's regional library but as a popular amateur historian and one of the town's biggest boosters (he has been known to glide around town on a Segway donning eighteenth-century regalia). He grew up attending School No. 3, where he learned Russian in the Soviet era and where, by his estimate, two-thirds of the students were Jewish. Most emigrated to Israel and the United States in the 1990s. When COVID-19 found its way to Ukraine in early 2020, halting public life and forcing his library to shutter, Vigurzhinsky had time on his hands. That April, he began filming videos, each with its own theme, about Tulchyn and sharing them with his five thousand Facebook friends, most of them homebound. Some viewers still live in Tulchyn. Others had long since moved away but tuned in for a taste of home.

Vladislav and I were first introduced by the administrators at Tulchyn's School No. 1. I had emailed them to ask about a black-and-white photo on their website showing the school building shortly after it was built. The photo had apparently come from Vladislav's personal archive. As Vladislav would later explain, a friend of his, who once worked at the municipal "wastepaper collection point," discovered the photo and salvaged it for Vladislav, a regular occurrence. After a few email exchanges, Vladislav pointed out a detail that I had somehow missed the first time I saw the photo: barbed wire in the lower-right corner, hinting at the wartime ghetto that once stood nearby. On the back, in pencil, was a single notation: "1948."

I had hoped to travel to Ukraine in June 2020, my first time back since leaving Chernivtsi as a young child. The plan was for a friend to meet me in Kyiv, where we would take a train to Vinnytsia and then travel to the places my family had described in their retellings. The pandemic, and an indefinite ban on foreigners entering Ukraine, put those plans in limbo. Vladislav's videos became the next-closest thing to being there in person. One day, I asked Vladislav if I could write about them.

"A great idea, write away," he emailed me in Ukrainian early one morning. "It will be interesting, or as the youths say, cool."

During the next few weeks, Vladislav sent me batches of photos that relate to Jewish life in Tulchyn. In my inbox, I soon found a postcard from 1910 showing Tulchyn's main synagogue, the Great Synagogue, which dwarfs the congregants pictured standing just outside it. It was forced to close in 1929 and has long since disappeared.[4] Vladislav also sent a watercolor painting of a synagogue that now houses the Museum of Local Lore. A third picture, taken in 1961, shows a "technical school of veterinary medicine" that was housed in another small former synagogue building. That building, too, has been razed. There are others, including hair-raising images of tanks rolling through the urban center.

Vladislav's fifteenth video tour is devoted to School No. 1, where a three-story brick addition now abuts the original structure, the first stop for Jews being sent to Pechera. Vladislav takes viewers to the yard behind it. Beyond a string of candy-colored tires that are halfway buried in the grass is what may well be Tulchyn's most historic site, where the town's fortress walls once stood. Today, no traces are left.[5] Nearby is a tower crane that presides over a stalled construction project, much to the chagrin of the locals.

As the weeks passed and more videos were added, I began to recognize the places I have long been hearing about—the cinema where Jews were humiliated in the early days of the German occupation, the abandoned brick shoe factory where my grandfather and fellow survivors found work after the war, the street my mother would take to get from my grandmother's store to her music school, the cathedral my grandfather lived beside for more than two decades.

When I was not watching Vladislav's dispatches, I wandered Tulchyn through the wonder of Google Maps. For weeks, I searched for the Voikova Street of my grandfather's boyhood, but there was no sign of it. Most street names have changed in recent decades. Lenin Street, which had been the town's main thoroughfare, is now named after Mykola Leontovych, the

Ukrainian composer and conductor. Kirov Street, where my mother and uncle lived as children, was renamed after one of Igor's closest childhood friends, Oleg Stepanyuka, a neighbor from the same apartment building who was killed at the age of twenty-two in the Soviet-Afghan War.

By sheer chance, I spotted an old placard with the name "Voikova Street" on one of the homes near School No. 1, in the eastern half of town. Voikova Street is now Romana Chaykovskoh Street. Compared to central Tulchyn, the streets here are much narrower. Some are unpaved. Many of the homes, topped with corrugated metal roofs, stand only feet apart. Others are separated by overgrown gardens. One bears my grandfather's old address and may well have been built on the same plot. I imagine my grandfather and his boyhood friends wading through a nearby creek, which appears to have long dried up. I picture him running through the town's dusty streets, and many years later, walking the same blocks beside his new bride, showing her the Jewish neighborhood that was no more.

A half-hour drive north is the village of Pechera, now billed as a regional tourist destination, where the former sanitorium building continues to operate as a rehabilitation clinic for adults with musculoskeletal disorders and injuries. It has undergone a facelift in recent decades. The two balconies above the front entrance, on the second and third floors, have been encased in glass. The building has been painted tea green, with olive-green stripes running down the corners of the façade. A satellite dish is affixed above the entryway. Two bronze lion statues now guard the entrance, which overlooks a round of shrubs and the stone fountain where Pechera's prisoners had once heaved their belongings. Entire sections of the wall that once contained the camp are missing, where support posts are the only remnants. The small plaque affixed near the front gate more than three decades ago now has a Star of David. The text has long since been changed to reflect the Jewish identities of the camp's victims.

The grounds surrounding the hospital are now known as Pechera Park, home to sixty species of plants including the 250-year-old lime trees that line the driveway. Standing on the banks of the Buh, at the foot of the stairs leading to the hospital, is an old marble statue: a woman beckoning visitors to the slow-moving waters. The park is still reputed for its healing powers. "Pechera is unique for its relief landscape, lack of industry, and mild climate," one of the hospital's senior clinicians recently wrote in a blog post.

"This is a little Switzerland: a clean ecological environment, an original historical park with an area of [forty-seven acres]—the place itself accelerates the regenerative processes in the body."[6]

In early 2020, the provincial government proposed closing and consolidating a handful of medical facilities, including the eighty-seven-room hospital in Pechera. The hospital's chief physician, seventy employees, former patients, and the wider Pechera community have vehemently opposed the plan and have openly wondered what might become of the property—and to whose benefit.[7]

International researchers have made appearances in recent years, as has an Israeli documentary filmmaker and the occasional busload of heritage travelers. In the 1990s, Moisei Beregovski's long-lost archive resurfaced in an unmarked box at the Vernadsky National Library of Ukraine. Recently, a musical group organized by University of Toronto professor Anna Shternshis and musician Pavel Lion resurrected a pair of songs from the collection—"Tulchin" and "My Mother's Grave," written by two Pechera child survivors—and set them to a variety of musical arrangements. In 2018, the group's album *Yiddish Glory* was nominated for a Grammy Award in the "Best World Music Album" category, believed to be only the second time that a Yiddish-language album has ever been considered. News of the nomination was covered by leading North American media outlets, which mention the Pechera camp. The plight of Tulchyn's Jews was a subplot to the popular Russian movie *Papa*, which still airs on Russian television stations in the United States (although it leaves much to be desired in the way of historical accuracy).[8]

The village's secrets are now out in the open. Yet local memory in Pechera seems to have vanished. Just outside the park, several small inns and resorts have opened, promising outdoor pools, kayaking on the Southern Buh, and historical sightseeing ("I liked everything except the coffee. Sorry, but brewed coffee should be delicious," reads one recent traveler's online review). The nearby Potocki watermill is a major attraction, as is the neo-Romanesque mausoleum, which now also serves as a Catholic church. Visitors snap photos of companions posing on the steps that lead from the park to the riverbanks. The right bank of the Buh is now a popular campground. In 2020, a music festival was planned not far from the former camp site. It is unsettling, even from behind a computer screen, to find people at leisure here, unaware of the events of 1941–44, which continue to grow more remote with each passing year. Even visiting Ukrainian journalists often omit the most significant chapter of the village's recent history in their dispatches.⁹

One need not go far to find similar examples. In mid-2000, U.S. scholars Marianne Hirsch and Leo Spitzer accompanied the son of a Holocaust survivor to the site of another infamous camp in northern Transnistria, Vapnyarka. They were joined by a Ukrainian translator and a local driver. The party of five left Chernivtsi and crossed the Buh at Mohyliv-Podilskyi before reaching Vapnyarka, a journey that took them six hours. They brought only a photocopy showing a cardboard model of three brick buildings that housed the prisoners, hoping it could help lead them to what remained of the site. The second-generation survivor making the trip with them, David Kessler, was the son of Dr. Arthur Kessler, the pre-war medical director of the Chernivtsi Hospital. Dr. Kessler was the Vapnyarka prisoner who discovered that the grass-pea fodder given to the inmate population as a cheap food source was also poisoning them, leading to a hunger strike. Growing up in Israel, Kessler heard only bits and pieces of his father's story. He noticed that the people who often visited his childhood home used crutches. Even his father's memoir was inaccessible to Kessler, having been written in German. "There are some things children should be spared knowing," his father would say. "One day the story will be told."

When the party arrived in Vapnyarka, they expected to find a sign leading to the former camp site. Instead, they were told time and time again that they were mistaken, that what they were looking for was the Tomashpil ghetto some twelve miles away. There was never a camp in Vapnyarka, the locals insisted. They then checked the town's army base, where after a lengthy wait, an officer noticed that one of the buildings depicted in the photo they had shown him was still standing. The other two had been torn down a few years earlier. They received permission to enter the base and found one of the three brick buildings they had been looking for near a playground. This building, they were told—the only one still standing— was now a kindergarten. As with other Holocaust sites in Ukraine, the presence of a camp in Vapnyarka had been forgotten, its memory wiped clean for both political and ideological reasons and by the passage of time. On the drive back to Chernivtsi, the travelers realized that they were perhaps the first outsiders since 1944 to see the remaining camp building for what it once was. But they were also disappointed that none of the town's inhabitants, not even on the army base, seemed the least bit interested in hearing about their discovery.[10]

In June 1988, while beginning to write her memoir, survivor Ruth Glasberg Gold received permission to return to Bershad. Her family had been deported to the ghetto established there from their native Chernivtsi (or Czernowitz and Cernăuți, as they knew it under Austria-Hungary and Romania, respectively). As she would write, "I felt a strong need to validate my previous existence as an ordinary child with love, family, and a home and also to validate the tragedy that followed, in order to stop the cycle of pain." The first person she encountered was an old man. When Gold stopped to ask if he could point her to the ghetto site—it had been the largest in Transnistria, with twenty-five thousand prisoners—he replied, "Ho, ho. What was, was!"

At the edge of town, Gold and her cousin identified what had been the Jewish cemetery, the place where victims' bodies were taken and left unburied during the war, including Ruth's brother and parents. They were disappointed to find only the grave markers for local Jews who had died more recently. There was also a stench, which as they would learn, was human waste from the town's outhouses that had been deposited near the site of the unmarked graves.

"Was there no dignity at all, no respect for the dead?" she later wrote.[11]

In 2009, a travel party headed by Jeffrey Veidlinger, then a professor with Indiana University, visited Pechera. They were led from site to site by survivors Sasha Kolodenker and Rita Shveibish. Standing on a footpath mere feet from the Buh, they looked on as visitors flocked to the river and its boulders. When a member of Veidlinger's team asked Kolodenker in Yiddish what he thought about the people standing ankle-deep in the Buh chit-chatting, romping through the waters, or passing by with a picnic basket, he replied, "Let them! Of course!" In the book *In the Shadow of the Shtetl*, published four years later, Veidlinger would write that Kolodenker's refrain was consistent with what other survivors of the Holocaust in Transnistria had told his team, that it was time to move on. "If all the killing sites of Ukraine were cordoned off," Veidlinger wrote, explaining the sentiment, "there would be almost no riverbanks, forests, cliffs, or ravines left to enjoy."[12]

Yet for Mikhail Bartik, the separation of place from memory is perhaps what he feared most in the late 1980s, when he began his decade-long crusade to pressure the Soviet government to recognize the camp and to begin honoring its victims. Bartik and others raised money to fence off the three-hundred-foot trenches in the woods and to erect additional monuments, some of them dedicated to deceased loved ones, others to entire communities of victims. Soviet authorities had no interest in maintaining the sites. Especially galling to Bartik was the lack of support for erecting signposts to help visitors reach the mass graves or for paving the gravel forest road leading to them, which was often obstructed by overgrowth and which few could locate. For the late Soviet government, and then Ukraine's, to burden the region's aging and shrinking Jewish population with the upkeep, he said, was an affront to the dignity of the victims.[13] Bartik and his wife, Ester, would eventually emigrate to Germany, as had many Jews from the former Soviet republics.

"People speak about Auschwitz, Dachau, this place and that," he would tell two interviewers in 1994 from his then-home in Tulchyn, while stifling a burst of emotion. "But there at least, they gave them something to eat once a day. . . . If they tattooed a number on me, at least I would know I have some worth. We didn't get tattoos. Our numbers are here: in our hearts."[14]

Notes

Abbreviations

GARF   Gosudarstvennyi arkhiv Rossiiskoi federatsii (State Archive of the Russian Federation)

USHMM   United States Holocaust Memorial Museum

VHA   USC Shoah Foundation Visual History Archive

Acknowledgments

1. At her request, I have used a pseudonym for my great-aunt, whom I call "Luba" in the book.

Prologue

1. Braverman, "The Fascists Entered," 91.

2. Garrard, "The Nazi Holocaust," 4.

3. Wiesel et al., "Executive Summary," 6.

4. John Mullan, "Week Three: Jonathan Safran Foer on the Origins of Everything Is Illuminated," *Guardian*, 20 March 2010, www.theguardian.com/books/2010/mar/20/jonathan-safran-foer-everything-illuminated.

5. Veidlinger, *In the Shadow of the Shtetl*, xiii–xiv, 2–3; Geissbühler, *Once upon a Time*, 23–24.

6. Hirsch and Spitzer, "Small Acts of Repair," 18–19.

7. "Mitzvah" is a Hebrew word that means commandment, but it also refers to doing a good deed.

Chapter 1

1. Joseph Goebbels's diaries, as quoted in Ancel, "The German-Romanian Relationship," 261.

2. Ancel, "The German-Romanian Relationship," 267–68.

3. Kruglov, "Jewish Losses in Ukraine," 274–75; Lower, *Nazi Empire-Building*, 72.

4. Ancel, "The German-Romanian Relationship," 253, 256, 265–68; Kaplan, *In Europe's Shadow*, 139; Deletant, *Hitler's Forgotten Ally*, 2.

5. Kaplan, *In Europe's Shadow*, 134.

6. Ancel, "The German-Romanian Relationship," 253.

7. Ioanid, *The Holocaust in Romania*, 281.

8. Kaplan, *In Europe's Shadow*, 134; Deletant, *Hitler's Forgotten Ally*, 62.

9. Ancel, "The German-Romanian Relationship," 257, 259, 264; Hilberg, *The Destruction of the European Jews*, 809.

10. Ancel, *Transnistria*, 430–33.

11. Kaplan, *In Europe's Shadow*, 137; Ioanid, *The Holocaust in Romania*, 12, 274.

12. Wiesel et al., "Roots of Romanian Antisemitism," 1–2.

13. Wiesel et al., "Solidarity and Rescue," 2.

14. Aron Hirt-Manheimer, introduction, in Jagendorf, *Jagendorf's Foundry*, xxi.

15. Valeriu Florin Dobrinescu, "Documente si marturii: Ion Antonescu vazut de contemporani [Documents and other evidence]," *Dosarele istoriei* 7, no. 6 (2002): 16, 18, as quoted in Deletant, *Hitler's Forgotten Ally*, 37–39.

16. Ancel, *The History of the Holocaust in Romania*, 8.

17. Wiesel et al., "The June/July 1940 Romanian Withdrawal," 12; Ioanid, *The Holocaust in Romania*, 118.

18. Ioanid, *The Holocaust in Romania*, 52–53.

19. Ioanid, *The Holocaust in Romania*, 61.

20. Ioanid, *The Holocaust in Romania*, 272.

21. Ancel, *The History of the Holocaust in Romania*, 552; 559.

22. Wiesel et al., "Executive Summary," 43.

23. Wiesel et al., "The Holocaust in Romania," 27–29.

24. Ofer, "Life in the Ghettos of Transnistria," 235.

25. Wiesel et al., "The Holocaust in Romania," 24.

26. Snyder, *Bloodlands*, 253.

27. Ioanid, *The Holocaust in Romania*, 175.

28. Ancel, *Transnistria*, 28–29.

29. Wiesel et al., "The Holocaust in Romania," 26–29.

30. Carp, *The Legionary Movement*, 15; Carp, *Transnistria*, 32; Hilberg, *The Destruction of the European Jews*, 810.

31. Jean Ancel, ed., *Documents Concerning the Fate of Romanian Jewry*, vol. 6 (New York: Beate Klarsfeld Foundation, 1986), 199–201, as quoted in Wiesel et al., "The Holocaust in Romania," 23–24.

32. Ancel, *Documents Concerning the Fate of Romanian Jewry*, 6:499, as quoted in Wiesel et al., "The Holocaust in Romania," 29–30.

33. Wiesel et al., "The Holocaust in Romania," 30.

34. Ioanid, *The Holocaust in Romania*, 63.

35. Ioanid, *The Holocaust in Romania*, 63–77.

36. Wiesel et al., "The Holocaust in Romania," 21–22.

37. Carp, *The Legionary Movement*, 15; Wiesel et al., "The Holocaust in Romania," 14.

38. Ioanid, *The Holocaust in Romania*, 123–24.

39. Hilberg, *The Destruction of the European Jews*, 822, table 8–21.

40. Deletant, "Romania," 166–67. The implications were enormous for the populace. For the Jewish communities that now found themselves outside the Romanian demarcation line and in the German zone of occupation, the war would spell near total destruction. Some individuals managed to survive by hiding. In the Romanian zone, the odds of survival were generally better. See Veidlinger, *In the Shadow of the Shtetl*, xviii, 161–62, 189, 232.

41. Ancel, *Transnistria*, 17–18; Veidlinger, *In the Shadow of the Shtetl*, 189.

42. Solonari, *A Satellite Empire*, 1n1. According to Solonari, Finland controlled a tiny territory in northwest Russia.

43. Wiesel et al., "The Holocaust in Romania," 44–45, 87; Ancel, *Transnistria*, 50.

44. Ancel, *Transnistria*, 56.

Chapter 2

1. Jakubowska, *Patrons of History*, 46; Potocka, *Dziennik*, 118, 149; Potocka, *Moje wlasne wspomnienia*, 312.

2. Schultz, "Health Resorts and Sanitoriums," 132.

3. Golbert, "Holocaust Sites in Ukraine," 230n70; Vynokurova, "The Fate of Bukovinian Jews," 21–22.

4. Carp, *Transnistria*, 337; Megargee, *USHMM Encyclopedia of Camps and Ghettos*, 742.

5. Veidlinger, *In the Shadow of the Shtetl*, 194; Ancel, *Transnistria*, 353.

6. Ancel, *Transnistria*, 88; Wiesel et al., "The Holocaust in Romania," 49.

7. Evgeniia Tsirulnikova, USC Shoah Foundation, VHA Interview 31784.

8. Carp, *Transnistria*, 425; Vynokurova, "The Fate of Bukovinian Jews," 21–22.

9. Carp, *Transnistria*, 242.

10. Golbert, "Holocaust Sites in Ukraine," 228.

11. Carp, *Transnistria*, 350; Golbert, "Holocaust Sites in Ukraine," 215, 228; Ioanid, *The Holocaust in Romania*, 192.

12. Abram Kaplan, USC Shoah Foundation, VHA Interview 34818.

13. Deletant, *Hitler's Forgotten Ally*, 175.

14. Carp, *Holocaust in Romania*, 218; Carp, *Transnistria*, 336.

15. Agmon et al., *Vinnitsa District*, 85.

16. Bronshteyn, *Dead Loop*, 264, transcribed from Bronshteyn's USC Shoah interview with Reizia Vainblat, USC Shoah Foundation, VHA Interview 30862.

17. Ancel, *Transnistria*, 41, 45.

18. Carp, *Transnistria*, 242.

19. Bronshteyn, *Dead Loop*, 276–77, transcribed from Bronshteyn's USC Shoah interview with Shelia Vaisman, USC Shoah Foundation, VHA Interview 31618.

20. Phone interview with author, 19 February 2020.

21. Sara Chernobilskaya, "The Forgotten Concentration Camp," *Novoe Russkoe Slovo* (New York), 21 January 2005.

22. United States Holocaust Memorial Museum, Jeff and Toby Herr Oral History Archive (hereafter USHMM), RG-50.226.0029, oral history interview with Riza Yankelevna Roitman; Golbert, "Holocaust Sites in Ukraine," 217.

23. Gosudarstvennyi arkhiv Rossiiskoi federatsii (State Archive of the Russian Federation; hereafter GARF), Fond 7021, op. 54, d. 1341, ll.163–65. Accessed through the European Holocaust Research Infrastructure, https://training.ehri-project.eu/eo9-testimony-survivors-liusia-sukharevich-and-mania-ribalova-9-may-1944.

24. USHMM, RG-50.226.0029, oral history interview with Riza Yankelevna Roitman.

25. Phone interview with Radu Ioanid, 19 February 2020. Ioanid points to the example of the massacres committed by Sonderkommando Russland in 1942. Afterward, Romania's Army Headquarters asked Antonescu whether they had permission to conduct them. In his response, Antonescu said that "it is not the Army's job to worry about this matter." For more on the Sonderkommando Russland events that Ioanid referenced, see Wiesel et al., "The Holocaust in Romania," 70.

26. Geissbühler, "What We Know about Romania and the Holocaust," 249–50.

27. Ancel, *Transnistria*, 44.

28. Paul Shapiro, *The Kishinev Ghetto*, 18.

29. Motl Braverman, interview by the author, Bellevue, Wash., 7 May 2012.

30. USHMM, RG-50.226.0029, oral history interview with Riza Yankelevna Roitman.

31. Mikhail Bartik, USC Shoah Foundation, VHA Interview 30959.

32. Arkadii Plotitskii, USC Shoah Foundation, VHA Interview 34591.

Chapter 3

1. Popoff, *Vasily Grossman*, 116.

2. Ilya Ehrenburg, *Memoirs, 1921–1941*, translated by Tatania Shebunina and Yvonne Kapp (Cleveland: World Publishing, 1964), as quoted in Popoff, *Vasily Grossman*, 117.

3. Popoff, *Vasily Grossman*, 117; Veidlinger, *In the Shadow of the Shteti*, 162–63.

4. Hilberg, *The Destruction of the European Jews*, 325.

5. Werth, *Russia at War*, 162.

6. Popoff, *Vasily Grossman*, 117.

7. Veidlinger, *In the Shadow of the Shtetl*, 189. According to scholar Vladimir Solonari, women comprised 70 percent of the population in parts of Transnistria. See Solonari, "Hating Soviets," 520. A version of this study appears in Solonari's *A Satellite Empire*.

8. Popoff, *Vasily Grossman*, 117; Pinchuk, "Soviet Media," 221–33.

9. Popoff, *Vasily Grossman*, 106, 114.

10. Altshuler, "The Distress of Jews," 80–81.

11. Veidlinger, *In the Shadow of the Shtetl*, 163.

12. USHMM, RG-50.226.0004, oral history interview with Mikhail Abramovich Bartik.

13. Boris Sandler, interviewed by the author, Bellevue, Wash., 28 October 2018.

14. Veidlinger, *In the Shadow of the Shtetl*, 163–65.

15. Yad Vashem, "The Untold Stories: The Murder Sites of the Jews in the Occupied Territories of the Former USSR," s.v. "Kirovograd," www.yadvashem.org /untoldstories/database/index.asp?cid=804.

16. Bergström, *Barbarossa*, 64.

17. Wallace Carroll, "It Takes a Russian to Beat a Russian," *Life*, 19 December 1949, 80–88.

18. Ioanid, *The Holocaust in Romania*, 177; Veidlinger, *In the Shadow of the Shtetl*, 165; Ancel, "The Romanian Campaigns," 125; Ofer, "Life in the Ghettos of Transnistria," 232.

19. Kogan-Rabinovich, "In the Inferno," 455–82.

20. Veidlinger, *In the Shadow of the Shtetl*, 8; Sokolova, "The Podolian Shtetl," 36–39, 47.

21. Veidlinger, *In the Shadow of the Shtetl*, 77, 188.

22. Veidlinger, *In the Shadow of the Shtetl*, 59–77.

23. Veidlinger, *In the Shadow of the Shtetl*, 44.

24. *YIVO Encyclopedia of Jews in Eastern Europe*, s.v. "Shtetl," www .yivoencyclopedia.org/article.aspx/Shtetl.

25. Bartal, "Imagined Geography," 181–82.

26. Veidlinger, *In the Shadow of the Shtetl*, 15.

27. Veidlinger, *In the Shadow of the Shtetl*, 137.

28. Veidlinger, *In the Shadow of the Shtetl*, 44.

29. Veidlinger, *In the Shadow of the Shtetl*, 34.

30. Subtelny, *Ukraine*, 90, 124, 189–90.

31. Reid, *Borderland*, 143–44.

32. Spector, *The Encyclopedia of Jewish Life*, 1340.

33. Dubnow, *History of the Jews in Russia and Poland*, 147–49. In his description of the events in Tulchyn, Dubnow relied on Natan Hanover's famous account of the massacre in *Yeven metsulah* [Abyss of despair], published in 1653. Historians have since concluded that Hanover "employed significant license" in reconstructing the episode. See Glaser, "The Heirs of Tul'chyn," 128–29.

34. Zinberg, *The German-Polish Cultural Center*, 125.

35. Dubnow, *History of the Jews in Russia and Poland*, 1:148. Beginning in the late nineteenth century, the story of the Tulchyn massacre would be adapted into books and plays, one of which was dramatized by the Yiddish Art Theatre in New York City in 1928. That year, the *New York Times* concluded, "Nothing on Broadway this season approaches the grandiose conception." See "Yiddish Art Theatre,"

New York Times, 30 September 1928, https://timesmachine.nytimes.com/timesma chine/1928/09/30/95841328.html?pageNumber=117. For more on the books and plays inspired by this episode of Tulchyn's history, see Slutsky, "Tulchin," 174.

36. Slutsky, "Tulchin," 174. Veidlinger, *In the Shadow of the Shtetl*, 25.

37. Spector, *The Encyclopedia of Jewish Life*, 1340.

38. Veidlinger, *In the Shadow of the Shtetl*, 33–34.

39. Veidlinger, *In the Shadow of the Shtetl*, 59, 189–90.

40. Mikhail Bartik, USC Shoah Foundation, VHA Interview 30959.

41. Bronshteyn, *Dead Loop*, 38–39, transcribed from Bronshteyn's USC Shoah interview with Riza Roitman, USC Shoah Foundation, VHA Interview 30990.

42. Veidlinger, *In the Shadow of the Shtetl*, 189.

43. Veidlinger, *In the Shadow of the Shtetl*, 36; Sokolova, "The Podolian Shtetl," 51.

44. Bronshteyn, *Dead Loop*, 130, transcribed from Bronshteyn's USC Shoah interview with Donia Presler, USC Shoah Foundation, VHA Interview 31670.

45. Ancel, *Transnistria*, 39.

46. Ancel, *Transnistria*, 24; Solonari, *A Satellite Empire*, 146, 150.

47. Ancel, *Transnistria*, 52.

48. Veidlinger, *In the Shadow of the Shtetl*, 48. Michman, *The Emergence of Jewish Ghettos*, 130.

49. Michman, *The Emergence of Jewish Ghettos*, 130–34; Ofer, "Life in the Ghettos of Transnistria," 236–37; Veidlinger, *In the Shadow of the Shtetl*, 166–67, 195–96; Spitzer, "Solidarity and Suffering," 107–9.

50. Mir-Tibon, "Am I My Brother's Keeper?," 129–30

51. Ancel, *Transnistria*, 53, 553, doc. 41.

52. Miron and Shulhani, *The Yad Vashem Encyclopedia of the Ghettos*, 851.

53. In their testimonies, some survivors, such as Svetlana Kogan-Rabinovich and Mikhail Bartik (in his VHA interview), recall that the Tulchyn ghetto was established on Volodarsky Street. According to Jeffrey Veidlinger, the ghetto was located on "'Beggars' street' in what had been a poor Jewish neighborhood." See: Veidlinger, *In the Shadow of the Shtetl*, 194. These assertions are shared by researcher Natalia Kolisnyk of Tulchyn's Museum of Local Lore, who writes that Volodarsky Street was part of the prewar Jewish neighborhood of Kaptsanovka (*kaptsn* is Yiddish for poor) and that the ghetto's former location encompasses today's School No. 1 and the bus station. See Tulchyn's official municipal website, "Holocaust Remembrance Day is celebrated around the world on January 27," 27 January 2020, http://tulchynska.gromada.org.ua/news/1580995840/. For more on Kaptsanovka, see Sokolova, "House-Building Tradition," 127–28.

54. Veidlinger, *In the Shadow of the Shtetl*, 194–96; Megargee, *USHMM Encyclopedia of Camps and Ghettos*, 807.

55. Ancel, *Transnistria*, 546.

56. Ancel, *Transnistria*, 53.

57. Garrard, "The Nazi Holocaust in the Soviet Union," 9.

58. Ancel, *Transnistria*, 40.

59. Wiesel et al., "The Holocaust in Romania," 41.

60. Solonari, "Hating Soviets," 519, 521.

61. Podolsky, "Collaboration in Ukraine," 190.

62. Eikel, "Division of Labor and Cooperation," 110.

63. Subtelny, *Ukraine*, 471.

64. Berkhoff, *Harvest of Despair*, 20–21, 29; Solonari, "Hating Soviets," 510–11.

65. Mikhail Bartik, USC Shoah Foundation, VHA Interview 30959.

66. Veidlinger, *In the Shadow of the Shtetl*, 208.

67. Wiesel et al., "The Holocaust in Romania," 45.

68. Office of the Historian, U.S. Department of State, "Foreign Relations of the United States Diplomatic Papers, 1941, Europe, Volume II," https://history.state.gov/historicaldocuments/frus1941v02/d862.

Chapter 4

1. Brönnimann, "The Global Climate Anomaly," 336–40.

2. Ancel, *Transnistria*, 70.

3. Ancel, *Transnistria*, 58, 75, 314.

4. Ancel, *Transnistria*, 59, 132–33, 145; Westermann, "Stone-Cold Killers," 1–2, 8–9.

5. Ancel, *Transnistria*, 57–58.

6. Ancel, *Transnistria*, 63; Ofer, "The Ghettos in Transnistria," 34.

7. There was some debate among survivors about the specific date on which they were deported. Some, including Etel and Motl, remembered it happening on 7 December. Others recalled being forced to leave Tulchyn on 13 December or on other days leading up to Hanukkah.

8. Kogan-Rabinovich, "In the Inferno," 463.

9. Kogan-Rabinovich, "In the Inferno," 463.

10. Miron and Shulhani, *The Yad Vashem Encyclopedia of the Ghettos during the Holocaust*, 851; Megargee, *USHMM Encyclopedia of Camps and Ghettos*, 807.

11. According to text on the school's old website, which has since been replaced, the school was founded in 1939.

12. Bronshteyn, *Dead Loop*, 258, transcribed from Bronshteyn's USC Shoah interview with Reizia Vainblat, USC Shoah Foundation, VHA Interview 30862.

13. Maftsir, *We Allow You to Die*.

14. Ancel, *Transnistria*, 345–46; Deletant, *Hitler's Forgotten Ally*, 175–76.

15. Ancel, *Transnistria*, 346.

16. Ancel, *Transnistria*, 314.

17. Maftsir, *We Allow You to Die*.

18. Ancel, *Transnistria*, 57.

19. Kogan-Rabinovich, "In the Inferno," 464.

20. Ancel, *Transnistria*, 395–96.

21. Maftsir, *We Allow You to Die*.

22. Bronshteyn, *Dead Loop*, 260, transcribed from Bronshteyn's USC Shoah interview with Reizia Vainblat, USC Shoah Foundation, VHA Interview 30862.

23. Bronshteyn, *Dead Loop*, 131, transcribed from Bronshteyn's USC Shoah interview with Donia Presler, USC Shoah Foundation, VHA Interview 31670.

24. Maftsir, *We Allow You to Die.*

25. USHMM, RG-50.226.0004, oral history Interview with Mikhail Abramovich Bartik.

26. Dvoichenko-Markov, "Gheorghe Duca," 79.

27. Dvoichenko-Markov, "Gheorghe Duca," 75–80; Malakov, *Po Bratslavshchine*, 113–25; Aftanazy, *Dzieje rezydencji na dawnych kresach Rzeczypospolitej*, 258.

28. Malakov, *Po Bratslavshchine*, 122–25; Aftanazy, *Dzieje rezydencji na dawnych kresach Rzeczypospolitej*, 259.

29. Aftanazy, *Dzieje rezydencji na dawnych kresach Rzeczypospolitej*, 258–59.

30. Urbański, *Z czarnego szlaku i tamtych rubiezy*, 37–41.

31. *Illustrated Encyclopedia of the Country*, National Museum in Krakow, s.v. "Napoleon Orda (1807–1883)," http://mnk.pl/exhibitions/napoleon-orda-1807–1883 -illustrated-encyclopaedia-of-the-country.

32. Radziwill, *One of the Radziwills*, 35–36.

33. Aftanazy, *Dzieje rezydencji na dawnych kresach Rzeczypospolitej*, 259.

34. Potocka, *Dziennik*, 118, 149; Potocka, *Moje wlasne wspomnienia*, 312.

35. Jakubowska, *Patrons of History*, 46n19.

36. Lednicki, *Reminiscences*, 57.

37. Urbański, *Z czarnego szlaku i tamtych rubiezy*, 41.

38. Maftsir, *We Allow You to Die.*

39. Arkadii Plotitskii, USC Shoah Foundation, VHA Interview 34591.

40. Arkadii Glinets, USC Shoah Foundation, VHA Interview 35116.

41. Solonari, "Hating Soviets," 520–21.

42. Dumitru, "Through the Eyes of Survivors," 211. According to survivors Mikhail and Ester Bartik, a classmate of theirs was raped by Germans within the camp. See Ester Bartik, VHA Interview 30987; Mikhail Bartik, USC Shoah Foundation, VHA Interview 30959.

43. Ancel, *Transnistria*, 174; Ofer, "Life in the Ghettos of Transnistria," 252; Solonari, *A Satellite Empire*, 148.

44. Ancel, *Transnistria*, 111.

45. Ester Bartik, USC Shoah Foundation, VHA Interview 30987.

46. Spitzer, "Solidarity and Suffering," 107–9.

47. Ancel, *Transnistria*, 51.

48. Ancel, *Transnistria*, 345, 386–87.

49. Garfinkle and Shevell, "Neurolathyrism in Vapniarka," 839–42.

50. Carp, *Transnistria*, 335.

51. Ioanid, *The Holocaust in Romania*, 182–86.

52. Carp, *Transnistria*, 257.

53. Yad Vashem, "The Untold Stories: The Murder Sites of the Jews in the Occupied Territories of the Former USSR," s.v. "Bratslav," www.yadvashem.org/untold stories/database/index.asp?cid=699; Carp, *Transnistria*, 257.

54. Megargee, *USHMM Encyclopedia of Camps and Ghettos*, 698–99; Veidlinger, *In the Shadow of the Shtetl*, 211.

55. Ester Bartik, USC Shoah Foundation, VHA Interview 30987.

56. Golbert, "Holocaust Sites in Ukraine," 232n87.

57. Allen, *The Fantastic Laboratory of Dr. Weigl*, 13–14, 21; David W. Tschanz, "Typhus Fever on the Eastern Front in World War I," Insects, Disease, and History, Montana State University, http://scarab.msu.montana.edu/historybug/wwi -tef.html.

58. Raisa Chernova, USC Shoah Foundation, VHA Interview 31077.

Chapter 5

1. Ofer, "The Ghettos in Transnistria," 45.

2. Megargee, *USHMM Encyclopedia of Camps and Ghettos*, 742. Speaking to Soviet investigators in May 1944 after the camp's liberation, two Pechera survivors stated that Zilberman (Tsimerman) was a Jew from Bukovyna. See GARF, Fond 7021, op. 54, d. 1341, ll.163–165, accessed through the European Holocaust Research Infrastructure, https://training.ehri-project.eu/eo9-testimony-survivors -liusia-sukharevich-and-mania-ribalova-9-may-1944.

3. Agmon et al., *Vinnitsa District*, 84.

4. Jagendorf, *Jagendorf's Foundry*, 68.

5. Ancel, *Transnistria*, 396–99; Carp, *Transnistria*, 319.

6. Gold, *Ruth's Journey*, 80.

7. Mikhail Bartik, USC Shoah Foundation, VHA Interview 30959.

8. Dumitru, *The State, Antisemitism, and Collaboration*, 194.

9. Ancel, *Transnistria*, 40.

10. Veidlinger, *In the Shadow of the Shtetl*, 216–17. One of these Romanians was said to have hanged two young Jewish sisters for wandering into the village to find bread. The same Romanian had apparently also turned his cellar into an elaborate dungeon. See Robert Rivkin, "This Pain Is Still Alive," *Russkiy Aktsent* [Russian accent] no. 1 (45), 1998, 4. (*Russkiy Aktsent* was a weekly Russian-language newspaper published in the United States and distributed in many U.S. cities.)

11. Ancel, *Transnistria*, 52.

12. Decades after this encounter, Motl continued to wonder how a child so young could have learned such language or internalized such hatred.

13. The Ms. Zhenya that Motl remembered may have been the same Zhenya Malina that Pechera survivor Donia Presler described in her USC Shoah Foundation interview. In Donia's retelling, the woman, also an ethnic German, fed and housed her sister and a friend during their escape to Tulchyn. Afterward, she

scolded the ghetto's Jews for refusing to help them. See Veidlinger, *In the Shadow of the Shtetl*, 216.

14. Etel's memories diverge from Motl's when it comes to this anecdote. Etel believes their trip took place much earlier than what Motl reported in his account. She believes they slept at Zhenya's home on New Year's Eve, as evidenced by the New Year's tree she saw. She also remembered German and Romanian soldiers entering the home for drinking and dancing, while she and Motl lay hiding under the daybed.

15. Arkadii Plotitskii, USC Shoah Foundation, VHA Interview 34591; Golbert, "Holocaust Sites in Ukraine," 216.

16. Golbert, "Holocaust Sites in Ukraine," 228n46.

17. USHMM, RG-50.226.0004, oral history Interview with Mikhail Abramovich Bartik.

18. Arkadii Plotitskii, USC Shoah Foundation, VHA Interview 34591.

19. Bronshteyn, *Dead Loop*, 274–75, transcribed from Bronshteyn's USC Shoah interview with Shelia Vaisman, USC Shoah Foundation, VHA Interview 31618.

20. Rivkin, "This Pain Is Still Alive," 4.

21. Ofer, "The Ghettos in Transnistria," 33, 36–37.

22. Ofer, "Life in the Ghettos of Transnistria," 246–47.

23. Arkadii Plotitskii, USC Shoah Foundation, VHA Interview 34591.

24. Bronshteyn, *Dead Loop*, 273–74, transcribed from Bronshteyn's USC Shoah interview with Shelia Vaisman, USC Shoah Foundation, VHA Interview 31618.

25. USHMM, RG-50.226.0004, oral history Interview with Mikhail Abramovich Bartik.

26. Ester Bartik, USC Shoah Foundation, VHA Interview 30987.

27. Ancel, *Transnistria*, 699, doc. 575.

28. Kogan-Rabinovich, "In the Inferno," 466.

29. Ester Bartik, USC Shoah Foundation, VHA Interview 30987.

30. Golbert, "Holocaust Sites in Ukraine," 215.

31. Maftsir, *We Allow You to Die*.

32. Evgeniia Tsirulnikova, USC Shoah Foundation, VHA Interview 31784.

33. Poliak, *Osenniye Listya Vospominaniy*.

34. Carp, *Transnistria*, 425n200.

35. Ioanid, *The Holocaust in Romania*, 217. In a phone interview with Radu Ioanid in winter 2020, he reemphasized to me that Pechera was not *among* the worst concentration sites in Transnistria, it was the worst.

36. Carp, *Transnistria*, 337.

37. Ofer, "Life in the Ghettos of Transnistria," 238; Deletant, "Ghetto Experience in Golta, Transnistria," 31.

38. Mir-Tibon, "Am I My Brother's Keeper?," 136–40.

39. Ofer, "Life in the Ghettos of Transnistria," 252.

40. Mir-Tibon, "Am I My Brother's Keeper?," 131, 141n13.

41. Mir-Tibon, "Am I My Brother's Keeper?," 135, 138.

42. Carp, *Transnistria*, 337.

43. Mir-Tibon, "Am I My Brother's Keeper?," 135–36. Gali Mir-Tibon is also the author of an Israeli novel called *The List of the Mothers*, published in 2017, which tells the story of single mothers deported to Pechera in 1942. Mir-Tibon speaks about her personal connection to the deportations in a video interview that can be found at http://ehpes.com/blog1/?p=10206.

44. Tibon, "Two-Front Battle," 157–59; Jagendorf, *Jagendorf's Foundry*, 100–1.

45. Jagendorf, *Jagendorf's Foundry*, 111.

46. Carp, *Transnistria*, 337.

47. Jagendorf, *Jagendorf's Foundry*, 111; Megargee, *USHMM Encyclopedia of Camps and Ghettos*, 742.

48. Records from the National Council for the Study of Securitate Archives, as quoted in Mir-Tibon, "Am I My Brother's Keeper?," 141n12.

49. Abram Kaplan, USC Shoah Foundation, VHA Interview 34818.

50. Arkadii Glinets, USC Shoah Foundation, VHA Interview 35116.

51. Carp, *Transnistria*, 337.

52. Poliak, *Osenniye Listya Vospominaniy*. Incidentally, this is almost identical to the rendition that survivor Riza Roitman performed for USC Shoah Foundation interviewer Moris Bronshteyn in 1997 and later transcribed in Bronshteyn's book of interview transcriptions. See Bronshteyn, *Dead Loop*, 48.

53. Evgeniia Tsirulnikova, USC Shoah Foundation, VHA Interview 31784.

54. Vynokurova, "The Fate of Bukovinian Jews," 23.

55. Abram Kaplan, USC Shoah Foundation, VHA Interview 34818.

Chapter 6

1. Angrick, "Forced Labor along the 'Straße der SS,'" 83; Angrick, "Annihilation and Labor," 196.

2. Lower, *Nazi Empire-Building*, 142–44.

3. Wiesel et al., "The Holocaust in Romania," 72.

4. Angrick, "Annihilation and Labor," 197–98.

5. Angrick, "Annihilation and Labor," 207.

6. Wiesel et al., "The Holocaust in Romania," 72–73; Ancel, *Transnistria*, 322–25.

7. Carp, *Transnistria*, 339.

8. Angrick, "Forced Labor along the 'Straße der SS,'" 89.

9. Carp, *Holocaust in Romania*, 281.

10. Carp, *Holocaust in Romania*, 340.

11. Ancel, *Transnistria*, 329.

12. Angrick, "Annihilation and Labor," 208.

13. Megargee, *USHMM Encyclopedia of Camps and Ghettos*, 743.

14. Angrick, "Forced Labor along the 'Straße der SS,'" 87.

15. Angrick, "Annihilation and Labor," 192–6, 207, 209.

16. Fradis-Milner to Rakhil Kovnator, *The Unknown Black Book*, 157–61.

17. Kovnator and Ehrenburg, "The Story of Rakhil Fradis-Milner," 73.

18. Fradis-Milner to Rakhil Kovnator, *The Unknown Black Book*, 160–61.

19. Robert Rivkin, "This Pain Is Still Alive," *Russkiy Aktsent* (Russian Accent), no. 1 (45), 1998, page 5.

20. Lower, *Nazi Empire-Building*, 149–50.

21. Carp, *Transnistria*, 341, 343.

22. Angrick, "Annihilation and Labor," 208–9.

23. Rivkin, "This Pain Is Still Alive," 5.

24. After moving to the Cincinnati area, Manya (now Manya Ganiyevva) wrote a memoir, which found its way to the U.S. Holocaust Memorial Museum and was later referenced in Jeffrey Veidlinger's *In the Shadow of the Shtetl*. See pages 186–87, 189–90, 193, 218. The Ukrainian scholar Boris Zabarko has also featured her testimony in his work.

25. Ancel, *Transnistria*, 322.

26. Angrick, "Annihilation and Labor," 211, table 5.1.

27. Rivkin, "This Pain Is Still Alive," 5. Manya's description matches a known event in December 1943, when 156 prisoners fled Talalaivka after hearing that a liquidation was planned, thirty of whom were shot. See Angrick, "Annihilation and Labor," 213, 222n97.

28. Agmon et al., *Vinnitsa District*, 88–90.

29. Agmon et al., *Vinnitsa District*, 86.

30. Agmon et al., *Vinnitsa District*, 88–89.

31. Agmon et al., *Vinnitsa District*, 89–90.

32. Evgeniia Tsirulnikova, USC Shoah Foundation, VHA Interview 31784.

33. Carp, *Transnistria*, 346.

34. Agmon et al., *Vinnitsa District*, 90.

35. Agmon et al. *Vinnitsa District*, 90.

36. Ancel, *Transnistria*, 817–18, doc. 1025. In his interview with the USC Shoah Foundation, Arkadii Plotitskii mentions that he and some other boys discovered a cache of food hidden in the sanitorium building's basement, which the Jewish committee's members had apparently kept for themselves while other prisoners died of hunger. They made the discovery in early 1944, just before the Red Army liberated the camp. Arkadii Plotitskii, USC Shoah Foundation, VHA Interview 34591.

37. Megargee, *USHMM Encyclopedia of Camps and Ghettos*, 743.

38. Evgeniia Tsirulnikova, USC Shoah Foundation, VHA Interview 31784.

39. Dumitru, "Through the Eyes of Survivors," 211.

40. Mikhail Bartik, USC Shoah Foundation, VHA Interview 30959.

41. Deuber, *Fading Traces*.

42. During his interview with the USC Shoah Foundation, Arkadii briefly mentions singing this song; the original was made popular in the early twentieth century by Russian writer Maxim Gorky's play *The Lower Depths*. For this passage,

I have included a few lines translated from the handwritten Russian lyrics recorded by Moisei Beregovski's team and stored at the Vernadsky National Library of Ukraine's Manuscript Institute, which are attributed to an unknown Pechera prisoner and match Arkadii's description. These lyrics are likely similar to the ones Arkadii learned from other prisoners and sang during his escapes. See Vernadsky National Library of Ukraine, Manuscript Institute, Fond 190, "Cabinet of Jewish Culture of the USSR Academy of Sciences," accessed through the Yad Vashem Archives, YVA, 0.76/31, "Untitled song by an unknown author"; Arkadii Plotitskii, USC Shoah Foundation, VHA Interview 34591.

43. USHMM, RG-50.632.0015, oral history interview with Rita Genekhovna Shveibish and Isaak Peisakhovich Shveibish.

44. Sokolova, "The Podolian Shtetl," 42, 67, fig. 4.

45. Lukin, *100 evreiskikh mestechek Ukrainy*, 258.

46. "Memoirs of Sofia Budman-Goikhman," Yad Vashem, "The Untold Stories: The Murder Sites of the Jews in the Occupied Territories of the Former USSR," www.yadvashem.org/untoldstories/database/writtenTestimonies.asp?cid =811&site_id=1114.

47. Lukin, *100 evreiskikh mestechek Ukrainy*, 258.

48. Veidlinger, *In the Shadow of the Shtetl*, 187

49. "Memoirs of Sofia Budman-Goikhman," www.yadvashem.org/untoldstories /database/writtenTestimonies.asp?cid=811&site_id=1114.

50. Yakov Driz, interview with Ella Levitskaya, Centropa, 2002, www .centropastudent.org/biography/yakov-driz.

51. Megargee, *USHMM Encyclopedia of Camps and Ghettos*, 801. Other depictions of the Tomashpil ghetto suggest that only barbed wired, and not a fence, marked the Tomashpil ghetto's boundary. See Veidlinger, *In the Shadow of the Shtetl*, 195.

52. Megargee, *USHMM Encyclopedia of Camps and Ghettos*, 801; Yad Vashem, "The Untold Stories: The Murder Sites of the Jews in the Occupied Territories of the Former USSR," s.v. "Tomashpol," www.yadvashem.org/untoldstories/database /index.asp?cid=811.

53. Ofer, "The Ghettos in Transnistria," 45; Ofer, "Life in the Ghettos of Transnistria," 271.

54. Aron Hirt-Manheimer, commentary to *Jagendorf's Foundry*, Jagendorf, xii; Jagendorf, *Jagendorf's Foundry*, 60.

55. Lukin, *100 evreiskikh mestechek Ukrainy*, 259.

56. Megargee, *USHMM Encyclopedia of Camps and Ghettos*, 801.

Chapter 7

1. An August 1941 ordinance stipulated that anyone caught transporting letters or money to Jews would face a jail sentence of three to five years, along with a fine. See Ancel, *Transnistria*, 52.

2. Ofer, "Life in the Ghettos of Transnistria," 249; Solonari, *A Satellite Empire*, 190.

3. Hilberg, *The Destruction of the European Jews*, 844.

4. Kaplan, *In Europe's Shadow*, 140

5. Ioanid, *The Holocaust in Romania*, 266.

6. Jean Ancel, ed., *Documents Concerning the Fate of Romanian Jewry during the Holocaust*, vol. 8 (New York: Beate Klarsfeld Foundation, 1986), 608, as quoted in Ioanid, *The Holocaust in Romania*, 266.

7. Jean Ancel, ed., *Documents Concerning the Fate of Romanian Jewry during the Holocaust*, vol. 10 (New York: Beate Klarsfeld Foundation, 1986), as quoted in Ioanid, *The Holocaust in Romania*, 247; Ioanid, *The Holocaust in Romania*, 247–48.

8. Deletant, *Hitler's Forgotten Ally*, 2.

9. Ancel, "The German-Romanian Relationship," 263–64.

10. Wiesel et al., "The Holocaust in Romania," 79–81.

11. Ofer, "Life in the Ghettos of Transnistria," 254.

12. Jagendorf, *Jagendorf's Foundry*, 103.

13. Megargee, *USHMM Encyclopedia of Camps and Ghettos*, 633, 812.

14. Leo Baeck Institute Archive, ME 1416.MM III 14, memoir by Gerhard Schreibrer, 30.

15. Jagendorf, *Jagendorf's Foundry*, 160.

16. Leo Baeck Institute Archive, ME 1416.MM III 14, memoir by Gerhard Schreibrer, 26.

17. Ofer, "Life in the Ghettos of Transnistria," 254–57.

18. Without the kindness of ethnic Ukrainians, few camp prisoners would have survived. In one recent study, scholars Diana Dumitru and Carter Johnson argue that Soviet policies of integration and inclusion enacted during the interwar period—a departure from rabid anti-Semitism of Tsarist Russia—had been internalized by the populace and was one of the reasons why local Ukrainians sometimes helped vulnerable Jews. This goodwill contrasted with the treatment of Jews in Bessarabia during the opening weeks of Romania's invasion. Dumitru and Johnson argue that unlike in the Soviet Union, Romanian policies enacted in Bessarabia after 1918 dehumanized and alienated Jews and ultimately led to the incitement of violence against them in the summer of 1941. See Dumitru, "Constructing Interethnic Conflict and Cooperation." In a direct rebuttal to this study, scholar Vladimir Solonari argues that while the local populations resisted calls for anti-Jewish violence in Transnistria during the war, the territory was very much still rife with anti-Semitism and that many locals believed Jews were responsible for the ills brought by the Soviet regime. He writes that it wasn't until the summer of 1942 that many Ukrainians finally turned on the occupiers. See Solonari, "Hating Soviets."

19. Solonari, *A Satellite Empire*, 150, 165, 188–90; Ancel, *Transnistria*, 24, 41.

20. Arkadii Plotitskii, USC Shoah Foundation, VHA Interview 34591.

21. Ofer, "Life in the Ghettos of Transnistria," 254, 272–73.

22. Megargee, *USHMM Encyclopedia of Camps and Ghettos*, 807.

23. Schreiber may not have been aware that Tulchyn's Jews weren't massacred but sent to Pechera instead.

24. Leo Baeck Institute Archive, ME 1416.MM III 14, memoir by Gerhard Schreibrer, 29. He notes that the ghetto ended at "an empty schoolhouse," likely School No. 1.

25. Leo Baeck Institute Archive, ME 1416.MM III 14, memoir by Gerhard Schreibrer, 29.

26. Leo Baeck Institute Archive, ME 1416.MM III 14, memoir by Gerhard Schreibrer, 31.

27. Ioanid, *The Holocaust in Romania*, 221.

28. Megargee, *USHMM Encyclopedia of Camps and Ghettos*, 657.

29. Megargee, *USHMM Encyclopedia of Camps and Ghettos*, 800.

30. Rosen, "The Djurin Ghetto," 136.

31. Megargee, *USHMM Encyclopedia of Camps and Ghettos*, 666.

32. Shachan, *Burning Ice*, 274.

33. Shachan, *Burning Ice*, 253.

34. Megargee, *USHMM Encyclopedia of Camps and Ghettos*, 667.

35. Lukin, *100 evreiskikh mestechek Ukrainy*, 514.

36. Ofer and Rosen, "An Account from Transnistria," 53.

37. Megargee, *USHMM Encyclopedia of Camps and Ghettos*, 667.

38. Rosen, "The Djurin Ghetto," 146–47.

39. Goodman, "Max Goodman," 133.

40. Rosen, "The Djurin Ghetto," 131–32.

41. Ofer and Rosen, "An Account from Transnistria," 59.

42. Kunstadt's self-published diary, under entry 9 January 1943, 7 A.M., page 220, as quoted in Rosen, "The Djurin Ghetto," 143.

43. Kunstadt's self-published diary, under entry 9 January 1943, 7 A.M., page 220, as quoted in Rosen, "The Djurin Ghetto," 144.

44. Barbulescu, "The Djurin Ghetto," 108–9.

45. Ofer and Rosen, "An Account from Transnistria," 60.

46. Kunstadt's self-published diary, under entry 6 May 1942, page 31, as quoted in Rosen, "The Djurin Ghetto," 139–40.

47. Kunstadt's self-published diary, under entry 6 May 1942, page 31, as quoted in Rosen, "The Djurin Ghetto," 141n25.

48. Korber, "Miriam Korber: Transnistria," 257. Excerpts from Korber's diary entries were translated from Miriam Korber Bercovici, *Jurnal de Ghetou: Djurin, Transnistria, 1941–1943* (Bucharest: Editura Kriterion, 1995).

49. Korber, "Miriam Korber: Transnistria," 252.

50. Korber, "Miriam Korber: Transnistria," 256–64.

51. Korber, "Miriam Korber: Transnistria," 267; Mir-Tibon, "Am I My Brother's Keeper?" 135.

52. Kunstadt's self-published diary, under entry 7 February 1943, 8 P.M., page 247, as quoted in Rosen, "The Djurin Ghetto," 142–43.

53. Kunstadt's self-published diary, under entry January 4, 1943, as quoted in Ofer, "Life in the Ghettos of Transnistria," 271n39.

54. Lukin, *100 evreiskikh mestechek Ukrainy*, 514.

55. Barbulescu, "The Djurin Ghetto," 108n64.

56. Barbulescu, "The Djurin Ghetto," 108.

57. Ester Bartik, USC Shoah Foundation, VHA Interview 30987.

58. Ghetto leaders in Mohyliv-Podilskyi fought to save their Jewish residents from similar assignments but failed. When work units returned to Mohyliv-Podilskyi from Tulchyn in early 1943, the Jewish leaders reported that these men "were half dead from having to dig peat by hand while standing in the frigid marshes." See Jagendorf, *Jagendorf's Foundry*, 160.

59. Megargee, *USHMM Encyclopedia of Camps and Ghettos*, 722; Ofer, "Life in the Ghettos of Transnistria," 249.

60. Leonid Krais, interview with Ella Levitskaya, Centropa, 2002, www.centropa.org/biography/leonid-krais.

61. Zigler, "My Liberation," 442.

62. Bronshteyn, *Dead Loop*, 326, 334.

63. Raisa Vorobeva, USC Shoah Foundation, VHA Interview 33753.

64. Bronshteyn, *Dead Loop*, 334–35.

65. Raisa Vorobeva, USC Shoah Foundation, VHA Interview 33753.

66. Goodman, "Max Goodman," 133.

67. Golbert, "Holocaust Sites in Ukraine," 228n48.

68. Agmon et al., *Vinnitsa District*, 90–91.

69. Poliak, *Osenniye Listya Vospominaniy*.

70. Golbert, "Holocaust Sites in Ukraine," 215–18.

71. Arkadii Plotitskii, USC Shoah Foundation, VHA Interview 34591.

72. Leshchinskaya, "These Were the First Living Jews," 164.

73. Lev Muchnik, interview with TBN and Helping Hand Coalition, 21 August 2013, www.youtube.com/watch?v=uFlDHGbCxiw.

74. Arkadii Plotitskii, USC Shoah Foundation, VHA Interview 34591.

75. Mikhail Bartik, USC Shoah Foundation, VHA Interview 30959.

76. Arkadii Plotitskii, USC Shoah Foundation, VHA Interview 34591.

77. Mikhail Bartik, USC Shoah Foundation, VHA Interview 30959.

78. Lev Muchnik, interview with TBN and Helping Hand Coalition, August 21, 2013, www.youtube.com/watch?v=uFlDHGbCxiw.

79. Poliak, *Osenniye Listya Vospominaniy*.

80. Rubenstein and Altman, *The Unknown Black Book*, 18.

81. Leshchinskaya, "These Were the First Living Jews," 164.

82. Deletant, *Hitler's Forgotten Ally*, 230–44.

83. Deletant, *Hitler's Forgotten Ally*, 230–44.

84. Douglas Martin, "King Michael of Romania, Who Ousted a Hitler Puppet, Dies at 96," *New York Times*, 5 December 2017, www.nytimes.com/2017/12/05/obituaries/king-michael-romania-dead.html.

85. Ioanid, *The Holocaust in Romania*, 270.
86. Ancel, "The German-Romanian Relationship and the Final Solution," 263.
87. Kaplan, *In Europe's Shadow*, 135.
88. Ancel, *The History of the Holocaust in Romania*, 556; 670n28.
89. Ioanid, *The Holocaust in Romania*, 289.
90. Veidlinger, *In the Shadow of the Shtetl*, 188.
91. Wiesel et al., "Trials of the War Criminals," 1.
92. Hirsch and Spitzer, "Small Acts of Repair," 20–21.
93. According to the International Commission on the Holocaust in Romania, plenty of "small fries" were also tried, and their trials were often more revelatory. See Wiesel et al., "Trials of the War Criminals," 23. Per an email with a researcher at the U.S. Holocaust Memorial Museum's National Institute for Holocaust Documentation, Stratulat may well have been tried if he survived the war, but he (the researcher) had not come across the name "Stratulat" in connection with a war crimes trial.
94. Penter, "Local Collaborators on Trial," 353.
95. Ofer and Rosen, "An Account from Transnistria," 65n11.
96. Aron Hirt-Manheimer, commentary, in Jagendorf, *Jagendorf's Foundry*, 190–91; Megargee, *USHMM Encyclopedia of Camps and Ghettos*, 757.
97. Records from the National Council for the Study of Securitate Archives, as quoted in Mir-Tibon, "Am I My Brother's Keeper?," 140.
98. Aron Hirt-Manheimer, commentary, in Jagendorf, *Jagendorf's Foundry*, 190–91.

Chapter 8

1. Popoff, *Vasily Grossman*, 112, 119, 141, 159, 161, 172–73.
2. Grossman, "Ukraine without Jews," 14.
3. Popoff, *Vasily Grossman*, 165–66.
4. Grossman, "Ukraine without Jews," 13.
5. Kruglov, "Jewish Losses in Ukraine," 273; Veidlinger, *In the Shadow of the Shtetl*, xv, xviii, 160–62.
6. After their liberation, another Pechera child survivor (Ester Bartik) and her sisters found a vacant home in the former Tulchyn ghetto that had been inhabited by deportees from Bukovyna, who had evidently left. Yet Ester and her family could not conceive of having an entire house to themselves after the crowded conditions of Pechera. They felt the urge to invite a survivor named Fanya and her daughter to share the house with them. See USHMM, RG-50.226.0005, oral history interview with Ester Yankelovna Bartik.
7. Manley, *To the Tashkent Station*, 257.
8. Ofer, "Life in the Ghettos of Transnistria," 232.
9. Veidlinger, *In the Shadow of the Shtetl*, 245–47.
10. Spector, *The Encyclopedia of Jewish Life*, 1340.

11. Veidlinger, *In the Shadow of the Shtetl*, 245–47.

12. Veidlinger, *In the Shadow of the Shtetl*, xviii, 14.

13. Ancel, *Transnistria*, 331.

14. Werb, "Fourteen Shoah Songbooks," 101, table 14; Lyudmila Sholochova, "The Phonoarchive of Jewish Folklore at the Vernadsky National Library of Ukraine," trans. Illia Labunka, https://old.archives.gov.ua/Eng/NB/Phonoarchive .php.

15. The musical album *Yiddish Glory* recently resurrected these songs to much acclaim. For the full English-language lyrics, see their website at www.yiddishglory .com/music. More background can be found in the epilogue.

16. Werb, "Fourteen Shoah Songbooks," 95.

17. Golbert, "Holocaust Sites in Ukraine," 216–17.

18. Garrard, "The Nazi Holocaust in the Soviet Union," 7n8.

19. Gitelman, "Soviet Reactions to the Holocaust," 10–13.

20. Gitelman, "Politics and the Historiography," 28.

21. Garrard, "The Nazi Holocaust in the Soviet Union," 4, 8–10.

22. Garrard, "The Nazi Holocaust in the Soviet Union," 6, 8–10.

23. See GARF, Fond 7021, op. 54, d. 1341, ll.163–65. Accessed through the European Holocaust Research Infrastructure, https://training.ehri-project.eu/e09 -testimony-survivors-liusia-sukharevich-and-mania-ribalova-9-may-1944.

24. USHMM, RG-50.226.0029, oral history interview with Riza Yankelevna Roitman.

25. Mikhail Bartik, USC Shoah Foundation, VHA Interview 30959.

26. Spector, *The Encyclopedia of Jewish Life*, 977.

27. Veidlinger, *In the Shadow*, 37–38.

28. Poliak, *Osenniye Listya Vospominaniy*.

29. Dean, *Collaboration in the Holocaust*, 158.

30. Penter, "Local Collaborators on Trial," 343, 357–58.

31. My grandfather Motl Braverman also alluded to this story, as did survivors Ester Bartik and Arkadii Plotitskii in their USC Shoah Foundation interviews.

32. Kogan-Rabinovich, "In the Inferno," 476n16.

33. Raisa Chernova, USC Shoah Foundation, VHA Interview 31077.

34. See GARF, Fond 7021, op. 54, d. 1341, ll.163–165, accessed through the European Holocaust Research Infrastructure, https://training.ehri-project.eu/e09 -testimony-survivors-liusia-sukharevich-and-mania-ribalova-9-may-1944. In separate testimony recorded decades later, survivor Donia Presler explained that Dr. Vishnevsky had evaded postwar prosecution. Each morning in the camp, he had forced fellow prisoners—sometimes with threats of violence—to clean the human waste that accumulated in the camp's corridors overnight. He argued that these efforts had stemmed further disease outbreaks and had apparently made his case convincingly and was acquitted. See Bronshteyn, *Dead Loop*, 136, transcribed from Bronshteyn's USC Shoah interview with Donia Presler, USC Shoah Foundation, VHA Interview 31670.

35. Kruglov, "Jewish Losses in Ukraine," 285, table 8.5; Veidlinger, *In the Shadow of the Shtetl*, 77, 188.

36. Slutsky, "Tulchin," 174.

37. USHMM, RG-50.632.0047, oral history interview with Rita Genekhovna Shveibish.

38. Veidlinger, *In the Shadow of the Shtetl*, 274.

39. Shternshis, introduction to *Soviet and Kosher*, xiii.

40. Veidlinger, *In the Shadow of the Shtetl*, 136–37.

41. In her testimony with the USC Shoah Foundation, survivor Evgeniia Tsirulnikova said that in her native Bratslav, few could believe that she had spent the war in a death camp. "Don't be ridiculous. No one who was sent to a camp remained alive," she was often told. See Evgeniia Tsirulnikova, USC Shoah Foundation, VHA Interview 31784.

42. Korey, "A Monument over Babi Yar?" 71.

43. Gitelman, "Soviet Reactions to the Holocaust," 7–8; Veidlinger, *In the Shadow of the Shtetl*, 230.

44. Ancel, *Transnistria*, 338.

45. Mikhail Bartik, USC Shoah Foundation, VHA Interview 30959.

46. Korey, "A Monument over Babi Yar?" 61–71.

47. Anthony Austin, "U.S. Unit, at Babi Yar, Stunned by Soviet Silence on Jews," *New York Times*, 4 August 1979, www.nytimes.com/1979/08/04/archives/us-unit-at-babi-yar-stunned-by-soviet-silence-on-jews-a-contrast-in.html.

48. Snyder, *Bloodlands*, 382–83.

49. Gershenson, *The Phantom Holocaust*, 231, 232n9.

50. Veidlinger, *In the Shadow of the Shtetl*, 183, 187.

51. For a glimpse into how researchers negotiated for access to Romanian records, see Shapiro, *The Kishinev Ghetto*, xi, 1–5; and Paul Shapiro, preface to Ioanid, *The Holocaust in Romania*, xi–xiv.

52. This term likely originated from Julius Fisher's 1969 book of the same name.

53. Golbert, "Holocaust Sites in Ukraine," 208–9; Veidlinger, *In the Shadow of the Shtetl*, 188. Recent studies by Israeli scholars, including Dalia Ofer, Sarah Rosen, and Gali Mir-Tibon—cited throughout this book—have expanded scholarship on life in the ghettos of northern Transnistria.

54. Ruth Glasberg Gold, "How Transnistria Was Added to the Map of Concentration Camps at the U.S. Holocaust Memorial Museum in Washington, D.C.," *Czernowitz-L Discussion Group* (blog), 2011, http://czernowitz.ehpes.com/stories/ruth-trans/. See http://czernowitz.ehpes.com/stories/ruth-trans/speech.html for a transcription of her speech.

55. Mikhail Bartik, USC Shoah Foundation, VHA Interview 30959.

56. Schultz, "Health resorts and sanitoriums," 133.

57. Mikhail Bartik, USC Shoah Foundation, VHA Interview 30959.

58. Hirsch and Spitzer, *Ghosts of Home*, 234.

59. *Megargee, USHMM Encyclopedia of Camps and Ghettos*, 632.

60. Carp, *Transnistria*, 207–8.

61. Carp, *Transnistria*, 213–14.

62. Ioanid, *The Holocaust in Romania*, 173.

63. Hirsch and Spitzer, *Ghosts of Home*, 234–35.

64. *YIVO Encyclopedia of Jews in Eastern Europe*, s.v. "Chernivtsi," https://yivoencyclopedia.org/article.aspx/Chernivtsi.

65. Leonid Bershidsky, "Russia Mourns a Crooner Who Always Found Political Favor," *Bloomberg Opinion*, 30 August 2018, www.bloomberg.com/opinion/articles/2018–08–31/russia-mourns-iosif-kobzon-who-sang-from-stalin-s-time-to-putin.

66. For a map of the Chernivtsi ghetto, see Hirsch and Spitzer, *Ghosts of Home*, 126, map 3.

67. In the article, Grossman writes that even in death, "people remained people," his way of combating the dehumanization of the Jewish victims in Treblinka. See Popoff, *Vasily Grossman*, 177.

68. Ofer, "Life in the Ghettos of Transnistria," 229.

69. United States Holocaust Memorial Museum, "Chernivtsi Jewish Survivors Organization affidavits," https://collections.ushmm.org/search/catalog/irn513149.

70. United States Holocaust Memorial Museum, "Significant Archival Collections from and relevant to the Former Soviet Union," 3 October 2013, www.ushmm.org/m/pdfs/20131004-significant-archival-collections-from-and-relevant-to-the-former-soviet-union.pdf.

Chapter 9

1. Susan Byrnes, "Eastside Attracts Russian Immigrants—New Roots in Bellevue," *Seattle Times*, 5 April 1995, https://archive.seattletimes.com/archive/?date=19950405&slug=2114194.

2. In 2003, the INS was supplanted by three new agencies within the Department of Homeland Security: United States Citizenship and Immigration Services, Immigration and Customs Enforcement, and Customs and Border Patrol.

3. Philippe Coumarianos, "Ukraine Introduces New Currency," *United Press International*, 2 September 1996, www.upi.com/Archives/1996/09/02/Ukraine-introduces-new-currency/6213841636800/.

4. Zvi Gitelman, "Glasnost, Perestroika and Antisemitism," *Foreign Affairs*, Spring 1991.

5. Daniel Hryhorczuk, "Environmental Illness a Mystery," *Chicago Tribune*, 5 February 1995, www.chicagotribune.com/news/ct-xpm-1995–02–05–9502050233-story.html.

6. The Israeli food writer Janna Gur wrote recently about the phenomenon of Ashkenazi-Bessarabian culinary crossover and its Turkish and Balkan influences in a recent piece for *Tablet* magazine; she also mentions the smokey eggplant dish

I grew up eating. See Janna Gur, "Jewish Culinary Crossroads," *Tablet*, July 19, 2020, www.tabletmag.com/sections/food/articles/jewish-culinary-crossroads.

7. Hirsch and Spitzer, *Ghosts of Home*, 127.

8. Hirsch and Spitzer, *Ghosts of Home*, 53–55.

9. Veidlinger, *In the Shadow of the Shtetl*, xiv.

10. Beckerman, *When They Come for Us*, 49–50.

11. Chervyakov, Gitelman, and Shapiro, "*E Pluribus Unum*?" 70, 71 table 4.6, 72.

12. Lea Zeltserman, "Defining Jewish Cuisine," *Tablet*, 11 April 2018, www
.tabletmag.com/sections/food/articles/defining-soviet-jewish-cuisine.

13. Sara Chernobilskaya, "The Forgotten Concentration Camp," *Novoe Russkoe Slovo* (New York), 21 January 2005.

Epilogue

1. Vladislav Vigurzhinsky, "Tulchyn Release 4: Pushkin Street, bazaar," 15 April 2020, www.youtube.com/watch?v=SEAcD4uUtt4.

2. Sokolova, "Jewish Sights," 278, fig 7.

3. Sue Surkes, "Ukraine's Jews Walk Narrow Line between Murderous Past and Uncertain Future," *Times of Israel*, 17 May 2017, www.timesofisrael.com/ukraines
-jews-walk-narrow-line-between-murderous-past-and-uncertain-future/.

4. Veidlinger, *In the Shadow of the Shtetl*, 117.

5. Vladislav Vigurzhinsky, "Tulchyn Release 15: School No. 1, Fortress, Jewish Quarter and Former Ghetto, Juliusz Słowacki," 30 April 2020, www.youtube.com
/watch?v=Tp8r2raokCM.

6. Interview with Mykola Korobko, the Spinoza Foundation for Journalists with Disabilities and Musculoskeletal Disorders, 2 July 2020, http://spinoza.in.ua/2020
/02/07/щоб-відновити-здоров'я-пацієнта-інк/.

7. Valentina Pustovit, "Residents of Pechera, Staff and Patients Are Set to Defend the Sanatorium in the Village," *Vlasno.info*, 28 January 2020, http://vlasno.info
/spetsproekti/1/health/item/34336-meshkantsi-pechery-kolektyv-ta-patsiien.

8. *Papa* stars Russian cinema icon Vladimir Mashkov as the provincial Jewish father Abram, whose son David, a musical prodigy, leaves prewar Tulchyn (the shtetl) for the Moscow Conservatory. David learns in 1943, while serving in the Red Army, that his father and all the Jews of Tulchyn's ghetto have been executed. He returns to liberate a smoldering Tulchyn but finds it almost beyond recognition. He is injured in combat sometime thereafter. In the movie's final scene, when David awakens on a medical train, he sees his father in a vision. At David's insistence, Abram recounts how Tulchyn's Jews were led from the ghetto to the town's train station—which does not actually exist and never has—thinking they would be "resettled" in Poland. Their belongings are collected by Russian-speaking locals wearing white armbands. In the meantime, the Germans are polishing their rifles. Viewers are left to infer that every Jewish resident was shot shortly thereafter.

Worth mentioning is that the play on which the movie is based (banned in the Soviet Union for more than three decades) has Abram hitting one of the local policemen with his son's childhood violin after hearing an anti-Semitic slight, an act of resistance that is omitted from the movie's final scene. For a brief discussion of *Papa* and Holocaust depictions in post-Soviet film, see Gershenson, *The Phantom Holocaust*, 79, 188, 220. For a more in-depth analysis, see Gershenson, "Ambivalence and Identity," 183–89.

9. "The Village of Pechera," 1 October 2014, *Inter TV*, www.youtube.com/watch ?v=dUjk2Ar86Sk.

10. Hirsch and Spitzer, "'There Was Never a Camp Here,'" 135–53. A version of this study appears in Hirsch and Spitzer's *Ghosts of Home*, 197–231.

11. Gold, *Ruth's Journey*, 310–11, 336–39. In his book *Erased: Vanishing Traces of Jewish Galicia in Present-Day Ukraine Holocaust*, scholar Omer Bartov finds similar indignities during his travels to western Ukraine, in what had been Eastern Galicia.

12. Veidlinger, *In the Shadow of the Shtetl*, 258–60. According to the Babyn Yar Holocaust Memorial Center, there are now an estimated three hundred mass burial sites in Vinnytsia Province, less than half of which are memorialized. See "Places of Memory," Babyn Yar Holocaust Memorial Center, 18 October 2018, http://babynyar.org/en/byhmc-news/posts/news/places-of-memory-vinnytsia -oblast.

13. Mikhail Bartik, USC Shoah Foundation, VHA Interview 30959.

14. USHMM, RG-50.226.0004, oral history Interview with Mikhail Abramov-ich Bartik.

Selected Bibliography

Archival Sources

Gosudarstvennyi arkhiv Rossiiskoi federatsii (GARF) (State Archive of the Russian Federation), Moscow

Fond 7021, "Archives of the Soviet Extraordinary State Commissions," op. 54, d. 1341,11.163–65: Testimony by Survivors Liusia Sukharevich and Mania Ribalova. Accessed through the European Holocaust Research Infrastructure, https://training.ehri-project.eu/e09-testimony-survivors -liusia-sukharevich-and-mania-ribalova-9-may-1944.

Leo Baeck Institute Archive

ME 1416.MM III 14, Memoir by Gerhard Schreibrer

United States Holocaust Memorial Museum, Washington, DC (USHMM)

The Jeff and Toby Herr Oral History Archive

RG-50.226.0005, Oral history interview with Ester Yankelovna Bartik, August 13, 1994.

RG-50.226.0004, Oral history Interview with Mikhail Abramovich Bartik, August 13, 1994.

RG-50.632.0047, Oral history interview with Rita Genekhovna Shveibish, July 12, 2006.

RG-50.632.0015, Oral history interview with Rita Genekhovna Shveibish and Isaak Peisakhovich Shveibish, July 21, 2005 and July 9, 2006.

RG-50.226.0029, Oral history interview with Riza Yankelevna Roitman, August 13, 1994.

USC Shoah Foundation Visual History Archive (VHA)

Abram Kaplan. Interview 34818. Interviewed by Moris Brohnstein. Mohyliv-Podolski, Ukraine, July 31, 1997.

Arkadii Glinets. Interview 35116. Interviewed by Moris Brohnstein. Mohyliv-Podolski, Ukraine, August 11, 1997.

Arkadii Plotitskii. Interview 34591. Interviewed by Moris Brohnstein. Tulchyn, Ukraine, July 25, 1997.

Donia Presler. Interview 31670. Interviewed by Moris Brohnstein. Tulchyn, Ukraine, May 18, 1997.

Ester Bartik. Interview 30987. Interviewed by Moris Brohnstein. Tulchyn, Ukraine, April 28, 1997.

Evgeniia Tsirulnikova. Interview 31784. Interviewed by Moris Brohnstein. Bratslav, Ukraine, May 21, 1997.

Mikhail Bartik. Interview 30959. Interviewed by Moris Brohnstein. Tulchyn, Ukraine, April 24, 1997.

Raisa Chernova. Interview 31077. Interviewed by Moris Brohnstein. Tulchyn, Ukraine, May 5, 1997.

Raisa Vorobeva. Interview 33753. Interviewed by Maxim Sofovich. Tulchyn, Ukraine, September 15, 1997.

Reizia Vainblat. Interview 30862. Interviewed by Moris Brohnstein. Tulchyn, Ukraine, April 25, 1997.

Riza Roitman. Interview 30990. Interviewed by Moris Brohnstein. Tulchyn, Ukraine, April 28, 1997.

Shelia Vaisman. Interview 31618. Interviewed by Moris Brohnstein. Bratslav, Ukraine, May 16, 1997.

Vernadsky National Library of Ukraine, Manuscript Institute

Fond 190, "Cabinet of Jewish Culture of the USSR Academy of Sciences," delo 148, p. 62 (old code B2235); accessed through the Yad Vashem Archives (YVA)

YVA 0.76/31, "Untitled song by an unknown author."

Other Survivor Accounts

Agmon, Pinchas, Anatoll Stepanenko, Yosef Maljar, and Faina Vinokurova, eds. *Vinnitskaia oblast: Katastrofa (Shoa) i soprotivlenie* [Vinnytsia Province: Catastrophe (Shoah) and resistance]. Tel Aviv and Kyiv: Ghetto Fighters' House, 1994.

Braverman, Motl. "The Fascists Entered and the Tragedy Began." In *Liudi ostaiutsia liudmi: Svidetel'stva uznikov fashistskikh lagerei-getto* [People remain people; Testimony from prisoners of fascist ghetto-camps], Vestnik 3, edited by G. L. Shabashkevich, 91–97. Chernivtsi, Ukraine: Eliezer Steinbarg Jewish Cultural Society, Association of Former Prisoners of the Fascist Camps and Ghettos of the Chernivtsi Oblast, Chernivtsi Oblast State Archive, 1994.

Bronshteyn, Moris. *Dead Loop*. Translated by Dmitri Sled. Self-published, 2015.

Fradis-Milner, Rakhil. Rakhil Fradis-Milner to Rakhil Kovnator, September 25, 1944. In *The Unknown Black Book: The Holocaust in the German-Occupied Soviet Territories*, edited by Joshua Rubenstein and Ilya Altman, 157–61. Bloomington: Indiana University Press, 2008.

Goodman, Max. "Max Goodman." In *Witnesses to the Holocaust: An Oral History*, edited by Rhoda G. Lewin, 132–33. Boston: Twayne Publishers, 1990.

Kogan-Rabinovich, Svetlana. "In the Inferno: The Dead Loop Concentration Camp." In *Before All Memory Is Lost: Women's Voices from the Holocaust.* Edited by Myrna Goldenberg, translated by Irina Sadovina, 455–82. Toronto, Ont.: Azrieli Foundation, 2017.

Korber, Miriam. "Miriam Korber: Transnistria." In *Young Writers' Diaries of the Holocaust*, edited by Alexandra Zapruder, 243–70. Translated by Julie Donat. 2nd ed. New Haven, Conn.: Yale University Press, 2015.

Kovnator, Rakhil, and Ilya Ehrenburg, eds. "The Story of Rakhil Fradis-Milner." In *The Complete Black Book of Russian Jewry*, edited by Ilya Ehrenburg and Vasily Grossman, translated and edited by David Patterson, 70–76. New Brunswick, N.J.: Transaction Publishers, 2001.

Leshchinskaya, Regina. "These Were the First Living Jews They Met during the War." In *Holocaust in the Ukraine*, edited by Boris Zabarko, translated by Marina Gubas, 161–65. Portland, Ore.: Vallentine Mitchell, 2005.

Poliak, Eva. *Osenniye Listya Vospominaniy* [Autumn leaves of memories]. Self-published, 2017.

Zigler, Etty. "My Liberation." In *Shattered! 50 Years of Silence: History and Voices of the Tragedy in Romania and Transnistria*, edited by Felicia Carmelly, 442–43. Toronto, Ont.: Abbeyfield Publishers, 1997.

Books, Articles, and Documentaries

Aftanazy, Roman. *Dzieje rezydencji na dawnych kresach Rzeczypospolitej* [The history of the great houses of the former borderlands of the Polish-Lithuanian Commonwealth]. T. 10, *Wojewodztwo braclawskie* [Bracław Voivodeship]. Wroclaw: Zakład Narodowy im. Ossolińskich, 1996.

Allen, Arthur. *The Fantastic Laboratory of Dr. Weigl: How Two Brave Scientists Battled Typhus and Sabotaged the Nazis.* New York: Norton, 2014.

Altshuler, Mordechai. "The Distress of Jews in the Soviet Union in the Wake of the Molotov-Ribbentrop Pact." *Yad Vashem Studies* 36, no. 2 (2008): 73–141.

Ancel, Jean. "The German-Romanian Relationship and the Final Solution." *Holocaust and Genocide Studies* 19, no. 2 (Fall 2005): 252–75.

———. *The History of the Holocaust in Romania.* Edited by Leon Volovici. Translated by Yaffah Murciano. Lincoln: University of Nebraska Press, 2011.

———. "The Romanian Campaigns of Mass Murder in Transnistria, 1941–1942." In *The Destruction of Romanian and Ukrainian Jews during the Antonescu Era*, edited by Randolph L. Braham, 87–133. New York: Rosenthal Institute for Holocaust Studies, 1997.

———. *Transnistria, 1941–1942: The Romanian Mass Murder Campaigns.* Vol. 1 of *History and Document Summaries.* Translated by Karen Gold and Rachel Garfinkel. Tel Aviv: Goldstein-Goren Diaspora Research Center, 2003.

Angrick, Andrej. "Annihilation and Labor: Jews and Thoroughfare IV in Central Ukraine." In *The Shoah in Ukraine: History, Testimony, Memorialization,* edited by Ray Brandon and Wendy Lower, 190–223. Bloomington: Indiana University Press, 2008.

———. "Forced Labor along the 'Straβe der SS.'" In *Forced and Slave Labor in Nazi-Dominated Europe: Symposium Presentations*, 83–92. Washington, D.C.: Center for Advanced Holocaust Studies, United States Holocaust Memorial Museum, 2004. www.ushmm.org/m/pdfs/Publication_OP _2004-02.pdf.

Barbulescu, Ana. "The Djurin Ghetto: Official Order, Internal Structure, and Networking Strategies." *Holocaust Studii și cercetări* 11, no. 12 (2019): 95–120.

Bartal, Israel. "Imagined Geography: The Shtetl, Myth, and Reality." In *The Shtetl: New Evaluations*, edited by Steven T. Katz, 179–92. New York: New York University Press, 2009.

Bartov, Omer. *Erased: Vanishing Traces of Jewish Galicia in Present-Day Ukraine Holocaust*. Princeton, N.J.: Princeton University Press, 2007.

Beckerman, Gal. *When They Come for Us, We'll Be Gone: The Epic Struggle to Save Soviet Jewry*. Boston: Houghton Mifflin Harcourt, 2010.

Bergström, Christer. *Barbarossa: The Air Battle, July–December 1941*. Burgess Hill, U.K.: Classic Publications, 2007.

Berkhoff, Karel. *Harvest of Despair: Life and Death in Ukraine under Nazi Rule*. Cambridge, Mass.: Belknap Press of Harvard University Press, 2004.

Brönnimann, Stefan. "The Global Climate Anomaly 1940–1942." *Weather* 60, no. 12 (2005): 336–42.

Carp, Matatias. *Holocaust in Romania: Facts and Documents on the Annihilation of Romania's Jews, 1940–1944*. Edited by Andrew L. Simon. Translated by Sean Murphy. Safety Harbor, Fla.: Simon Publications, 2000. https://isurvived.org/2Postings/HolocaustRomania-carp.pdf.

———. *The Legionary Movement and the Rebellion*. Vol. 1, *Cartea Neagră: Fapte si Documente Suferintele Evreilor din Romania, 1940–1944* [The black book: The sufferings of the Jews from Romania, 1940–1944]. Translated by Gerda Tanner. Bucharest: The Socec & Co. S. A. R Publishing House, 1946. http://survivors-romania.org/pdf_doc/black_book_1.pdf.

———. *Transnistria*. Vol. 3, *Cartea Neagră: Fapte si Documente Suferintele Evreilor din Romania, 1940–1944* [The black book: The sufferings of the Jews from Romania, 1940–1944]. Bucharest: Societatea Nationala de Editura si Arte Grafice Dacia Traiana, 1947. http://survivors-romania.org/pdf_doc/black _book_3.pdf.

Chervyakov, Valeriy, Zvi Gitelman, and Vladimir Shapiro. "*E Pluribus Unum?* Post-Soviet Jewish Identities and Their Implications for Communal Reconstruction." In *Jewish Life after the USSR*, edited by Zvi Gitelman, Musya Glants, and Marshal I. Goldman, 61–75. Bloomington: Indiana University Press, 2003.

Dean, Martin. *Collaboration in the Holocaust: Crimes of the Local Police in Belorussia and Ukraine, 1941–44*. New York: St. Martin's, 2003.

Deletant, Dennis. "Ghetto Experience in Golta, Transnistria, 1942–1944." *Holocaust and Genocide Studies* 18, no. 1 (Spring 2004): 1–26.

———. *Hitler's Forgotten Ally: Ion Antonescu and His Regime, Romania 1940–1944.* Basingstoke, U.K.: Palgrave Macmillan, 2006.

———. "Romania." In *Joining Hitler's Crusade: European Nations and the Invasion of the Soviet Union, 1941,* edited by David Stahel, 46–78. Cambridge, U.K.: Cambridge University Press, 2018.

Deuber, Walo, dir. *Fading Traces: Postscripts from a Landscape of Memory.* New York: Filmakers Library, 2001.

Dubnow, Simon. *From the Beginning until the Death of Alexander I (1825).* Vol. 1, *History of the Jews in Russia and Poland: From the Earliest Times until the Present Day.* Translated by Israel Friedlaender. Philadelphia: Jewish Publication Society of America, 1916.

Dumitru, Diana. "Constructing Interethnic Conflict and Cooperation: Why Some People Harmed Jews and Others Helped Them during the Holocaust in Romania." *World Politics* 63, no. 1 (2011): 1–42.

———. *The State, Antisemitism, and Collaboration in the Holocaust: The Borderlands of Romania and the Soviet Union.* New York: Cambridge University Press, 2016.

———. "Through the Eyes of Survivors: Jewish-Gentile Relations in Bessarabia and Transnistria during the Holocaust." In *Eradicating Differences: The Treatment of Minorities in Nazi-Dominated Europe,* edited by Anton Weiss-Wendt, 203–28. Newcastle, U.K.: Cambridge Scholars Publishing.

Dvoichenko-Markov, Demetrius, "Gheorghe Duca Hospodar of Moldavia and Hetman of the Ukraine, 1678–1684," *Balkan Studies* 31, no. 1 (1990): 73–86.

Ehrenburg, Ilya, and Vasily Grossman, eds. *The Black Book: The Ruthless Murder of Jews by German Fascist Invaders throughout the Temporarily Occupied Regions of the Soviet Union and in the Death Camps of Poland during the War of 1941–1945.* Translated by John Glad and James Levine. New York: Holocaust Library, 1980.

Eikel, Markus. "Division of Labor and Cooperation: The Local Administration under German Occupation in Central and Eastern Ukraine, 1941–1944." In *The Holocaust in Ukraine: New Sources and Perspectives: Conference Presentations,* 101–20. Washington, D.C.: Center for Advanced Holocaust Studies, United States Holocaust Memorial Museum, 2013. www.ushmm.org/m/pdfs/20130500-holocaust-in-ukraine.pdf.

Garfinkle, Jarred, Frederick Andermann, and Michael I. Shevell. "Neurolathyrism in Vapniarka: Medical Heroism in a Concentration Camp." *Canadian Journal of Neurological Sciences/Journal Canadien Des Sciences Neurologiques* 38, no. 6 (2011): 839–44.

Garrard, John. "The Nazi Holocaust in the Soviet Union: Interpreting Newly Opened Russian Archives." *East European Jewish Affairs* 25, no. 2 (1995): 3–40.

Geissbühler, Simon. *Once upon a Time Never Comes Again: The Traces of the Shtetl in Southern Podolia (Ukraine)*. Bern: Projekt 36, 2014.

———. "What We Know about Romania and the Holocaust—and Why It Matters." In *Romania and the Holocaust: Events—Contexts—Aftermath*, edited by Simon Geissbühler, 241–66. Stuttgart: Ibidem-Verlag, 2016.

Gershenson, Olga. "Ambivalence and Identity in Russian Jewish Cinema." In *Jewishness: Expression, Identity and Representation*, edited by Simon J. Bronner, 175–94. Oxford: Littman Library of Jewish Civilization, 2008.

———. *The Phantom Holocaust: Soviet Cinema and Jewish Catastrophe*. New Brunswick, N.J.: Rutgers University Press, 2013.

Gitelman, Zvi. "Politics and the Historiography of the Holocaust in the Soviet Union." In *Confronting the Holocaust in the USSR: Bitter Legacy*, edited by Zvi Gitelman, 14–42. Bloomington: Indiana University Press, 1997.

———. "Soviet Reactions to the Holocaust, 1945–1991." In *The Holocaust in the Soviet Union: Studies and Sources on the Destruction of the Jews in the Nazi-Occupied Territories of the USSR, 1941–1945*, edited by Lucjan Dobroszycki and Jeffrey Gurock, 3–28. Armonk, N.Y.: M. E. Sharp, 1993.

Glaser, Amelia M. "The Heirs of Tul'chyn: A Modernist Reappraisal of Historical Narrative." In *Stories of Khmelnytsky: Competing Literary Legacies of the 1648 Ukrainian Cossack Uprising*, edited by Amelia M. Glaser, 127–38. Stanford: Stanford University Press, 2015.

Golbert, Rebecca L. "Holocaust Sites in Ukraine: Pechora and the Politics of Memorialization." *Holocaust and Genocide Studies* 18, no. 2 (Fall 2004): 205–33.

Gold, Ruth Glasberg. *Ruth's Journey: A Survivor's Memoir*. Gainesville: University Press of Florida, 1996.

Grossman, Vasily. "Ukraine without Jews." Translated by Polly Zavadivker. *Jewish Quarterly* 58, no. 1 (January 2011): 12–18.

Hilberg, Raul. *The Destruction of the European Jews*. 3rd ed. New Haven, Conn:. Yale University Press, 2003.

Hirsch, Marianne, and Leo Spitzer. *Ghosts of Home: The Afterlife of Czernowitz in Jewish Memory*. Berkeley: University of California Press, 2010.

———. "Small Acts of Repair. The Unclaimed Legacy of the Romanian Holocaust." *Journal of Literature and Trauma Studies* 4, no. 1–2 (2016): 13–42.

———. "'There Was Never a Camp Here': Searching for Vapniarka." In *Locating Memory: Photographic Acts*, edited by Annette Kuhn and Kirsten Emiko McAllister, 135–54. New York: Berghahn Books, 2006.

Ioanid, Radu. *The Holocaust in Romania: The Destruction of the Jews and Gypsies under the Antonescu Regime: 1940–1944*. Chicago: Ivan R. Dee, 2008.

Jagendorf, Siegfried. *Jagendorf's Foundry: Memoir of the Romanian Holocaust, 1941–1944*. Edited by Aron Hirt-Manheimer. New York: HarperCollins, 1991.

Jakubowska, Longina. *Patrons of History: Nobility, Capital and Political Transitions in Poland.* New York: Routledge, 2016.

Kaplan, Robert D. *In Europe's Shadow: Two Cold Wars and a Thirty-Year Journey through Romania and Beyond.* New York: Random House, 2016.

Korey, William. "A Monument over Babi Yar?" In *The Holocaust in the Soviet Union: Studies and Sources on the Destruction of the Jews in the Nazi-Occupied Territories of the USSR, 1941–1945,* edited by Lucjan Dobroszycki and Jeffrey Gurock, 61–76. Armonk, N.Y.: M. E. Sharpe, 1993.

Kruglov, Alexander. "Jewish Losses in Ukraine." In *The Shoah in Ukraine: History, Testimony, Memorialization,* edited by Ray Brandon and Wendy Lower, 272–90. Bloomington: Indiana University Press, 2008.

Lednicki, Waclaw. *Reminiscences: The Adventures of a Modern Gil Blas during the Last War.* The Hague: Mouton, 1971.

Lower, Wendy. *Nazi Empire-Building and the Holocaust in Ukraine.* Chapel Hill: University of North Carolina Press, 2005.

Lukin, V., A. Sokolova, and B. Khaymovich, eds. *100 evreiskikh mestechek Ukrainy: istoricheskii putevoditel'* [100 shtetls of Ukraine: Historical guide]. Vypusk 2, *Podiliia.* St. Petersburg: Ezro, 2000.

Maftsir, Boris, dir. *We Allow You to Die: Searching for the Unknown Holocaust in the Former Soviet Union.* Israel: 2016. https://movie-discovery.com/movie/we-allow-you-to-die-en/1042.

Malakov, D. V. *Po Bratslavshchine: Ot Vinnitsy do Tulchina* [By Bratslavshchina: From Vinnytsia to Tulchin]. Moscow: Iskusstvo, 1982.

Manley, Rebecca. *To the Tashkent Station: Evacuation and Survival in the Soviet Union at War.* Ithaca, N.Y.: Cornell University Press, 2009.

Megargee, Geoffrey, Joseph White, and Mel Hecker, eds. *The United States Holocaust Memorial Museum Encyclopedia of Camps and Ghettos, 1933–1945.* Vol. 3, *Camps and Ghettos under European Regimes Aligned with Nazi Germany.* Bloomington: Indiana University Press, 2018.

Michman, Dan. *The Emergence of Jewish Ghettos during the Holocaust.* Translated by Lenn J. Schramm. New York: Cambridge University Press, 2011.

Mir-Tibon, Gali. "'Am I My Brother's Keeper?': Jewish Committees in the Ghettos of the Mogilev District and the Romanian Authorities in Transnistria, 1941–1944." In *The Ghettos in Global History: 1500 to the Present,* edited by Wendy Z. Goldman and Joe William Trotter Jr., 127–47. Abingdon, U.K.: Routledge, 2018.

Miron, Guy, and Shlomit Shulhani, eds. *The Yad Vashem Encyclopedia of the Ghettos during the Holocaust.* Jerusalem: Yad Vashem, 2009.

Ofer, Dalia. "Life in the Ghettos of Transnistria." *Yad Vashem Studies* 25 (1996): 229–74.

———. "The Ghettos in Transnistria and Ghettos under German Occupation in Eastern Europe. A Comparative Approach." In *Im Ghetto 1939–1945: Neue Forschungen zu Alltag und Umfeld* [In the ghetto 1939–1945: New research on everyday life and the environment], edited by Christoph Dieckmann and Babette Quinkert, 30–54. Göttingen: Wallstein, 2009.

Ofer, Dalia, and Sarah Rosen. "An Account from Transnistria: The Diary of Lipman Kunstadt, a Social Critic from Within." *In Beyond Camps and Forced Labour: Proceedings of the Sixth International Conference*, edited by Suzanne Bardgett, Christine Schmidt, and Dan Stone, 49–66. Cham: Palgrave Macmillan, 2020.

Penter, Tanjya. "Local Collaborators on Trial. Soviet War Crimes Trials under Stalin (1943–1953). In *Cahiers du Monde russe* 49, no. 2–3 (2008): 341–64.

Pinchuk, Ben-Zion. "Soviet Media on the Fate of Jews in Nazi-Occupied Territory (1939–1941)." *Yad Vashem Studies* 11 (1974): 221–33.

Podolsky, Anatoly. "Collaboration in Ukraine during the Holocaust: Aspects of Historiography and Research." In *The Holocaust in Ukraine: New Sources and Perspectives: Conference Presentations*, 187–98. Washington, D.C.: Center for Advanced Holocaust Studies, United States Holocaust Memorial Museum, 2013. www.ushmm.org/m/pdfs/20130500-holocaust-in-ukraine.pdf.

Popoff, Alexandra. *Vasily Grossman and the Soviet Century*. New Haven, Conn.: Yale University Press, 2019.

Potocka, Janina. *Dziennik 1914–1919* [Diary 1914–1919]. In *Peczara*. Lomianki, Poland: Wydawnictwo LTW, 2014.

Potocka, Zofia. *Moje wlasne wspomnienia* [My own memories]. In *Peczara*. Lomianki, Poland: Wydawnictwo LTW, 2014.

Radziwill, Michael. *One of the Radziwills*. London: J. Murray, 1971.

Reid, Anna. *Borderland: A Journey through the History of Ukraine*. New York: Basic Books, 1997.

Rosen, Sarah. "The Djurin Ghetto in Transnistria through the Lens of Kunstadt's Diary." In *Romania and the Holocaust: Events—Contexts—Aftermath*, edited by Simon Geissbühler, 131–50. Stuttgart: Ibidem-Verlag, 2016.

Schultz, Heinrich. "Health Resorts and Sanitoriums." In *Encyclopedia of Ukraine*. Vol. 2, *G–K*. Edited by Volodymyr Kubiyovych. Toronto: University of Toronto Press, 1988.

Shachan, Avigdor. *Burning Ice: The Ghettos of Transnistria*. Boulder, Colo.: East European Monographs, 1996.

Shapiro, Paul A. *The Kishinev Ghetto, 1941–1942: A Documentary History of the Holocaust in Romania's Contested Borderlands*. Tuscaloosa: University of Alabama Press, 2015.

Shternshis, Anna. *Soviet and Kosher: Jewish Popular Culture in the Soviet Union, 1923–1939*. Bloomington: Indiana University Press, 2006.

Slutsky, Yehuda. "Tulchin." In *Encyclopaedia Judaica*. Vol. 20, *To–Wei*. 2nd ed. Edited by Michael Berenbaum and Fred Skolnik. Detroit: MacMillan Reference USA, 2017.

Snyder, Timothy. *Bloodlands: Europe between Hitler and Stalin*. New York: Basic Books, 2010.

Sokolova, Alla. "House-Building Tradition of the Shtetl in Memorials and Memories (Based on Materials of Field Studies in Podolia)." *East European Jewish Affairs* 41, no. 3 (December 2011): 111–35.

———. "Jewish Sights: Exoticization of Places and Objects as a Way of Presenting Local 'Jewish Antiquity' By the Inhabitants of Little Towns." In *Jewish Space in Central and Eastern Europe: Day-to-Day History*, edited by Jurgita Šiaučiūnaitė-Verbickienė and Larisa Lempertienė, 261–80. Newcastle, U.K.: Cambridge Scholars Publishing, 2007.

———. "The Podolian Shtetl as Architectural Phenomenon." In *The Shtetl: Image and Reality: Papers of the Second Mendel Friedman International Conference on Yiddish*, edited by Gennady Estraikh and Mikhail Krutikov, 36–79. Translated by Alexander Ivanov. Oxford: Legenda, 2000.

Solonari, Vladimir. *A Satellite Empire: Romanian Rule in Southwestern Ukraine, 1941–1944*. Ithaca, N.Y.: Cornell University Press, 2019.

———. "Hating Soviets—Killing Jews: How Antisemitic Were Local Perpetrators in Southern Ukraine, 1941–42?" *Kritika: Explorations in Russian and Eurasian History* 15, no. 3 (Summer 2014): 505–33.

Spector, Shmuel, and Geoffrey Wigoder, eds. *The Encyclopedia of Jewish Life before and during the Holocaust*. 3 vols. New York: New York University Press.

Spencer, Peter S., and H. H. Schaumburg. "Lathyrism: A Neurotoxic Disease." *Neurobehavioral Toxicology and Teratology* 5, no. 6 (November-December 1983): 625–29.

Spitzer, Leo. "'Solidarity and Suffering': Lager Vapniarka among the Camps of Transnistria." In *Witnessing Unbound: Holocaust Representation and the Origins of Memory*, edited by Henri Lustiger Thaler and Habbo Knoch, 105–30. Detroit: Wayne State University Press, 2017.

Subtelny, Orest. *Ukraine: A History*. 4th ed. Toronto: University of Toronto Press, 2009.

Stampfer, Shaul. "What Actually Happened to the Jews of Ukraine in 1648?" *Jewish History* 17, no. 2 (May 2003): 207–27.

Tibon, Gali. "Two-Front Battle: Opposition in the Ghettos of the Mogilev District in Transnistria: 1941–1944." In *Romania and the Holocaust: Events—Contexts—Aftermath*, edited by Simon Geissbühler, 151–70. Stuttgart: Ibidem-Verlag, 2016.

Urbański, Antoni. *Z czarnego szlaku i tamtych rubieży: zabytki polskie przepadłe na Podolu, Wołyniu, Ukrainie* [From the black trail and distant outposts: Polish historical monuments lost in Podolia, Volhynia, and Ukraine]. Wyd.2. Warszawa: Dom Ksiazki Polskiej, Spolka Akcyjna, 1928.

Veidlinger, Jeffrey. *In the Shadow of the Shtetl: Small-Town Jewish Life in Soviet Ukraine*. Bloomington: Indiana University Press, 2013.

Vynokurova, Faina. "The Fate of Bukovinian Jews in the Ghettos and Camps of Transnistria, 1941–1944: A Review of the Source Documents at the Vinnytsa Oblast State Archive." *Holocaust and Modernity* 2, no. 8 (2010): 18–26.

Werb, Bret. "Fourteen Shoah Songbooks." *Musica Judaica* 20 (2013): 39–116.

Werth, Alexander. *Russia at War, 1941–1945.* New York: Dutton, 1964.

Westermann, Edward B. "Stone-Cold Killers or Drunk with Murder? Alcohol and Atrocity during the Holocaust." *Holocaust and Genocide Studies* 30, no. 1 (Spring 2016): 1–19.

Wiesel, Elie, Tuvia Friling, Lya Benjamin, Radu Ioanid, and Mihail E. Ionescu, eds. "Executive Summary." In *Final Report of the International Commission on the Holocaust in Romania,* 2004. www.yadvashem.org/yv/pdfdrupal/en /report/english/executive_summary.pdf.

———. "Roots of Romanian Antisemitism." In *Final Report of the International Commission on the Holocaust in Romania,* 2004. www.yadvashem.org/yv /pdfdrupal/en/report/english/1.1_Roots_of_Romanian_Antisemitism .pdf.

———. "Solidarity and Rescue: Romanian Righteous among the Nations." In *Final Report of the International Commission on the Holocaust in Romania,* 2004. www.yadvashem.org/yv/pdf-drupal/en/report/english/1.11_Soli darity_and_Rescue.pdf.

———. "The Holocaust in Romania." In *Final Report of the International Commission on the Holocaust in Romania,* 2004. www.yadvashem.org/yv/pdf -drupal/en/report/english/1.5_he_olocaustin_omania.pdf.

———. "The June/July 1940 Romanian Withdrawal from Bessarabia and Northern Bukovyna and Its Consequences on Interethnic Relations in Romania." In *Final Report of the International Commission on the Holocaust in Romania,* 2004. www.yadvashem.org/yv/pdfdrupal/en/report/english/1.3 _The_1940_Romanian_withdrawal.pdf.

———. "Trials of War Criminals. In *Final Report of the International Commission on the Holocaust in Romania,* 2004. www.yadvashem.org/yv /pdfdrupal/en/report/english/1.12_Trials_of_War_Criminals.pdf.

Zinberg, Israel. *The German-Polish Cultural Center.* Vol. 7, *A History of Jewish Literature.* Translated and edited by Bernard Martin. Cincinnati: Hebrew Union College Press, 1975.

Index

Italicized page numbers indicate illustrative matter.
Country names reflect current (2021) boundaries.

CPSIA information can be obtained
at www.ICGtesting.com
Printed in the USA
LVHW021255080322
712890LV00002B/313